'Lara Marlowe's book has the depth and breadth of a documentary and the subtlety and insight of a novel. If you wish to understand the war in Ukraine, and why and how the Ukrainians are fighting with such valour and tenacity, then read this vivid, moving and affirmative testimony.'
– John Banville, novelist and winner of the Booker Prize for *The Sea*

'Unsparing but tender, filled with love and pain, this extraordinary book gives voice to a new generation of Ukrainians whose lives have been interrupted by the Russian war machine.'
– Yaroslav Trofimov, Chief Foreign Affairs Correspondent for the *Wall Street Journal* and author of *Our Enemies Will Vanish*

'Lara Marlowe has taken us deep into the psyche of Ukrainians who will sacrifice almost anything to resist Russian occupation. We celebrate with Lt Yulia Mykytenko when she triumphs, and weep with her in the face of tragedy. This is an intimate portrait of a remarkable individual and an essential chronicle of the war in Ukraine.'
– Lindsey Hilsum, International Editor for Channel 4 News and author of *I Brought the War with Me*

'This extraordinary book captures the reality of this terrible war through the voice of a remarkable young woman who has chosen to fight for her country. Vivid in its depiction of the human cost of the conflict, intelligent in its explanation of causes and consequences, I recommend this book to anyone who wants to understand what is at stake in Ukraine.'
– Fergal Keane, BBC Foreign Correspondent and author of *The Madness: A Memoir of War, Fear and PTSD*

'*How Good It Is I Have No Fear of Dying* is extraordinary. Lieutenant Yulia Mykytenko embodies the fighting spirit, defiance, and resilience that have come to define Ukraine. People around the world will look to the next generation of Ukrainians, like Lieutenant Mykytenko, for inspiration. This account provides a gritty, on-the-ground perspective to complement the numerous analyses of the Russo-Ukrainian war. Lara Marlowe excels as an interviewer by allowing Lieutenant Mykytenko to share her story in her own words, offering a Ukrainian perspective that is too often overlooked.'
– Christopher Miller, Chief Ukraine Correspondent for the *Financial Times* and author of *The War Came To Us: Life And Death In Ukraine*

'A defiant dispatch from the crucible of Ukraine, *How Good It Is I Have No Fear of Dying* brings an illuminating vision of an ongoing war, a portrait of bravery and endurance amidst the dirge of battle.'
– Nico Walker, author of *Cherry*

'In Ukraine, war has made of women warriors, of daughters heroes, of widows avengers. The book you are holding is more than a muscular and gripping personal narrative from the front line of the 21st-century's bloodiest European conflict: it is an irreplaceable chronicle of a modern war in which women command soldiers, fight over the last machine gun at a recruitment centre and pick out wedding dresses during lulls between battles.'
– Anna Badkhen, author of *Bright Unbearable Reality*, longlisted for the 2022 National Book Award

HOW GOOD IT IS I HAVE NO FEAR OF DYING

LIEUTENANT YULIA MYKYTENKO'S FIGHT FOR UKRAINE

LARA MARLOWE

MELVILLE HOUSE
BROOKLYN · LONDON

How Good It Is I Have No Fear of Dying
Lieutenant Yulia Mykytenko's Fight for Ukraine

First published in 2024 by Head of Zeus, United Kingdom
Copyright © 2024 by Lara Marlowe
First Melville House printing: October 2024

Melville House Publishing
46 John Street
Brooklyn, NY 11201

mhpbooks.com
@melvillehouse

ISBN: 978-1-68589-187-9
ISBN: 978-1-68589-188-6 (eBook)

Library of Congress Control Number: 2024945918

Printed in the United States of America

1 3 5 7 9 10 8 6 4 2

A catalog record for this book is available from the Library of Congress

For all my brothers and sisters in the Ukrainian army, and in memory of my fallen comrades.

Yulia Mykytenko

War is the father of all and the king of all; some he has marked out to be gods and some to be men, some he has made slaves and some free.

Heraclitus

Contents

Author's Note

The word Donbas is an abbreviation for Donetsk coal basin, which comprises the eastern Ukrainian oblasts of Luhansk and Donetsk.

The word oblast means province or region in Ukrainian and Russian.

Russia invaded Crimea and Donbas in 2014 and launched the full-scale invasion of Ukraine on 24 February 2022. Where the text clearly alludes to the 2022 invasion, we have sometimes dropped the prefix 'full-scale'.

I

The Russians Are Coming

Fate is not chosen... It is accepted, whatever it is. And when it is not accepted, it chooses us by force.

Vasyl Stus, from *Camp Notebook*, 1981/82

Zakytne, a small village on the Siverskyi Donets river, Donbas. 15 January 2024

Last night I ordered my front squad to abandon their dugout. They had been under fire for twenty-four hours and they couldn't even launch a drone to see where they were being shelled from, so there was no point keeping them there. My boys had to load up drones and laptops, two-way radios, ammunition and assault rifles and trudge five kilometres in the dark, like pack animals, back to our base camp. They didn't say much when they got here. Soldiers rarely do.

I told them to get some sleep, because we will go out tonight with shovels and dig a new shelter, a kilometre in from the last one, where our infantry can provide better cover. If we had more time, and if I thought we'd be able to hold the new position, we would line it with wood and carry supplies there, to make it comfortable for the drone pilots.

While this is going on, our section of the front line is virtually blind. The Russians will keep advancing, sneaky bastards. They and we use tanks and armoured vehicles only in exceptional circumstances, because expensive armour is so vulnerable to drones. Technically drones are called UAVs, Unmanned Aerial Vehicles, but we call them birds.

I command a twenty-five-man drone reconnaissance platoon and my drones are my babies. We've had four or five dozen of them but eventually they get shot down or you send them on a suicide mission. The serial numbers are too long to remember, so we give every drone a name. When I tell the boys that Bonnie or Clyde fell, they know which drone I mean. The little ones are called Joy or Dream or Bars, which means snow leopard. I named one Jane, after my favourite writer, Jane Austen.

The Russians had to change their strategy, and so did we. Their drones and minefields are a big part of the reason why our counter-offensive failed last year. With a drone, you see everything. We set up a workshop in our derelict house where the boys weld explosive charges onto FPV or first-person-view drones. With a $500 FPV, you can destroy a tank that cost millions. It's a revolution in warfare and it won't change until the Russians or we are totally successful at confusing them with electronic counter-measures, or zapping them with lasers. The Russians are ahead of us in electronic warfare, which worries me a lot. Our commanders say we'll be able to advance once we have air cover from the F-16 fighter jets that NATO has promised us. Well, maybe. Until that happens, low-tech is king.

It has become a truism that the front line is static, but that's not exactly right. The Russians are coming. Slowly, surely, inexorably, they've been moving into our section of the front line near Lyman for months now. They send out small groups of men at night: convicts, or the least educated, or Ukrainian separatists, whom they consider highly expendable. Sometimes there are only two or three soldiers, at most twenty. We see them walking in single file through the grey zone between their line and ours, looking straight ahead like zombies, even when we fire on them. After 100 metres they stop, dig a foxhole and stay there. They gradually move more men forward and fortify the position until they're ready to stage an assault. When they do that, we fire on them, which reveals our camouflaged positions to the Russians' drones. Then they pound us with artillery. We fire back, but our artillery shells are rationed. The Russians fire at least five shells for every one of ours.

The units to the east and west of us have taken casualties. It will be our turn soon. Yesterday the enemy fired a BM-27 Uragan multiple rocket launcher at our base camp, which is really just a smashed-up village in Donetsk, near the regional border with Luhansk. One rocket hit the billet across the street. No one was wounded. At five o'clock this morning, a Lancet suicide drone exploded in front of our dilapidated house. I think the Russians were aiming for the tanks, but the drone fell short and broke the windows in our four-by-fours and army lorries.

I expect they'll break through the line soon, and we'll have to pack up and move again, like we did last year when Wagner mercenaries moved up from Soledar towards our previous base camp at Zvanivka. If we don't move, they'll pulverize us with artillery.

I am First Lieutenant Yulia Mykytenko, a Ukrainian woman, aged twenty-eight. This is my life now and for the foreseeable future, trying to stay alive and protect my men, while Russian forces eat away at Donbas.

Let me tell you how I got here.

Vyshneve, a dormitory town south-west of Kyiv. 4.30 a.m., 24 February 2022

The first explosion jolts me into the no man's land between sleep and waking. For a moment I think I am back in eastern Ukraine. I try to dismiss the noise as a routine artillery bombardment. Two years on the front in Donbas taught me to put up with shelling as one puts up with bad weather. I ignore the impulse to get up, turn in bed and pull the pillow over my head. My mind and body feel as if they are wrapped in cotton wool. Then there is a second explosion, followed by a third and a fourth. My mother Tamara's apartment, which has been my home since I was nine years old, and which is still my permanent address, is near two airports in the suburbs of Kyiv, Hostomel and Zhulyany. The Russians are bombing the airports.

I pull on a bathrobe and stagger into the living room. Tamara is up too. We embrace sleepily.

'It's started,' I tell her.

'I know,' she says. 'I'll make coffee.'

My family has seen too much drama to panic now. Tamara's training as a psychotherapist taught her how to stay calm.

We turn on the central heating and sit on the sofa in our night clothes, glued to Ukrainian television. War is often more auditory than visual. Our apartment is on the ground floor and we cannot see the aircraft bombing the airports. The pre-dawn darkness flickers from black to light grey each time an explosion lights up the horizon. The Russians attack Hostomel with cruise missiles, followed by helicopter gunships.

Hostomel has a very long runway that can accommodate the largest transport aircraft. The Russians intend to use it as an air bridge for an assault on Kyiv. The Ukrainians destroy the runway and kill about 300 Russian paratroopers on the first day. The following day, the Russians will seize Hostomel and surrounding villages, so they'll be just a few kilometres from our home.

'Shall we go up to the roof, Mama? We might be able to see the bombing.'

'Crazy girl! We need to call Svitlana and your brother and figure out what we are going to do.'

My aunt Svitlana is sixty-seven years old, ten years older than Tamara, and lives near a military base just outside Chernihiv, 140 kilometres to the north and on the invasion route from Belarus.

'It is very loud,' Svitlana complains over the telephone. We can hear explosions in the background.

'Go to the basement, Titka Svitlana,' I tell her, using the Ukrainian word for 'aunty'. Five years in the Ukrainian army have made me bossy, especially under bombardment.

Svitlana is stubborn. 'I don't want to. I'm too old and I'm not afraid to die.'

'Please, Titka. If you won't go to the basement, at least go into the bathroom, so you have two walls between you and the explosions.'

Then we call my younger brother, Bohdan. He is living in Lazarivka, about 80 kilometres to the west in Zhytomyr oblast, in the brick dacha that belonged to our late paternal grandmother, Lyuba.

'It's quiet here, for now,' Bohdan says. 'If the Russians come, I expect they'll loot the shop, but there's not much I can do about that. We've got plenty of food in the meantime. What are you two going to do? Why don't you come to Zhytomyr? I guess I'll join the Territorial Defence Forces. What do you think?'

'Bohdan, they want people with military experience,' I say. 'You're only twenty-two and you can't even remember how to hold a gun. I think you'd get in the way.'

Bohdan sounds crushed. 'I had a few months of cadet training, back in 2014. I'll give it a try. What about you, Sis?'

I tell my brother I'll ask Tamara to take me to the recruitment centre as soon as the bombing lets up. The moment I realized the full-scale invasion had started, I knew what my dead husband and father would expect of me.

A small voice argues with itself inside me. *This will be more dangerous than the last time. You could stay with Tamara and Bohdan in Lazarivka. It would reassure them, and the army wouldn't notice your absence.* But the opposing argument is stronger. *You are a commissioned officer. They trained you at the military academy. You have years of experience. Do you think you could live with yourself if you didn't volunteer?*

We move to the kitchen, with the radio on in the background.

'This is going to be a long day,' I say to Tamara. 'We'd better have some breakfast. After that, I want you to drive me to the recruitment centre at Svyatoshyn. I'll get a few things together. You should pack too, and go stay with Bohdan in the dacha. You may have to protect him from the Russians, because they'll be on the lookout for young men. If they take Kyiv, things will get very nasty. You'll be safer in the country. Take all the family documents – birth and death certificates, bank papers, property deeds. Take clean underwear, warm clothes, any medicines you might need.'

Tamara doesn't mind me bossing her around. 'What about the cats?' she asks, referring to our three moggies, Khoma, Ryzhyi and Symirochka.

'Take them with you. I know how much you love them, and they'll help you relax when things are stressful. They'll love being out in the country. You and the cats will be safer with Bohdan, far from Kyiv.'

In Donbas, it always makes me sad to see famished pets wandering the streets of deserted villages. I brought Khoma and Symirochka back from Donbas in 2018. Ryzhyi found us in Vyshneve. They are all street cats. When I return to the eastern front in June 2022, I adopt a black and white kitten called Villi. He lives with my platoon in our crumbling house at base camp. When I go on a mission or on leave, the boys look after him for me. It's an order.

While Tamara and I organize the logistics of our departure, excerpts of two speeches play over and over on the radio and television. President Volodymyr Zelenskiy had recorded a short, emotional address to the people of Russia the previous night, knowing the invasion was about to start. Zelenskiy says Putin refused to take his telephone calls. The attacks we are hearing are 'the beginning of a big war on the European continent', he says.

In another of several speeches on the 24th, Zelenskiy invokes Winston Churchill, saying the blasts are 'the sound of a new Iron Curtain, which has come down and is closing Russia off from the civilized world'. He tells European leaders in a video-conference that evening, 'This may be the last time you see me alive.'

If Russia tries to take Ukraine away from its citizens, Zelenskiy warns, 'We will defend ourselves. Not attack, but defend ourselves. And when you attack us, you will see our faces, not our backs, but our faces.'

Zelenskiy goes on to say the 'disaster' will carry a very high price, that the people of Russia will lose their money, reputation, quality of life and freedom. Most of all, he says, they will lose their loved ones and themselves. He insists that Ukraine is not a threat to Russia. He alludes to the violation of the Budapest Memorandum.

Independent Ukraine signed the memorandum in 1994, the year before I was born. Russia, the United States, the United Kingdom, China and France promised to guarantee Ukraine's security if we gave up our nuclear weapons. It's grotesque; Russia, which is supposed to be co-guarantor of our security, is now invading the whole country. The treaty isn't worth the paper it's written on. When Russia invaded Crimea and Donbas in 2014, NATO didn't lift a finger, and I don't expect them to do much now. It's almost laughable. Every country in the world will learn the lesson. If you have nuclear weapons, nobody messes with you. If you give them up, you get invaded.

Zelenskiy appeals to the citizens of the Russian Federation to force their president to 'stop now, before it is too late'. It is already too late.

Now it is Putin's turn. He seems to make the same address over and over. In his long, rambling lecture of 12 July 2021, the Russian dictator said Ukraine never existed, that Lenin made it up. He made a similar speech three days ago. The message is always the same: Ukraine and Russia are one country, one people. Russia has done so much for Ukraine, and Ukrainians are ungrateful. The Bolsheviks, Stalin and the West tore Ukraine from the body of Russia. Now NATO uses Ukraine to threaten Russia. Russia is the victim, not the aggressor.

Putin's speech is much longer than Zelenskiy's, and more old-fashioned. I don't take much of it in that morning, but later, on a slow day, I go back and read it on the Kremlin website.

Putin devotes about a third of his speech to the sins of the United States and the West. With Putin, it is always about history. Not history as it happened, but his distorted vision of the past. He laments the bombardment of Belgrade in 1999, the invasion of Iraq in 2003, US support for the uprising against the Syrian dictator Bashar al-Assad in the 2010s and the overthrow of the Libyan dictator Muammar Gaddafi.

For thirty years, Putin says, Russia has tried to come to an equitable agreement with NATO about security in Europe. 'We invariably faced either cynical deception and lies or attempts at pressure and blackmail, while the North Atlantic Alliance continued to expand despite our protests and concerns.' He is the aggrieved party. 'What is the explanation for this contemptuous and disdainful attitude to our interests and absolutely legitimate demands?' he asks.

It is true that fourteen former Warsaw Pact members have joined NATO since the fall of the Soviet Union, and that NATO promised in 2008 that Georgia and Ukraine could eventually join too. But Putin claims in the same speech to respect the independence of post-Soviet states. These countries flocked like frightened chicks to hide in NATO's skirts because they are scarred by centuries of Russian and Soviet imperialism.

Without going into detail, Putin harks back to US Secretary of State James Baker's promise to Mikhail Gorbachev after the fall of the Berlin Wall: that if the dying Soviet Union allowed East and West Germany to reunite, NATO would move 'not one inch' eastwards. 'They have deceived us … they have played us,' Putin says. 'Where is justice and truth here? Just lies and hypocrisy all around.'

Putin's main argument boils down to 'NATO made me do it'. It sounds absurd to Ukrainians, but that narrative has gained wide currency in much of the world, including within large swathes of the population in Western countries whose leaders support Ukraine.

'Any further expansion of the North Atlantic Alliance's infra-structure or the ongoing efforts to gain a military foothold on the Ukrainian territory are unacceptable to us,' Putin continues. He is claiming the right of veto over Ukraine's ability to join an alliance with any power other than Russia. 'The problem is that in territories adjacent to Russia, which I have to note is our historical land, a hostile "anti-Russia" is taking shape. Fully controlled from the outside, it is doing everything to attract NATO armed forces and obtain cutting-edge weapons.'

Note the reference to 'our historical land'. Putin simply does not accept Ukraine's independence. And he refuses to admit that Ukraine wants NATO as much or more than NATO wants Ukraine. An amendment to Ukraine's constitution in 2019 made joining NATO and the European Union our main foreign policy goal.

No Putin speech would be complete without a riff on the Great Patriotic War, as Russians call the Second World War. He repeats three times that Russia is fighting Nazis in Ukraine. Then he threatens to use nuclear weapons.

'Today's Russia remains one of the most powerful nuclear states,' Putin says, as if anyone could forget it. 'Moreover, it has a certain advantage in several cutting-edge weapons. In this context, there should be no doubt … that any potential aggres-sor will face defeat and ominous consequences should it directly attack our country ... No matter who tries to stand in our way or ... create threats for our country and our people, they must know that Russia will respond immediately, and the consequences will be such as you have never seen in your history.'

Such as you have never seen in your history. One doesn't know whether to laugh or tremble in trepidation.

Russia cannot survive unless Ukraine reverts to its former status as a Russian colony or satellite, Putin says. 'For our country, it is a matter of life and death, a matter of our historical future as a nation. This is not an exaggeration; this is a fact. It is not only a very real threat to our interests but to the very existence of our state and to its sovereignty... Russia cannot feel safe, develop and exist while facing a permanent threat from the territory of today's Ukraine.'

Minutes after the speech is broadcast, Putin launches more than 150 cruise and ballistic missiles from land, sea and air at Ukrainian cities. And he says *we* are threatening *him*.

Putin twice refers to a 'genocide' being perpetrated against Russian-speakers in Donbas. The idea that we committed 'genocide' by opposing the 2014 invasion and subsequent takeover of an integral part of our country by Ukraine's former colonial power is particularly absurd. I have been there. During my years in the eastern region, I saw a minority of corrupt, thuggish Russian-backed separatists torture and kill my brothers-in-arms.

Putin cloaks his violation of the United Nations Charter in legalese, going so far as to invoke as justification the right to self-defence, enshrined in article 51, Chapter VII of the charter. He says he is answering an appeal from the so-called People's Republics of Luhansk and Donetsk, the puppet regimes he set up in Donbas.

The Russian dictator alternates threats to use nuclear weapons with gems of Putinspeak. The gravity of events and the Orwellian quality of his invasion speech overcome my usual reluctance to listen to his mendacious verbiage. 'It is not our plan to occupy Ukrainian territory. We do not intend to impose anything on anyone by force... Freedom guides our policy.' He claims to perpetuate 'the culture and values' of Russian ancestors while he is killing Ukrainians, adding that 'having truth and justice on our side is what makes us truly strong'.

Russia is launching attacks over all Ukraine, descending from our northern border with Belarus, coming up from Crimea to the south and from Russia to the east. We fear it is only a matter of time before they reach Kyiv.

After daybreak there are longer pauses between detonations. At around eight o'clock I tell Tamara it is time to go. I put on my dog tags, which are on a chain with my dead husband Illia's wedding band and my own wedding ring. I pack a duffle bag with several changes of thermal underwear because it is very cold, uniforms, soap, toothpaste, toilet paper and my sleeping bag.

We get stuck in an enormous traffic jam created by hundreds of thousands of residents of Kyiv fleeing westward. Zelenskiy's first speech since the beginning of the onslaught comes on the radio shortly before nine o'clock.

'Today, Putin started a war against Ukraine, and against the entire democratic world,' Zelenskiy says. 'He wants to destroy our country, and everything we have been building. But we know the strength of the Ukrainian people. You are indomitable. You are Ukrainians.'

'Whatever you think of Zelenskiy, he has a way with words,' Tamara says. Her eyes scan the horizon, watching for aircraft or missiles.

'If Zelenskiy has found the fighting spirit today, it's a good thing,' I tell my mother. 'But he's a chameleon. He shares responsibility for this disaster. The army isn't ready because he campaigned for the presidency on promises of ending the war in Donbas.'

It is reported later that when the British and Americans offered to rescue Zelenskiy so that he could set up a government in exile, he replied, 'I need ammunition, not a ride.' In the West, people believe Zelenskiy galvanized the country and saved us from capitulation. Frankly, I think we would have fought even if he had left the country. Ukrainians have an anarchical, rebellious streak. Unlike Russians, we are individualistic. We know how to take the initiative. That is our biggest strength. We don't depend on the authorities. The country would not have collapsed.

'How are you feeling?' Tamara asks while we sit in traffic on the way to the recruitment centre. When Bohdan and I were children, she used to punish us for bad grades, but, to be fair, most parents did then. She apologizes for it now. Since she became a psychotherapist, Tamara worries more about our emotional and mental well-being. That brought us closer to her. My mother is my confidante, though we rarely have time for a heart-to-heart talk.

'To be honest, I'm relieved,' I tell her.

'What do you mean?'

I tell my mother that it makes things clearer for me, that I've had a hard time in the six months since I left the military. I had forgotten how to be a civilian. I joined the army straight out of university. For years I missed things like going shopping, wearing make-up, soaking in a hot bath, going to restaurants. But when I came back, these things seemed frivolous and alien to me, and no one understood. I missed my brothers-in-arms, and, I suppose, the excitement of battle. In Donbas, everything is black and white. Civilian life is grey. I was unsure of myself, like a blind person tapping with a cane, trying to find the way forward.

My departure from the military started out well enough. I went to Zakynthos in Greece for a week with my boyfriend, Mykyta. I'd been outside Ukraine before, but only for professional reasons. I had never taken a real holiday abroad. When I was in the army, I had to write reports and obtain permission for everything. Suddenly there was no need for that. I was free to do anything I wanted. Mykyta and I rented a car and drove all over the island. I was happy…

And then I wonder if Mykyta is all right. He's at the military academy in Lviv, which must be a target.

'Are you okay?' I text my sort of boyfriend. We met at the Ivan Bohun Military Lyceum (high school) in Kyiv, where I was put in charge of the first female platoon after my husband died. We started a serious relationship, and we were close.

'Woken up by air raid sirens,' Mykyta texts back. 'Things okay so far, but edgy. And you?'

'Tamara driving me to recruitment centre now. I want to go back to Donbas. More later. Love Yulia.'

'There. That's done,' I say out loud. 'Mykyta is a nice guy, but he's too young for me… We tried.'

'Do you love him?'

'I guess not, Mama. I'm not sure I can love anyone after Illia.'

'Give it time,' she says.

It takes a full-scale invasion for me to realize that the relationship with Mykyta is over. There is no dramatic break-up. We just drift apart. The war becomes an excuse to end it. He understands that I have other priorities, and he accepts it. We're still friends. Mykyta is a lieutenant now, like me, in a newly created brigade in Kyiv. Sometimes he asks me questions about the service and relationships in the unit, how he should behave as a commander. I have more experience and he needs support and advice.

I was depressed when I got back from Greece. I didn't know what to do with my life. I had resigned from the military because I didn't like the authorities, the president, the minister of defence. When I was in Donetsk between 2016 and 2018, we didn't have enough ammunition. That last winter, I remember my commanding officer saying, 'We're being shelled and bombed. We don't have anything to fire back. Are we supposed to use snowballs?'

After Zelenskiy signed the Steinmeier Formula in October 2019, the government actually paid soldiers not to fire back at the Russians. This was the follow-on to the Minsk I and II accords, thought up by the then foreign minister of Germany, Frank-Walter Steinmeier, who is Germany's president now.

After Steinmeier, you got a bonus of 5,000 hryvnia added to your salary if you didn't fight back. The military were enraged. Our defence minister, Lieutenant General Andriy Taran, had what I can only call a Soviet mindset. He was distant and uncommunicative. I thought they were destroying the army from the inside, that we were going back to the pro-Russian time before the 2014 revolution, to Yanukovych and the Party of Regions. Like Tato, I feared that Ukraine was doomed to be under Russia's boot again.

Tato, Dad in Ukrainian, was my father, Mykola, who died in 2020. Twenty-two years have passed since my parents divorced. Mykola was not a good husband, but Tamara never had another man and she never spoke ill of him. She is usually silent when his name comes up.

'Sometimes I wonder if I inherited a depressive gene from Tato,' I say to Tamara. 'Maybe it was sparked by what I saw in Donbas, or by the deaths of Illia and Tato. I found myself alone in your apartment while you were working on some kind of international psychotherapists' project in western Ukraine. Mykyta went back to being a cadet at the military academy. I didn't know what to do after five years of service. I had grown accustomed to the army, and I was used to strict rules. Suddenly I needed to take decisions and find a job, which I had never done before. I was lost. To tell the truth, I was suicidal.'

'Oh Yulia! Why didn't you call me?' Tamara is upset. A tear rolls down her cheek, the first I've seen on this terrible day.

'Don't worry, I'm okay now. You were busy, and I had to get through it on my own. It didn't last long, just a month or two.' It helped that I landed a job at Veteranius last October, helping veterans reintegrate into civilian life through information technology. It pulled me out of my depression. I enjoyed the work, and it was almost as if I was still in the army. I had become a civilian, but I was in touch with the military.'

Tamara is more worried about the present. She says, 'I don't know what is going to happen. I guess nobody knows, not Putin, not Zelenskiy, and certainly not us. You children are all I care about, and I want you to be safe. I'm uneasy about you going back to the army.'

'Of course you are. But I have to be there. I'd hate myself if I wasn't. I expected something like this, because the conflict was frozen.'

Despite the compromises he made, Zelenskiy didn't manage to make peace with Russia. He talked about giving autonomy to Donbas six months after he was elected, but he didn't have the political support to go through with it. The troops were furious when he agreed to dismantle some Ukrainian positions under the Steinmeier Formula, regardless of the fact that the Russians did not dismantle the positions they were supposed to. Then he announced that he would end conscription and that Ukrainian troops couldn't respond to Russian shelling, so as not to provoke them. I was sure that Putin would interpret these measures as signs of weakness and so would attack us. It was obvious for people in the military.

But most people just wanted to get on with their lives, jobs, families and mortgages. Nobody wanted to see a looming disaster. Many things were neglected. There were no troops at the border. There was no mobilization. My comrades who were in Donbas in 2021 said they told the government that things were heating up, but the government ignored it. The army on the ground knew the invasion would happen. When the intelligence services warned Zelenskiy in November 2021 that Russia was going to attack, he said, 'No, it's not going to happen.'

The rest of the world forgets that the war with Russia really started in 2014, with the invasion of Crimea and Donbas. We had already lost 14,500 lives before 24 February 2022. There were already more than a million refugees.

This wasn't the first time Russia had massed troops on our borders. Joe Biden and Boris Johnson were the only ones who believed Putin was about to invade. Zelenskiy was sceptical. He asked the Biden administration to tone down predictions because he was afraid they would create panic and destroy our economy.

Zelenskiy was so confident that he attended the Munich security conference just five days before the full-scale invasion. French president Emmanuel Macron went to Moscow to see Putin a couple of weeks earlier, saying that dialogue could prevent a conflict. There was a lot of hoping for the best.

Like many of my comrades, I expected an invasion, but not this soon. I thought there would be more signs of movement, that the Russians would prepare field hospitals and blood banks, which are first necessities for an invading army. There was none of that. I underestimated Putin's lack of concern for the well-being of his soldiers. I thought Putin was bluffing, and now I'm shocked too.

The 10-kilometre journey from Vyshneve to Svyatoshyn, both commuter towns west of Kyiv, takes us two hours because we are caught up in the exodus of fleeing civilians. We hear on the radio that there is heavy fighting around Sumy and Kharkiv in the north-east, in Mariupol in the south-east, in Kherson to the south and at Hostomel airport, just north of us. The Russians have captured the nuclear power plant at Chornobyl.

We finally arrive at the recruitment centre. Tamara plans to drive on to Zhytomyr oblast to be with Bohdan. 'Mama, stay with me for a while,' I say. 'Maybe things will calm down and it will be good for you to have a break from driving. We may not see each other for a long time.'

We are surprised by the size of the crowd at the recruitment centre. There are hundreds of men packed inside, and hundreds more outside. I make a mental note of the men around me so I can stop newcomers from jumping the queue, and I begin to wait, with Tamara beside me. We are the only women except for those processing applications inside. At lunchtime, Tamara brings sandwiches and coffee from a nearby café, so I don't lose my place in the queue.

'I think I should go now,' Tamara finally says. 'I don't want to be on the road after dark.' She takes me in her arms and says, 'I love you, Yulia.'

'I love you too, Mama.' For a split second I am a little girl again, terrified at the prospect of losing her. War holds so many unforeseen dangers. I am probably as worried about Tamara as she is about me. I feel a sob start to rise inside me and stifle it. Tamara is crying.

'Stop, Mama, please. They're staring at us.'

I am going through a rebellious phase, and I have dyed my hair bright pink. I don't want to draw any more attention to myself than I already have. The men have noticed me anyway because I'm a woman. I don't want them to see me crying.

The staff cannot cope with the sheer number of volunteers with military experience. They don't know what to do with me because I am a woman, so I wait. When I get hungry again, I ask someone to save my place while I buy food.

Some men are sent straight to the front line. More keep arriving to replace them. I ignore my fellow volunteers at first, but when we realize it is going to be a long night, we start talking about our military experience, about what brigades we want to join, where we want to fight. They seem impressed to learn that I spent two years in Donbas.

For the few first nights, I put two chairs together and sleep on them in my sleeping bag.

'So, why did Putin do this?' a large, bald man called Kostya, who is sleeping on the floor near me, asks just as I am about to fall asleep. Most of the men have brought bedding with them. The centre turns off the fluorescent strip lighting late at night, but light comes from the emergency exit signs and the screens of dozens of smartphones. Kostya stares at the ceiling and directs his question to no one in particular. 'I can't believe this is only about NATO,' he says.

'I think Putin wants our mineral wealth,' says a young scientist with black hair, a goatee beard and wire-rim glasses who is trying to find a comfortable position on the row of chairs behind me. 'There's a superpower race for rare earth metals and critical minerals. They're essential for the energy transition and for digital technology. And guess what? China and Russia are cornering the market. Ukraine has huge resources, especially in Donbas. Our agreement with the European Union includes a section on cooperation in mining. I think Putin wants to prevent that and seize our resources for Russia.'

'There may be some truth in that,' says Serhiy, a software programmer in his thirties. 'But I think that, most of all, Putin is afraid of our example. The last thing he wants is to have a successful democracy where people can say and do what they want to, where citizens vote in free and fair elections, right on his doorstep. The example would be a permanent incitement to rebellion in Russia.'

The conversation interests me, so I join in. 'There can be more than one reason,' I say. 'You may all be right, but I think the most important reason is Putin's obsession with history. He talks about it all the time. He thinks he is the reincarnation of Peter I. He says he is reconstituting Novorossiya, founded by Catherine II in 1764. When the separatists in Luhansk and Donetsk declared independence in 2014, they even called themselves Novorossiya. I think Putin's tirades against the European Union and NATO are just excuses. He can't stand it that Kyiv is hundreds of years older than Moscow. To be as great as they pretend to be, the Russians need historical roots that they don't have, but which we do. They must have Ukraine as part of their history, to proclaim their greatness.'

'You're right that it's about history, but I think it's about more recent history,' says Oleksii, a schoolteacher. 'Putin talks all the time about the Great Patriotic War. He talked about it in his speech this morning. He's stuck in a time warp, and he thinks he's refighting the Second World War. That's why he spouts all this rubbish about denazifying Ukraine. He wasn't even born then, for heaven's sake!'

Another volunteer, a man with grey hair whom the others call 'Grandpa', joins in. 'It's obvious to me,' Grandpa says. 'He wants to reconstruct the Soviet Union. Ukraine's independence in August 1991 was the nail in the coffin of the Soviet Union, which collapsed four months later. They never forgave us. In 1992 the Duma said Khrushchev had violated the law by giving Crimea to Ukraine. Putin says the fall of the Soviet Union was the greatest tragedy of the twentieth century. He's trying to reverse it.'

The officials at the recruitment centre are so overwhelmed that I volunteer to help them on the second day by filling out forms for the men who are joining up. There is still a lot of fighting in the Kyiv region, and we occasionally hear explosions. In the middle of the second night, in another television address, Zelenskiy summarizes casualties so far. At least 137 Ukrainians, civilians and military, have been killed, he says. More than 300 others have been wounded.

One reason I joined up was because I wanted a weapon. I had an AK-74 while I was in the army, but I had to give it back when I completed my contract in August 2021. For me, being under occupation without a weapon is the biggest nightmare. I wanted a gun to protect myself and my mother. I couldn't just sit in the apartment and wait for Russian tanks to drive down our street.

My instinct is right, because within days of the invasion it is impossible to buy firearms or body armour anywhere in Ukraine.

I am not the only one who feels this way. There is practically a stampede when they start handing out weapons at the recruitment centre. I am surprised to see another young woman ahead of me. She is about thirty years old, wears make-up and has long, painted fingernails. She has signed up for the Territorial Defence Forces.

The army recruiter holds up a Soviet-made PK machine gun.

'Give it to me!' says the young woman with the fingernails.

'I'm sorry. This is the last one and I promised it to this gentleman,' the recruiter says, nodding towards a middle-aged man who waits to one side.

'But I attended courses! I know how to use it!' the woman says, her voice rising.

'Here it is, Ivan,' the recruiter says, ignoring the woman and handing the machine gun to the man.

Ivan looks apologetically at Fingernails, but she doesn't give up. Everyone is watching and there's a stunned silence when she tries to wrest the machine gun from him.

'Give it to me. It's mine!' she shouts. Ivan bursts out laughing.

'I am a gentleman, as well as a trained machine gunner,' he says with an enormous grin. 'So I will give it to you. Thank you for making my day. I think the Russians are stupid to invade a country where girls are fighting for machine guns!' Everyone laughs now.

'Look how many of us there are,' says Ivan, sweeping an arm at the hundreds of men massed in the large hall. He is charismatic and speaks loudly so everyone can hear. 'Sister, brothers, you give me hope. We will defeat the invaders. *Slava Ukraini!*'

'*Heroyam slava!*' the crowd shout in unison before cheering the gallant machine gunner. Some have tears in their eyes.

We follow the war news on our smartphones. It is clear from day one that our Western backers will not send troops or become involved, because they're afraid of 'escalation'. We will drag the words 'risk of escalation' behind us like a ball and chain for years. What is the point of our allies helping us if they cannot do it wholeheartedly? Sometimes I think it would have been more merciful to let us be overrun. We need ammunition and armoured vehicles, aircraft and missiles. We are grateful, of course, but they always send too little, too late. Then they complain that we are not winning fast enough.

After four or five days, the recruitment centre offers me a position in the security unit that runs the centre. I accept, because areas on the outskirts of Kyiv such as Bucha, just 20 kilometres away, are occupied by the Russians. It is important to me to be near Tamara and our home in the event she needs protection. I wait until the Russians withdraw from the Kyiv and Zhytomyr oblasts in April to request transfer to the eastern front.

My unit operates a military refuelling station, so there are large fuel tanks next to the underground air raid shelter. Local women and the clerks in the recruitment centre run to the shelter every time the air raid sirens sound, which is several times a day. I don't like the shelter because I'm afraid the Russians will bomb the fuel tanks and there will be a huge explosion. I wear a uniform, and a big jacket against the cold. When I pull a knitted cap over my hair and most of my face, it is easy to mistake me for a man. Nobody notices when I follow the men into the recruitment centre, instead of going to the shelter.

Most of my compatriots divide their lives into before and after 24 February 2022. I already know what it is like to be at war with Russia. For me, the full-scale invasion marks the resumption of normal life. When I rejoin the army, I know I am in the right place. It seems perfectly natural. Not the war, but to be in the army. I cannot imagine doing anything else. It is a relief for me to be on active duty.

II

Return to Bucha

Ukraine is crying quietly
With tears and blood...
The executioner builds his tomorrow
On the human sorrow...
Ukraine is crying bitterly
And sobs heavily,
She washes with her tears
Her sons who died.
Mother Ukraine is crying,
Every mother weeps,
When she lets her son go
To gain freedom...

Taras Shevchenko, 'Ukraine Is
Crying Quietly', in *Testament*, 1848

Bucha, 30 kilometres north-west of Kyiv. April 2022

When Russian troops retreat from Bucha after a month-long
occupation, they leave behind a trail of bodies, many of them

mutilated, tortured and burned beyond recognition: 458 civilians in all, killed by bullets.

There are bodies lying face down in the street, some with their hands and feet tied, shot in the temple. A row of corpses, their wrists bound behind them with plastic restraints, lie crumpled against a wall after a firing squad-style execution. In transcripts of wire intercepts, Russian soldiers refer to the hunting down of individuals whose names appear on lists, to their arrest, torture and execution as *zachistka* or cleansing. Bodies are found in basements, in yards and in mass graves. Some have had their ears cut off and teeth extracted. Some have been flattened by Russian tanks. A soldier was heard boasting of shooting two Ukrainians through their apartment window. People who ventured out for food and water lie where Russian snipers felled them, clutching shopping bags.

A gynaecologist recounts having surgically reconstructed the ruptured genitalia of a twelve-year-old girl who was gang-raped by Russian soldiers after they shot dead her parents and the family dog. An image of a naked woman found dead, wrapped in a fur coat in the basement where she was raped, her hair matted with blood, makes a deep impression on me.

More than a year later, when I return home on leave from the eastern front, I will visit Tamara in our apartment in Vyshneve. She has been hired by the Ukrainian government to treat citizens traumatized by war, including female former prisoners who have been raped by Russian troops. Female soldiers, like me.

'If I have to choose between death and captivity, I will choose death, because I do not want to be tortured,' I say.

'Oh Yulia, I'll be devastated if anything happens to you! It's true that captivity is more dangerous for women. I can't lie to you; many women prisoners are raped, and it is hell for them. But you must tell yourself that the most important thing is to stay alive, that you can recover.'

'That is the thing I fear most. I could stand physical torture, but I would rather die than be raped.'

'Dreadful as these things are, you will be stronger if you prepare yourself mentally,' Tamara says. 'Women patients told me how they preserved themselves in prison. They stopped all hygiene. No washing, tooth-brushing or hair-combing. They smeared excrement over their bodies. It was their only hope of preventing their jailers from raping them, and it worked. They told me they did this.'

Evidence of atrocities at Bucha mounted in the hours following the retreat of Russian forces on 1 April. The killing started much earlier. The town's mayor, Anatoliy Fedoruk, told reporters on 7 March that dogs were already tearing bodies apart in the streets. In a February 2024 television interview with the American far-right presenter Tucker Carlson, Putin would claim that the former British prime minister Boris Johnson had sabotaged a peace deal in the spring of 2022. But there was no peace deal on the table. The extent of the horrors in Bucha led Zelenskiy to abandon peace negotiations in Istanbul, and all talk of accepting neutrality to end the war. Evidence of war crimes in Bucha also caused the suspension of Russia's membership of the United Nations Human Rights Council. The European Union stepped up economic sanctions against Russia and offered to fast-track Ukraine's application to join the EU.

Putin denies that Russian forces committed war crimes in

Bucha. He and the governments of China, Cuba, Nicaragua and Venezuela claim that the images of corpses, mass graves and underground dungeons have been faked. Amnesty International, Human Rights Watch, the BBC and the *New York Times* authenticate them.

The Ukrainian government holds the Russian 64th motorized rifle brigade responsible for most of the atrocities. Putin responds by elevating the 64th to Guards status on 18 April. They committed war crimes and Putin decorates them for 'professionalism'. It is his way of showing contempt for the Ukrainians and Americans and their posse of war crimes lawyers; his way of showing that he doesn't give a damn what anyone thinks of Russia's assault on Ukraine.

Russian nationalists communicating on the Telegram messenger service exhort Russian soldiers to rape more Ukrainian women, prostitute Ukrainian prisoners of war and commit mass murder. They market T-shirts emblazoned with the letter Z, the symbol of the Russian invasion, and the words 'Slaughter in Bucha; We Can Do It Again'.

Once the bodies are collected and buried, my army unit is assigned to conduct night patrols through Bucha, Hostomel and Irpin. We are supposed to catch collaborators, marauders and deserters. I saw devastated towns in eastern Ukraine between 2016 and 2018, but driving with comrades in a Humvee through Bucha's silent, darkened streets lined with gutted buildings affects me differently. Bucha was the scene of my early childhood.

When I enter Bucha on patrol a few nights after the Russian retreat, I do not recognize the place where I spent the first five years of my life, and which I have visited innumerable times since. Those shops and houses that are not reduced to rubble are scarred and blackened. Burned-out vehicles line the streets. Nothing seems to be in the right place. There is an other-world-liness about the disorder and destruction. I feel numbed, as if I have entered a parallel universe.

Tamara and I worried a lot about Viktoria and Oleh, our former neighbours and closest friends in Bucha, while the Russians were there. Viktoria was my nanny from the age of three until I was five. She is one of my sweetest memories from a child-hood that was often unhappy. She rang several times during the Russian occupation and said three words before hanging up: 'I am alive.' We assumed she wanted to reassure us without giving the Russians a pretext to arrest her.

Back in the late 1990s, it was Viktoria who dressed me and combed my hair, with infinite tenderness, before walking me to the local kindergarten after Tamara went to work in the morning. When I was in a school play, Viktoria made my costume. I feasted on the sticky buns she baked, and pulled apart the warm, doughy loaves she made for our congregation at the Good News Baptist Church. I often slept over at Viktoria and Oleh's apartment, in the same five-storey complex where we lived. My favourite toy, a bunny, stayed in their home. I spent summer holidays with them. She was Titka Viktoria, Aunty Viktoria, and we were very close. Because Viktoria and Oleh had no children of their own, I was like a surrogate daughter to them. Viktoria is more traditional than my own mother. She loves handicrafts and gardening and taught me to plant flowers and dry them between the pages of the Bible. From her, I learned to love Ukrainian embroidered clothing known as *vyshyvanka*.

After my unit is assigned to patrol Bucha, I go to Viktoria and Oleh's apartment block at the first opportunity. Tamara and Bohdan are still in Zhytomyr, so they have not been able to visit. Viktoria's brief phone calls have stopped and I haven't been able to reach her. I am worried.

The building where my family once lived is run down and the windows are broken, but it is still standing. I can see Viktoria's potted plants on the first-floor balcony. I leave my comrades waiting in the Humvee and bound up the stairs in a welter of emotion, wearing my camouflage uniform, carrying my assault rifle and a bag of vegetables that Tamara has sent from the garden in Zhytomyr. There is no electricity, so I don't bother ringing the doorbell. I knock softly, because I don't want to frighten Viktoria.

I recognize the sound of Viktoria's gentle footfall. A shadow falls across the peephole and I know she is there on the other side. The door swings open and Viktoria throws herself into my arms. It is years since I have seen her. She seems smaller, diminished.

'Yulia,' she cries, 'Oh Yulia!' with tears streaming down her face. Viktoria leads me by the hand into the living room, where a large photograph of Oleh sits on the coffee table, the corner of the frame crossed diagonally with a black sash. Despite the war, their friends and neighbours have brought sympathy bouquets which wilt in vases.

'Oleh?' I ask, knowing the answer.

Viktoria looks at the framed photograph as if addressing her dead husband. 'He helped many people survive the occupation.' Oleh smiles back from the picture. He was a kind, uncomplicated man, a labourer.

'The Russians made their headquarters in the kindergarten, the one that you attended. They rounded up townspeople and held them prisoner in the schoolyard at gunpoint. People were desperate, cold and hungry. Some of them were ill. Oleh thought the Russians would not hurt him, because his father was Russian. He tried to negotiate with them for food, medicine and water. They were moody and often drunk. They shot him dead in front of me, for no apparent reason.' Weeks have passed and Viktoria is calm as she tells me what happened. Serene. In a way almost happy.

I hold Viktoria's hand and try to comfort her. She does not answer. I see a lump go up and down in her throat as she swallows hard.

'Dear Titka Viktoria, you must see a counsellor, someone kind, like Mama. It will help you to talk about it. There are so many people grieving.'

'No, no. It really isn't necessary,' Viktoria says, shaking her head. 'I have my church, my faith and my memories. Oleh is with God.'

Oleh's black Labrador, Graf, sits on the floor looking up at Viktoria.

'Would you like to see Oleh's grave?' Viktoria asks.

'Of course.' I think momentarily of my comrades waiting in the vehicle outside and decide it doesn't matter. I would do the same for them.

Viktoria has aged a great deal. She seems older than Tamara now, though she's a decade younger. She moves slowly, gathering up her coat and keys for the short walk to the cemetery. Graf follows close behind us. What a strange picture we must make, the uniformed army lieutenant toting an assault rifle and the solemn Ukrainian housewife, walking arm in arm through the desolate streets of Bucha, trailed by an arthritic black dog.

Oleh's grave has a granite slab with the same photograph I saw in the apartment engraved on it, the same wilting flowers. Small blue and yellow Ukrainian flags are stuck in the ground around its contours. Viktoria stares at the earthen mound with an almost beatific smile. Her eyes are watery, but no tears fall now. She appears to be in communion with the grave, not alone, but in denial.

'Do you like his headstone? I was lucky to get it made so quickly. The local stonemason has been overwhelmed with orders since the Russians pulled out... Oleh was a good man. He is at peace and with God now,' Viktoria says, repeating her words in the apartment. I do not know if I believe it, but she does.

'Do you want to see Andriy's grave?' she asks after a few minutes.

'Andriy? Is he dead too?' Andriy was a childhood friend to me, just a few years older, handsome with dark hair and eyes.

'Andriy helped set up the Territorial Defence Force in Bucha,' Viktoria says. 'He enrolled a lot of people from our church. He was such a quiet man; you would not have thought he could be so brave. He and his comrades were the first ones shot at the beginning of the occupation. They'd been captured and tried to escape. We found their bodies on the ground, near the city council building. His widow was devastated.'

I remember now seeing a video recorded by the resistance. Six or eight men are shown running across the street with their hands tied and the Russians chasing them. I was still at the recruitment centre, just 20 kilometres away, and we were horrified by it. I saw the town hall, but I didn't recognize Andriy.

'That is so sad, Viktoria.'

My childhood nanny shrugs, as if to say it doesn't matter.

'And ye shall hear of wars and rumours of wars: see that ye be not troubled: for all these things must come to pass, but the end is not yet,' Viktoria says, quoting the Gospel. 'Signs of the times,' she adds. 'Our Lord will come soon.'

The Russians shot so many Ukrainian men in Bucha that I suspect it was a deliberate strategy, to reduce the pool for mobilization. I think they wanted to eliminate the male population, so that only women survived. I shudder to think what they might do to my little brother.

But instead of seizing Kyiv, the glittering first prize, the Russians have been driven out of the region. Commentators said they brutalized Bucha for revenge, after taking heavy losses at Hostomel airport, five and a half kilometres away, and losing an entire column of armoured vehicles on Vokzalna Street.

In Bucha and elsewhere, Ukrainians demonstrate the skills they learned from NATO advisers, destroying the first and last tank or armoured vehicle in a column with Javelin shoulder-fired anti-tank missiles which the United States gave us long before the invasion. The rest of the column is trapped and easily picked off, one tank or vehicle at a time. Javelins become a sort of cult weapon. I've heard of people naming pets Javelin, their baby sons and daughters Javelin or Javelina. There are Javelin toys for children, Javelin T-shirts and online memes of saints cradling Javelins. By 2023, we will have more than 5,000 American Javelins and as many British NLAWs, which stands for Next-generation Light Anti-tank Weapons. The NLAWs are smaller and lighter than the Javelins, and easy to transport. You can learn how to use one in less than a day.

On patrol in Bucha and Irpin, I decipher graffiti that has been spray-painted in Russian. It says things like 'You don't need to live this well' and 'Why is there so much luxury here?' Bucha and Irpin were affluent commuter towns. The Russian soldiers were poor, and they discovered the comfortable homes of the Ukrainian middle class. Some had never seen flush toilets, which they mistook for spring wells. I think they were jealous in a primitive, vengeful way. They must have had approval from their superiors, but it also came from the envy and hatred inside them. It reminds me of the way the Soviet army went on the rampage in Berlin at the end of the Second World War. The Soviets raped tens of thousands of German women. They stole watches and underwear.

Driving through Bucha at night is an eerie experience. The jagged outlines of destroyed buildings stand black against the sky. Suddenly I see a lone electric light bulb burning inside a house.

'Look! There on the right. Someone has batteries or a generator. Let's have a look,' I say to my comrades in the Humvee.

We park a few dozen metres from the house and advance slowly, crouching with assault rifles at the ready. The yard and house are a shambles, very dirty and neglected. 'Stay on the path. Watch out for mines and unexploded ordnance,' I say.

'They must be squatters,' I think out loud.

'With a generator?' says one of my soldiers. 'Seems unlikely.'

'Look there,' another soldier whispers, pointing. Discarded cardboard and khaki-coloured foil packaging marked 'military rations' in Russian are scattered around the yard.

I gesture to my soldiers to be quiet as we climb the steps

and slip through the front door. The entrance and hallway are stacked high with appliances: refrigerators, washing machines, microwaves, televisions – things that obviously don't belong there. At the end of the corridor is a room where two Ukrainian men talk while they warm themselves in front of a fire. When they see us standing in the doorway, the younger one reaches for a gun on the table.

'Drop it! Hands up!' I shout. I and the two soldiers behind me move into the room while the others stand guard outside. Our sights are trained on the two men. I am wearing a helmet and flak jacket and the place is poorly lit, so they probably do not realize I am a woman until they hear my voice. I'm not sure which surprises them more; Ukrainian troops bursting into their hideout, or the fact that they are being apprehended by a woman. They hold up their hands.

'What is all this stuff?' I ask, gesturing at the appliances that surround us.

'We're shopkeepers here in Bucha,' says the man who tried to reach for the gun. 'We ordered a lot of merchandise before the war, and we brought it here for safekeeping.'

We cannot help laughing at their preposterous story. They look more like thieves than shopkeepers to me. 'And the Russian rations in the yard?' I ask.

'There was no food during the occupation. We bought them from the soldiers,' the other man says.

'Handcuff them,' I tell my men. 'Call the police and the National Guard to come and arrest them.'

We spend an uneasy hour waiting with our prisoners. What if more Russian collaborators show up? There are only four of us. What if we are ambushed? The younger one wants to make conversation, but we ignore him. I suspect they betrayed members of the resistance to the occupiers, probably out of greed rather than ideology. The Russians must have rewarded them by giving them carte blanche to steal. Many collaborators fled with their Russian masters, but these two stayed behind. Greed may have done for them; they didn't want to leave their booty.

Another night we are driving down the little road between Bucha and Hostomel. The towns in the area are surrounded by forests. We move slowly and shine torches into the woods. We see movement among the trees, stop the vehicle and get out. There are only two of us tonight, so we radio for reinforcements. Two more comrades arrive and we move into the forest, again watching out for landmines. We find three grimy, shabbily dressed men huddled in a small encampment amid the pine trees. At first we think they might be homeless civilians. But they answer in Russian, with Russian accents. We train our guns on them and they raise their hands above their heads.

'Kneel on the ground,' I tell them. 'Give us your documents.'

'We have no documents,' one of the men mumbles.

'You are Russian deserters?'

'Yes,' he nods sheepishly.

'How did you end up here?'

'We are against the war. We did not want to kill Ukrainians.'

You wanted to save your skins, and it was more dangerous to keep fighting than to desert, I think to myself.

'We threw our uniforms away and we put on whatever clothes we could find. Please, madam, have mercy. We are very hungry. Do you have food?' the deserter says.

Again, we radio the police and National Guard to fetch them. I give them some rations from the back of the Humvee, with mixed feelings. They are victims of Putin's misrule, like us.

They probably did not want to be sent to Ukraine, but they are nonetheless the enemy. They may have killed Ukrainian soldiers or civilians.

The deserters throw themselves on the rations like starving dogs.

I am tired of doing patrols in Kyiv oblast and I long to return to the brigade I served with for two years from 2016. I telephone my friend Mila, a paramedic the same age as me. She joined the 54th mechanized brigade when my late husband Illia and I did. Unlike me, Mila never left Donbas. She has served there continuously since 2016 and knows the entire brigade and then some.

I tell Mila that I want to return to the eastern front and ask if there is a platoon up for grabs. She knows of two vacancies. The observation unit needs a commander, but the sergeant is jealous of his turf and could be a problem. The other opening is to command a UAV aerial reconnaissance platoon.

'Nobody goes on foot patrols with binoculars anymore,' Mila says. 'We launch drones from dugouts on the front line and watch the enemy that way.'

Mila remembers how keen I was on drones when we were stationed near Svitlodarsk in 2017. 'You were the first person I heard talking about them. You told everyone it was crazy to risk soldiers' lives when we could do reconnaissance with winged machines,' she says, urging me to apply to command the drone unit. I thank her profusely.

The battalion has been temporarily assigned to the base at Maryinka, just south-east of Donetsk city. Mila praises the new company commander, Captain Dmytro, describing him as young, intelligent and a great guy. She tells me how to reach him. He accepts my candidacy with enthusiasm. All I have to do now is wait.

One night my unit is assigned to staff a checkpoint outside the high walls of a factory in the Kyiv region. It is a proper checkpoint with a small guard house and a stove which warms us. There is nothing to indicate what is produced in the factory. Like the good soldiers we are, we do not ask.

Around midnight we hear the whoosh of a missile. The air pressure changes. The windows in the guard house implode, propelling razor-sharp pieces of glass into the room. Our body armour protects us, but a comrade is cut on the hand. The missile explodes a few hundred metres beyond us. We are thrown to the floor by the power of the blast, which is the loudest noise I have ever heard. I think of a high-rise building collapsing, or dozens of cargo containers being dropped from a great height onto a concrete surface. We rush to a nearby shelter. The next morning, I learn that the Russians have attacked the Neptune anti-ship missile factory. It may be vengeance, for the Neptune factory is a link in one of the war's more colourful sagas.

On the evening of 13 April, the Ukrainian military reported that two Neptune missiles hit the Russian missile cruiser *Moskva*, the flagship of the Russian Black Sea fleet, south of Odesa and east of Zmiinyi or Snake Island. The missiles started a fire which reached the warship's ammunition store. It blew up, sinking the vessel the following morning. Russia did not admit that the *Moskva* had been struck by Ukrainian missiles, only that a fire on board detonated munitions. Moscow initially said all crew had been evacuated. A court in Sevastopol later confirmed the deaths of seventeen missing crew members, though there were rumours of far more casualties. The *Moskva* was the largest Soviet or Russian warship to be sunk since the Second World War, and the first Russian flagship sunk since the Russo-Japanese war of 1905.

Two days before the *Moskva* sank, the Ukrainian postal service issued a million postage stamps showing a Ukrainian soldier standing on the shoreline, giving the finger to the *Moskva*. The stamp commemorated an incident on the first day of the war, when the *Moskva* ordered a thirteen-man Ukrainian border guard unit on Snake Island, near the Danube delta in the Black Sea, to surrender. Their commander, border guard Roman Hrybov, responded, 'Russian warship, go fuck yourself.'

Hrybov's words became a slogan, printed on T-shirts, billboards and protest banners, as well as on the commemorative stamp. He and his comrades were taken prisoner and later released. The sinking of the *Moskva* was a huge morale boost for Ukraine and a humiliation for Putin. Experiencing the missile strike on the Neptune factory makes me feel almost personally involved in the story of the bullying warship that got its just desserts.

We are encouraged by every act of heroism in those early weeks of the war. Several times, Ukrainians risked their lives to block Russian tanks and armoured personnel carriers with their bodies. There was nearly always someone with a smartphone to record instances of bravery. The videos were relayed millions of times on social media platforms and shown on television screens around the world.

Videos from Kherson warmed my heart, all the more so because the city fell on 2 March as a result of treachery. General

Serhiy Kryvoruchko, the head of the security service SBU in Kherson, and his deputy, Colonel Ihor Sadokhin, had let the Russians drive up from Crimea unopposed. But Kherson's citizens refused to passively accept Russian rule. They continued to show that they did not want to live under occupation, that they wanted the Ukrainian army. They demonstrated in large numbers, waving flags and banners, knowing the Russians might shoot them. I thought: *This is the way it is when people work together for the same goal, in unity, in the hope of stopping the occupiers.* Such feelings were extremely powerful for the first six months of the war. People were truly resisting. I was inspired by this and felt proud of my compatriots.

When Kherson was liberated on 9 November 2022, Ukraine exploded with joy. I was back in Donetsk oblast by then, and I watched the scenes of cheering, flag-waving Ukrainians throwing flowers and kissing our troops as they drove into the city. I envied the way the soldiers were welcomed, because I have served only in the Kyiv and Donetsk oblasts during active fighting, and none of the units I have served with have been greeted like heroes.

When the Russians moved into Luhansk and Donetsk in 2014, only a few people there protested. We liberated several towns during my first tour of duty in Donetsk, but I had the impression that people did not really want us there. Some even considered us to be occupiers. It was terribly demoralizing.

We call the people in Donbas who are sitting on the fence or waiting for the Russians to liberate them *pochekuny* or 'waiters'. There is even a meme that represents them. The fat, Buddha-like creature looks like a sitting bear. He wears a T-shirt and twiddles his thumbs. The Russians have their own word for 'waiters': *zhduny*, for Ukrainians in Crimea who hope for the return of Crimea to Ukrainian rule.

Few of the 'waiters' express their opinions openly. Most stay silent. I don't try to talk to them. Many inhabitants of Donbas tolerate us because they understand that it is in their economic interest to have us deployed there. Some of the local residents cheer for Ukraine. They are glad to see us, and they say so, but I fear they are a minority. Each time we lose territory, I worry about these people. I am afraid that their neighbours will denounce them as pro-Ukrainian, and they will be punished by the Russians.

The pro-Ukrainians I talk to in Donbas claim that 80 per cent of the people they know are waiting for the Russians. I'm not sure that is a reliable statistic, but in Luhansk and Donetsk, the 'waiters' certainly make up a higher percentage of the population than elsewhere in Ukraine.

Yet as the war wears on, I have begun to see the attitude of the 'waiters' changing. The Russians use the locals as front-line cannon fodder. Pro-Russian Ukrainian fighters are not valued or honoured. They receive no benefits or status. I have no definitive proof that public opinion in Donbas is changing. My perception is based on conversations I have had and what I see in interviews and on social media.

Most of the pro-Ukrainian people in Donbas fled westwards, which partly explains why the proportion of pro-Russian 'waiters' is so high there. Another reason is that the Soviet Union forcibly settled ethnic Russians in Donbas between the two world wars, to work in the mines and industry. Many of the 'waiters' are their descendants. If you want to know whether you are dealing with a Russian, we say, ask where the person's grandparents are buried.

The Soviets disrupted millions of lives through mass deportations of indigenous populations – for example the Tatars of Crimea, whom they replaced with ethnic Russian settlers.

One of the most pro-Ukrainian communities in Donetsk is called Zvanivka, where I was stationed for six months in 2022/23. Its inhabitants are an ethnic and linguistic sub-group of Ukrainians called Boykos. The Soviets forcibly moved them from western Ukraine to the east in 1951, because they were suspected of anti-Soviet agitation, and because the USSR made a deal giving their land to Communist Poland.

The area that was populated by Ukrainians from the west of the country remains very different from the rest of Donetsk. The inhabitants speak Ukrainian and welcome our troops.

We need heroic deeds to keep up our morale, because the life-blood of our nation is seeping away in the form of millions of refugees, an entire generation of children.

Most of my relatives volunteer right away for the Territorial Defence Forces or the army. All stay in Ukraine. My brother Bohdan joins the TDF and tries to join the army, but they won't take him because he has no military experience. I ask him to stay with Tamara because she needs support, which unfortunately I cannot give her.

I have a few acquaintances who flee abroad, mostly women and children. Everyone has his or her reasons for leaving. It would be wrong for me to judge a woman who wants to save her children. I don't think they are doing anything bad. Although I am not a mother, I can understand what it must be like. They are afraid. But I cannot understand why Ukrainian refugees do not return now that most of the country has stabilized. Yes, there are air raid sirens and drone attacks, but this has become the new normal. Going to the basement or shelter is a routine part of everyday life. I do not understand why people refuse to return to their homeland.

It annoys me when Ukrainians living abroad complain. For example, I read articles about problems between Ukrainian refugees and the social services in Germany. They can take your child away from you if you slap him or her. There may be cultural differences, but I'm sorry; if you leave your homeland and move to another country, you must obey their rules. It reminds me of Russians who go abroad and try to recreate their own little version of Russia.

A soldier in my platoon has a wife and two children who are refugees in Scotland. Scottish social services require them to make a video call every week to their father who is fighting in the east. I think this is so that children do not lose contact with their homeland, so they will want to return one day. This is mandatory and it's a good thing.

There are Ukrainians who stay in western Europe because they earn more money there, which is shameful to me. I've been scandalized to learn from Ukrainian officials that thousands of pro-Russian Ukrainians who had lived under occupation in Crimea and Donbas – and accepted Russian passports – travelled through Russia to EU member states because they could not resist the opportunity to settle in prosperous countries and obtain social welfare payments by claiming to be refugees. It's an awkward issue, because the majority of refugees have fled out of fear for their own safety and the safety of their children. Security is a long-term issue, because after the war Ukraine will not feel economically, politically or militarily safe for a very long time. There will be thousands of mines and pieces of ordnance lying around. And we will always fear another Russian onslaught.

While I am patrolling Bucha and the outskirts of Kyiv, the Russians double-down with a vengeance on the south and east of the country.

Mariupol is, along with Bucha, where Russia shows its true face in the first months of the full-scale invasion. The siege of Mariupol starts on 24 February and lasts for eighty-six days. An estimated 25,000 Ukrainians are killed. Three brave journalists – the cameraman and director Mstyslav Chernov, photographer Evgeniy Maloletka and producer Vasilisa Stepanenko – risk their lives to record the destruction of the city for the Associated Press. They share the 2023 Pulitzer Prize for Public Service and their film, *20 Days in Mariupol*, wins the Oscar for best documentary in March 2024.

On 9 March 2022, the Russians bomb a maternity and children's hospital in Mariupol. Maloletka's photograph of a pregnant woman, Iryna Kalinina, being carried out on a stretcher is seen around the world. She dies from shrapnel wounds and her baby boy is stillborn. She and her husband Ivan had intended to call him Miron, from the Russian word for peace. The Russians claim the photograph is faked, just as they claimed that the corpses in Bucha were actors who, after the photographs were taken, got up and walked away.

I am frustrated to be stuck in Kyiv oblast, where it is relatively quiet, rather than fighting in Mariupol where the war is raging. War resembles normal life in that way; one is rarely in the right place at the right time.

I visited Mariupol three times, in 2015, 2018 and 2019. I liked the city's architecture and its busy port on the Sea of Azov. In the spring of 2015, I went there to spend a weekend with Illia, who had been based nearby at Shyrokyne since the war started in 2014. We got engaged that weekend in Mariupol. In 2018, I scattered Illia's ashes at Shyrokyne, because it was a special place to him. I returned to stay with friends the following year. When you see a city that has been important in your life being flattened in relentless bombardments, it hurts as if that city were a person you loved.

If I had fought in Mariupol, I might have been killed or captured, like the soldiers who took refuge in the Azovstal steel plant. Survivors of the siege were taken to Olenivka prison in Donbas, where more than fifty were killed and about one hundred wounded in an explosion on 29 July 2022. The Russians claimed the prison was hit by a US-made HIMARS (High Mobility Artillery Rocket System), but a UN report says it was not. We think the Russians bombed the prison wing to hide their ill-treatment of Ukrainian prisoners. Those who have been released in exchanges say they were tortured, crowded into small cells and deprived of food and water. When the explosion happened, the Russians provided no medical care for the wounded.

From Kyiv to Donetsk oblast. June 2022

My request to be transferred back to the 54th mechanized brigade in Donetsk oblast makes its way slowly through the army bureaucracy. It always takes more time to transfer an officer than an enlisted man or woman, but it seems to happen much faster for my male colleagues. I may be paranoid, but I wonder if the delay is a question of my skills or my gender. After all, I am qualified to command a motorized infantry unit, a much-needed speciality.

I call Mila to tell her I am returning. Between packing for front-line duty and saying farewells, I start watching the defence

ministry's videos for drone operators, on the Prometheus education platform. My soldiers in Donbas will help me master the
technical nuances. They are new to it too, so we'll learn together.

The women's veterans' group Veteranka helps me buy a
second-hand Mercedes four-wheel drive vehicle to rejoin my
battalion. It isn't practical to travel by train, because I am carrying a lot of equipment. I want to contribute something useful to
my brigade, so I drive the vehicle to Donetsk oblast and it stays
with us. I still drive it around the combat zone. Volunteers from
Veteranka pack the vehicle with sought-after items, including
camouflage nets, petrol and drones. I am like Father Christmas
arriving with a sleigh full of presents at an important time in
the battle.

I drive for ten hours from Kyiv to Donetsk oblast. The last
part of the journey is cross-country, off-road. I am alone. I am
alert for the entire time, thinking about the front line, which is
very unstable. I check constantly whether this or that road is
safe, if it has been captured. And I listen to the vehicle's engine,
which is not new.

Although I know where I am going and have been in touch
with my welcoming commanding officer, I am a little nervous. I
have been away from Donbas for four years. I am afraid I may
have lost my touch as an officer. Will the staff accept me? What
should I say to Captain Dmytro when I arrive?

I need not have worried. The soldiers who served with me
during my previous tour of duty in Donbas are glad to see me.
'We've been waiting for you. What took you so long? It's about
time!' they say. In the end, it is very easy, like coming home.

III

Return to Donbas

Don't send us back to our parents
We don't want them to see us like this
Let them think of the little children they miss
And remember us as naughty adolescents.

Boys with bruised knees and toy slingshots
With Fs on tests and armfuls of apples
Stolen from the neighbours' orchards.
Let our parents hope that one day we will come back
Let them hope that we are still somewhere...

But today we are still digging
This precious Ukrainian soil
This sweet and dear land.
With sapper shovels we are writing together
All over her body
The last poem of Ukrainian literature.
We are still alive. We are still here.

Ukrainian army private Borys Humenyuk,
'Testament', 2014. Humenyuk has been
missing in action since 2022.

Donetsk oblast. Summer 2022

After he annexed Crimea in the immediate aftermath of the 2013/14 Maidan revolution, Putin started the creeping annexation of Ukraine's two easternmost regions, the oblasts of Luhansk and Donetsk. Both share borders with Russia and together comprise Donbas, an abbreviation for Donetsk coal basin.

The war started here in the spring of 2014 with rent-a-mob demonstrations by pro-Russian separatists and a huge influx of Russian 'tourists', who were in fact intelligence officers and military without insignia; the same 'little green men' who had invaded Crimea. Exerting control over all of Donetsk and Luhansk was Putin's minimum war objective.

During my first tour of duty in Donetsk oblast between 2016 and 2018, the war settled into a frozen conflict. When I returned in June 2022, the shelling was more intense but everyday life on the front line had otherwise changed little. The attitude of my comrades towards me as a woman had, however, changed a great deal. It is easier now for a woman to integrate smoothly into the army. Soldiers no longer question my presence. Captain Dmytro, the commander of my company, whose call sign is Shaman or medicine man, leads by example, prompting his men to shed any bias they have against women in the combat zone.

My platoon, known informally as the Hellish Hornets, is one of five in Captain Dmytro's company of 128 soldiers. Going up the hierarchy, there are several companies in our battalion, and several battalions in our brigade of about 4,000. Almost everything happens at company level. Additional units who are not officially part of our brigade nonetheless fight in our front-line positions, under the leadership of our commanders. They include Territorial Defence, National Guard and border guard units, and their numbers are increasing. The soldier count is fluid. It is not written in stone that my company must number 128 soldiers. Sometimes we are more, sometimes less. Except for the assault fighters, everyone can multi-task. We are much more flexible than the Russians.

In June and July 2022, my company is stationed at Maryinka, just west of Donetsk city. Morale and motivation run high, and we are eager to attack Russian lines. With Captain Dmytro's blessing, I enrol in a class for officers about how to lead an assault. The class is given by combat-proven officers on the training base at Kurakhove, 20 kilometres west of Maryinka. Assault is the most dangerous military operation, the feat that every warrior dreams of. I feel certain my dead husband and father would have encouraged me to sign up.

'When Russia steals territory from your country, the only way to get it back is to fight for it,' Major Mykhailo exhorts us on the first day of assault class. 'You must attack them, stage assaults, many assaults, go on the offensive. Russia occupies 20 per cent of our country. We need daring and dramatic action… The question we all grapple with is how do you stage an assault without dying? That is the riddle that everyone wants to solve. The more combat you have witnessed, the more obvious the dilemma. Territory cannot be regained without sacrifice, but the human cost of an assault can be prohibitive, especially when one is fighting for a few hundred metres.'

Major Mykhailo emphasizes the importance of preparation. 'You must have a plan. You must know where you are going, how many of the enemy you are facing, what kind of weapons he has. Russian air defences make it too dangerous for us to fly our scarce fighter bombers, and our air defences mostly deter the Russians from flying theirs, so you'll have to stage assaults without air support. You'll rely on aerial reconnaissance from drone units like Lieutenant Mykytenko's Hellish Hornets,' he says, nodding to me on the front row. I am happy to have our role recognized, but a little embarrassed to be singled out from my classmates.

'Your soldiers must know how to take decisions in the heat of battle,' the major continues. 'And if at some point it becomes apparent that contact with the enemy is futile, the commander must make the crucial decision to retreat. Every assault is different. Sometimes the enemy is weak and does not fight back. Sometimes he is fierce and fights to the last bullet. You must adjust your response, know when to engage the artillery, call in reinforcements, or wait until the enemy runs out of ammunition.'

A few months later, surprise offensives in the Kharkiv and Kherson oblasts, in the north-east and south of the country, will liberate nearly 75,000 square kilometres of Russian-occupied territory. Though I and my comrades are frustrated not to participate, we know we have contributed by holding the line in Donbas. Collectively, we are flush with victory. We still believe that little Ukraine can defeat giant Russia. We feel the Armed Forces of Ukraine are invincible.

One of the best things about the assault training is getting to know Andriy, a sergeant who is two years older than me and who has since become my right-hand man in the platoon. Although it is not official, I consider Andriy to be my deputy commander. He is intelligent, hard-working and totally reliable. Before the war, he built websites as an IT expert. I think that's how he developed such a strategic brain. He is also interested in people and knows how to put them at ease. Soldiers come to him with their problems. He is a little on the shy side, but he is

a good communicator and I can ask him to deal with soldiers
or officials when I don't want to.

*

In July 2022, my company moves 175 kilometres northwards to
the village of Zvanivka, above Bakhmut and Soledar and facing
Russian troops who have recently seized the city of Lysychansk.
Zvanivka is populated by Boykos.

I continue to study drone tutorials online in my spare time,
but my ambition to command an assault group lingers. Captain
Dmytro sends such units on raids against Russian lines fairly
often. I ask if he would consider sending me on a mission.

'Are you sure you are ready, Lieutenant?'

'I want to go, sir.'

'I know that, but are you sure you are ready? Wanting to go
and being physically and mentally prepared are not the same
thing. I know you are a brave soldier, but an assault mission
is unique. It takes extraordinary self-control to advance in the
face of enemy fire, to shoot men dead at close range. Why don't
you think about it and let me know when you are certain?'

Captain Dmytro does not say explicitly that he is reluctant
to entrust an assault group to me, but that is my impression.
Perhaps there is a latent notion of chivalry behind it. Or perhaps
he doesn't want to send an officer without experience of close
combat. I curse my indecisiveness. No matter how strong and
ambitious a woman is, self-doubt seems to worm its way into
her. I wonder if I am up to the responsibility of leading men into
a direct confrontation with the enemy, because when you stage
an assault, there are always dead and wounded soldiers. I know
that if something did not go according to plan, I would always
blame myself.

During our first months in Zvanivka, we manage to push Russian forces back far enough that their artillery cannot reach us easily. But they still hit us on occasion.

I am so exhausted after a difficult night in the dugout spent watching the Russian lines that, on returning to our billet, I collapse in a deep, dreamless sleep. The next thing I know, two soldiers burst into my room shouting, 'The ceiling collapsed! The ceiling collapsed!'

'What's going on?' I ask sleepily.

'Our house has taken a direct hit! An artillery shell exploded in the kitchen. Are you all right, Lieutenant? The outside wall was blown away, and part of the roof has caved in. Petro managed to dig himself out, but Ruslan's leg is buried under the rubble.'

'I'm fine,' I say, scrambling out of bed and pulling on my uniform, flak jacket and helmet, in case the Russians fire more shells at us. The air is thick with grey powder dust, which coats everything. I brush off as much as I can as I rush out. 'Dig Ruslan out as fast as you can. I'll run to the transport platoon for a vehicle to take them to the infirmary.'

Fortunately, my men have received only minor injuries. But they still laugh about my ability to sleep through an artillery strike. Some of them call me 'Yulia-who-sleeps-through-shellfire'.

Our house is so badly damaged that we must find another billet, a task that falls to me as platoon commander. When we can, we rent from local people. When that is not possible, we move into a derelict building, of which there is no shortage in Donbas.

I wear my flak jacket only if I am on duty, on patrol or on a mission, when contact with the enemy is likely. I don't wear it all the time, even though we're in a combat zone, because it would drive you crazy to carry so much weight. During my first tour of duty in Donetsk, my flak jacket and helmet weighed more than ten kilos. Before I return in 2022, I look at other soldiers' gear and buy a light flak jacket. It's made of pressed polyester and, with the helmet, weighs only three and a half kilos. It wouldn't stop a round from an assault rifle, but I am not often that close to the enemy. I still wear the heavy flak jacket when I'm in danger of being wounded by shellfire.

Assault units wear the heavier flak jackets to protect them from AK-74 rounds. If you're on a stealth mission that doesn't involve a lot of skirmishes, you don't wear the heavy one because you can damage your body carrying so much weight. The army provides heavy-duty armour. The lighter, self-purchased flak jackets are not very effective. It's always a trade-off between efficiency and protection. I run with drones often, to launch them from open spaces away from tree branches, sometimes under shellfire. We also have to catch the drone when it returns from its flight mission. It's hard to run in a heavy flak jacket.

In the first months of the war, we were all more careful and alert, but vigilance makes you tired, and you let the rules slide. A lot of people get wounded because of this. Some have died because of carelessness. You start believing in your lucky star and you stop protecting yourself. In Kyiv, people are so fed up with air raid sirens that they no longer react. They believe in the Patriot and IRIS-T air defence systems the Americans and Germans gave us. They stop going to shelters. Consequently, the number of casualties has increased. Kyiv is the only city with top-notch anti-air defences, so it's not so serious if people don't react to alarms there. But the same weariness affects other towns and cities with little or no air defences to shoot down incoming drones and missiles.

Zvanivka, Donetsk oblast. 9 September 2022

Captain Dmytro is an exceptional soldier, trained at Odesa Military Academy. He is able to command respect while remaining a funny guy, honest and close to his men. He isn't a typical commander at all, not the least bit bureaucratic.

Captain Dmytro departs with an assault group of several dozen men before dawn on an autumn morning. Each time an assault unit leaves without me, I feel inadequate and a little left out. We have been shelling a front-line village called Spirne from which the Russians appear to have retreated. Captain Dmytro wants to make sure they have really gone, to clear the village of mines and booby traps and set up an advance position. This is what the ground war in Donbas is like: painstakingly slow, one village at a time.

My drone pilots watch the Humvees advance into the grey zone and stop in the abandoned village. The grey zone is the area between our foxholes and trenches and the Russians' foxholes and trenches, and it is teeming with landmines. Witnessing such a mission in real time is one of the most nerve-wracking tasks in the military. You are not in danger, but you experience the danger to your comrades, and you are anxious for them. If they get into trouble, it is your job to call in artillery, send reinforcements or stage a rescue.

It is painful for me to watch the video relay. I see Captain Dmytro, tall, handsome and charismatic, standing between two gutted houses giving orders. An artillery shell explodes and the image is obscured by smoke, dust and flames. Survivors see the bodies of their commander and his men scattered into pieces. Close to a dozen soldiers are killed in the barrage and nearly thirty are wounded. It is a terrible day for our company.

The number 200 has been used to designate dead soldiers

since the Soviet war in Afghanistan. The number 300 is the military's code for the wounded.

'Captain Dmytro 200,' comes the devastating news over the walkie-talkie. One can hear distress in the radio operator's voice. 'About one dozen 200. About thirty 300.'

Survivors race away in the Humvees, feeling sick at leaving their dead comrades behind. Fighting is so heavy that we are unable to retrieve the bodies of Dmytro and the others for two weeks.

I take an armoured vehicle to a pre-designated point to evacuate the wounded, who are brought out by other survivors. Vlad, one of my drone pilots, is with them. Though he is not wounded, he is clearly in shock. 'Oleksandr, Oleksandr, Oleksandr,' he murmurs. Oleksandr was Vlad's best friend, from another platoon in our company, and he died alongside Captain Dmytro. 'We have to go back to get Oleksandr,' Vlad keeps saying.

'I'm sorry. We cannot.' I try to express it firmly but soothingly. Each time, Vlad repeats his plea with more insistence.

Captain Dmytro was twenty-six years old, a year younger than me. He was the best commander I ever had.

We patrol 50 kilometres of the front line with our drones. Each drone can detect enemy movement within 10 to 15 kilometres. We observe the front line in real time, act as spotters for Ukrainian artillery and watch Russian assault units for signs of an imminent attack on our trenches. Rescuing the dead and wounded is a big part of my job. I and my drone pilots watch the fighting and see when our soldiers are killed or wounded. Then we must find the right moment to go in and fetch them.

It is my responsibility to decide when to send in an evacuation crew, and I often go with them.

We launch smaller drones from the trenches, Chinese Mavics and FPVs, all four-rotor quadcopters. The Mavics cost between $1,500 and $2,000 for the day-time variety, and at least $2,400 with night vision. If you are motivated, you can learn to fly one in a few days.

The best drone pilots are the ones who lose the fewest drones. You need to know how to navigate danger to the bird. All pilots lose drones, but if you understand how the antenna works, and how the enemy's anti-drone system functions, you don't lose as many.

As I said earlier, the FPVs are much cheaper, about $500 apiece. With the FPV, the pilot wears a visor over his eyes and sees everything the drone sees. We don't use them for reconnaissance but for kamikaze missions. Sometimes our artillery cannot reach or fire on the Russians because of obstacles such as terrain features, or because the Russians are too close to our own soldiers during an assault, or simply because we are short of artillery shells. In those cases, we use drones to drop grenades on them. If the Russians are not killed, at least they run away.

I have two soldiers who adapt drones with a soldering iron, in a workshop in our position. They even make their own explosives. We can attach anything that explodes to a drone. These days, we don't often get a chance to blow up a tank or a BMP armoured fighting vehicle. (BMP stands for *Boyevaya Mashina Pekhoty*, Russian for 'infantry combat vehicle'.) We mainly use the kamikaze drones to attack infantry soldiers. The drone transmits images of the target in real time, hovering and watching like a hawk from above. When the pilot decides the moment is right, the drone swoops down on its prey, crashing into it and exploding. A skilled FPV pilot can drop a grenade into an open tank hatch or pursue a fleeing enemy. FPVs follow soldiers on the battlefield like whining mosquitos. I have seen video of a Russian soldier trying to beat off an FPV with a stick.

There are tens of thousands of FPVs in Ukraine. Unfortunately, the Russians have more than we do, fresh off Russian assembly lines. Private companies produce them in Ukraine, but the state does not buy as many as it should, and they usually buy the day drones because they are cheaper. A night-vision FPV costs about $1,000 for a single-use kamikaze drone.

So Russians and Ukrainians are killing each other with cheap, mostly Chinese, drones that explode munitions onto troops when they crash: a cross between medieval flamethrowers and space-age technology. The Middle Ages meet the twenty-first century in the trenches of Donbas.

The historical comparison I hear most often is with the First World War. Erich Maria Remarque's classic *All Quiet on the Western Front* was required reading when I was in school. I re-read it during my first tour of duty in Donbas. A century later, life in trenches and dugouts had not changed much. The cold, dirt, danger, rats and lack of sleep are the same. It is not a good idea to take an anti-war book to a combat zone, but I appreciate the fact that Remarque does not romanticize war.

Some nights, dozens of drones laden with explosives are dispatched against Russian and Ukrainian cities. Air defence systems shoot down most of them, but the attacks maintain an atmosphere of insecurity. Operations inside Russia are the responsibility of the Ukrainian military intelligence agency HUR (*Holovne upravlinnia rozvidky Ministerstva oborony Ukrainy*), which has close ties with the US Central Intelligence Agency. The drone operations against targets in Moscow and elsewhere in Russia are highly classified, so I know little about them. I do know they are Ukrainian-made drones launched from inside Russia and that they travel great distances to reach their targets.

By late 2023, my platoon has more FPV pilots than drones. The Chinese say they will restrict exports to 'maintain world peace', no doubt as a favour to Russia. Ukraine's ability to step up its own weapons production, and to invent new technologies, may determine the course of the war. At the beginning of 2024, Russia is reportedly able to produce or buy 100,000 drones monthly, while Ukraine can manufacture or obtain only half that many.

The arrival of new birds is always a morale-booster. In a good week near the end of 2023, my platoon receives two new Mavics and a very large Ukrainian agricultural drone. It is not a kamikaze drone like the FPVs, but it can carry and throw grenades. Some of my men have trained on it, and we have been promised more of the large drones soon.

I am told that soldiers in Western armies don't collect money for their units the way we do. All army units in Ukraine have been doing this since the war started in 2014. The defence ministry provides the bulk of our funding, but we don't expect the military to cover all our expenses. My platoon has a separate account that we use to fix cars, pay for software and maintenance for our drones, and pay rent on our derelict house and for our Starlink internet service.

In addition to asking family, friends and the wider public for donations, every soldier gives a portion of his or her salary for the cause. Every man in my platoon contributes 6,000 hryvnia, about €150, to our shared Hellish Hornets bank account each month. My base salary as a lieutenant is 26,000 hryvnia, but I receive an additional 100,000 monthly as a front-line bonus, for a total salary equivalent to just over €3,000 per month. I donate to other units as well as my own. I guess you could say I'm a true believer.

I think the Ukrainian army is unique in its efforts at self-financing. I raise money on my Facebook page for the Hellish Hornets, mostly for night-vision drones and the basic needs of the platoon. I ask readers to buy a Hellish Hornet jumper or emblem or contribute even the cost of a cup of coffee to the cause. In the first two years of the war, we bring in close to a million hryvnia (more than €24,000). There have been a few big donations, including a supporter who purchased a €4,600 drone for us.

We and the Russians fight each other with the same ageing Soviet weaponry. It sounds crazy, but I know for certain that from 2014 until 2019, while we were fighting each other in Donbas, the Russians were still selling us spare parts for our old BMPs.

Most of the Russians' Soviet weaponry is more recent than ours, and they are ahead of us in electronic warfare and better equipped for night fighting. We have BMP-1s, which were first used in the 1973 Arab–Israeli war. They have Afghan war-era BMP-2s, which are slightly more effective and have a better gun. They also have BMP-3s, which were extensively redesigned and came into service in 1987. And they have newer, modified tanks with better protection than ours. The Kornet is their best anti-tank guided missile.

Whatever modifications and improvements the Russians have made to the old Soviet arsenal, it cannot compare with the Western weapons we receive. The problem is we don't have enough Western weapons and the Soviet weapons we have are old and worn out.

The T-90, the Russians' best tank, doesn't hold a candle to the Abrams, Challengers and Leopards we finally obtained from the West. Unfortunately, the quality of these tanks is not matched by quantity. Analysts said we needed at least 300 Western tanks for our counter-offensive in 2023. We received only half that number. When the Americans gave us thirty-one Abrams tanks in September 2023, they seemed to think we ought to win the war overnight. The previous year, they had refused to send tanks because they didn't want to antagonize Putin.

Personally, I have a weakness for HIMARS, the American High Mobility Artillery Rocket Systems which made such a difference when they arrived in Ukraine in the summer of 2022. My drone pilots sometimes provide coordinates for HIMARS strikes, and they are extremely effective and accurate.

Some soldiers, for example artillery officers, travel elsewhere in Ukraine or in Europe for weapons training. Mostly we improvise and learn to use new weapons on the battlefield. Ukrainian Special Forces got American M-16 assault rifles, but regular infantry did not. We don't really need them because we have AK-47s and AK-74s – again the same weapons as the Russians – which are easier to work with in the trenches. From America we also received grenades and armoured personnel carriers. The Italians sent mines. We have the Krab tracked gun howitzer which was designed in Poland but has a South Korean chassis and a British turret. We have British M777 155-millimetre towed howitzers. The British also sent us their Paladin air defence system as a protection against Russian drones. My platoon doesn't have artillery, but I see all this at work. The unit next to us has French Caesar self-propelled howitzers.

Napoleon allegedly said that an army marches on its stomach. Our leaders have understood how important food is, and they take care of us. I cannot complain about the food. We have military rations for the dugouts, for when we go on a mission or move from one area to the next, but we could not survive on them. Company headquarters sends regular ingredients that we cook. We take turns cooking within the platoon, though I prefer to wash dishes.

In summer we receive a variety of fresh fruit and vegetables; tomatoes, cucumbers and apples in the autumn. In the cold months they give us pickled onions, cabbage, grain, biscuits, oats, buckwheat, rice, peas, sugar, some meat – pork or chicken fillets or thighs – and we are always supplied with drinking water.

Ukrainian civilians, mainly women and children, prepare fresh food for us in volunteer centres and seal it in vacuum packages. Sometimes people drive out to our base camp with food and supplies, but usually they send it via Nova Poshta, a private nationwide delivery company which is used to ship equipment, food and supplies to the front. In October 2023, the Russians fire a rocket at the Nova Poshta office in Kharkiv, killing six postal workers.

Ukrainians are so generous with gifts of food and supplies, especially around New Year's, that I post advice on my Facebook page on 30 December 2023 on what to send and what not to send. First of all, I ask, please do not send Olivier salad, the concoction of eggs, meat, potatoes, vegetables and mayonnaise which originated under the Russian empire and is traditionally served at New Year's. A Ukrainian company donated eleven tonnes of Olivier salad to front-line troops. It's a terrible idea because it spoils rapidly and we don't have refrigerators. I joke that the best use for it would be to dump it on the FR – our polite abbreviation for 'fucking Russians' – to sicken them with the stench.

For my platoon, I receive a gift of ten kilos each of chicken thighs, fish and pork, most of which spoils before we can eat it. Dried or pickled vegetables and vacuum-packed and tinned meat are much better.

I ask well-wishers not to send knitted socks because they make your feet sweat. We prefer expensive thermal socks that let your feet breathe. We love getting chemical hand-warmers, which you place in gloves or boots to warm your hands and feet.

I ask the public not to send shaving toiletries, because I don't know a single soldier who shaves unless he's on leave. We don't have running water, so no razors or shaving cream. We don't need underwear either. Someone sent big boxer shorts which I wear with T-shirts in the summer. Avoid clothes in general, because soldiers have no dressers or cupboards and can keep only what they carry in their backpack.

We need tea and coffee. The army doesn't give us coffee and the tea leaves they send are poor quality and a nuisance to brew. Tea bags are much better. Tissues, including 'wet tissues' and so-called 'dry showers' which are like sealed, moist sponges soaked in soap, are good for personal hygiene in the trenches. We need disinfectant and home-made trench candles, also known as Hindenburg lights. These clever inventions originated in the First World War and are made by pouring wax into a tin can with a wick, surrounded by a spiral of corrugated cardboard. We use them for light in the trenches and dugouts. They provide some warmth as well.

I ask well-wishers to send pet food, because many units have rescued dogs and cats in the combat zone. Pet toys are also a much-appreciated gift.

No matter how good your weapons, if a mission is poorly planned, you are in trouble. I am on duty one day in October 2022 when an assault on Russian lines by men from my company goes badly wrong.

The commander who replaced Captain Dmytro sends out five of our old BMP-1 infantry fighting vehicles. It's a stupid thing to do, because convoys of large vehicles are a clear and easy target. Three people die in the assault and three of our BMPs are destroyed. It is the fault of the commander, who defies logic and recent experience by sending out so many BMPs at one time.

Yehor, a driver and mechanic whom I know from my company, is driving one of the BMP-1s. We watch the assault via drone link and see the rocket explode. The soldiers on top of the vehicle are thrown off by the blast but survive. We aren't sure about Yehor, though, because we can't see that well. We think maybe he was wounded and crawled into a sewage pipe visible on images relayed by the drone.

We wait several days in a forward position for things to calm down enough to safely go and search for Yehor. I am on duty with a squad of seven: me and six men, and there are other infantrymen with us. We are near the enemy and are visible, so I decide we should advance at night. We wait and sleep for a time in the basement of a disused industrial building and go out on foot again in the early morning, under cover of fog. Along the way, we stop at the first bombed-out BMP-1, whose driver has been killed, his body torn in half. The infantrymen take him back. We continue to the second destroyed BMP-1, still hoping we might find Yehor alive.

When we get there, we find a lot of personal items and weapons scattered on the ground. We open the vehicle and find Yehor inside. His neck is broken, and he has bled a great deal. His legs are torn. It takes a long time to extricate his body, which is trapped in the wreckage. When we pull on his torso, we hear muscles tearing.

We had intended to go farther, to the third destroyed BMP-1, to retrieve the body of the third dead soldier. At the very least, we hoped to retrieve pieces, limbs or bones, so the army could do a DNA test and provide certainty to the family. Unfortunately, we cannot reach the spot. There are anti-personnel mines. The wind is blowing, the fog is lifting, the day grows brighter. We must still walk several kilometres carrying Yehor's heavy body, so I make the decision to turn back. We take the personal items of the soldiers and their machine guns and carry Yehor's body to the evacuation point so that a vehicle can fetch him. We send the coordinates to the commander and return to base camp in Zvanivka village.

My friend Mila, the medic who first introduced me to Captain Dmytro, lives across the street in Zvanivka. We are the only women in an otherwise all-male company, which has strengthened our friendship. I trust her totally. We help each other a lot. For example, when Mila conducts a rescue, I tell her which vehicle to take because I and my drone pilots know what the roads are like and where the greatest danger is. Sometimes a pick-up truck is enough, but for some roads you need an armoured vehicle.

Mila has been in the combat zone for eight years and she is exhausted. She was a close friend of Yehor and I fear his death will break her. I feel it is my responsibility to tell her the bad news.

'Did you find Yehor?' Mila asks anxiously when she sees me. I nod 'Yes' but find it difficult to speak.

'He's dead, isn't he?' Mila slumps over in her chair and puts her head in her hands. Few things are worse than seeing a friend cry.

'It was very quick. His neck was broken by the impact. It must have killed him instantly,' I say.

'Yehor loved me, but I couldn't return his love and he accepted my friendship.' Mila is sobbing. She has always been very open about the fact that she is a lesbian.

'He was very dear to me. He was the only man who ever really loved me, and I rejected him. Oh, Yulia, this hurts so badly.'

I give Mila leave so she can attend Yehor's funeral. For some time after, she keeps to herself. She is usually a happy, sociable person but she becomes sad and withdrawn.

My brothers-in-arms don't often talk about their families or share pictures of their wives and children. Perhaps they want to preserve their privacy, or fear appearing weak if they show emotion. In the combat zone, we are closer than family. It's not that we care less about those we have left at home, but their presence is less immediate, less urgent a priority. Fighting together creates an almost mystical bond between us.

Mainly we talk about the war: about the situation, our mission, developments in our sector, our tasks. We talk about how we can improve interaction with other units, problems with communications. For example, our reconnaissance group covers the front line and we always seem to be short of walkie-talkies, which makes it difficult for us.

Officially we are not allowed to drink, but it is understandable that soldiers in a very difficult situation find it hard to do without alcohol. We drink a certain amount, but we don't get drunk, not in the company I'm in. Sometimes – not during missions, not during tasks – we get together and talk over a drink, sitting cross-legged on the floor in a circle. We do this to remember Captain Dmytro and Yehor, and sometimes on birthdays. I have lost more than twenty brothers-in-arms since I returned to the front in June 2022.

When a soldier from my platoon is killed, I always call the family, which is difficult. Some commanders are reluctant to do it because they live with their people all the time and it can be very emotional for them. If the commanding officer doesn't want to make the phone call, an officer who is a psychologist talks to the family. Another option – the official way – is for the unit to report through the conscription office where the soldier was recruited. That's what the commander does if he doesn't have the courage to give the bad news directly to the family. The recruitment office tells the family either that the soldier is missing or that he has been killed.

We have a lot of people who are officially missing, and the commander doesn't call the families and tell them what happened, although he knows the truth. We cannot say the person is dead unless we have retrieved the body. In February 2024, Zelenskiy announces that 31,000 Ukrainian soldiers have been killed in the first two years of war. He does not say how many are missing.

The saddest thing is when we know where the bodies are, but

it is too dangerous to try to reach them. Sometimes, even if we take back territory, we cannot get the bodies because the enemy took them away first. In the best-case scenario they become part of the exchange fund, so they can be traded for Russian bodies. A soldier in our company was killed and his body was exchanged a year later. Russian and Ukrainian headquarters organize the exchanges in the grey zone between our front lines. For more than a year after the full-scale invasion the exchanges took place in Zaporizhzhia oblast. Since late 2023 they have been moved to the north-easternmost oblast of Sumy. Vehicles carrying soldiers' remains are marked with the figure 200, so the enemy does not fire on them. I find it strange that we are civilized enough to exchange our dead, but not civilized enough to stop killing each other.

At worst, especially when we were dealing with Yevgeny Prigozhin's Wagner militia, the Russians take our soldiers' bodies in the hope of obtaining reinforcements. A Russian prisoner told us that if a body was very mutilated but had Ukrainian tattoos, they would burn off the tattoos so they could send the body to Russia and claim he was a Wagner mercenary. The higher their casualties, the more new recruits they could ask for.

I'm not sure what the Russians do with the bodies of our dead comrades. Maybe they send them to relatives of missing men, saying this was your son or husband. I heard on Radio Free Europe that the Russians don't do DNA tests and that sometimes bodies are sent to a remote village and the parents see that it is not their son, but they have to bury the person because it's the only way to obtain compensation from the government. Compensation is usually a new Lada car.

If there is any doubt about identity, the Ukrainian army always orders a DNA test. Compensation has increased dramatically, from one million hryvnia when the war started in

2014 to fifteen million hryvnia – nearly €355,000 – now. It's a lot of money, and there is resentment between those who lost loved ones in the first eight years of the war and the relatives of those who have died since the 2022 invasion. No matter what the compensation, it doesn't make up for losing your son, daughter or husband.

Don't ever let anyone tell you that war is not about death. We live with death day and night. I try not to dwell on blood and torn bodies, because if I let myself think about what I have seen it will sap my strength and energy. It will engulf me.

It doesn't take long for the 128 or so men and women in our company to conclude that the commander who is sent to replace Captain Dmytro is a disaster. We debate among ourselves whether he is incompetent because he drinks or if he drinks because he is incompetent. He has a washed-out, unhealthy complexion and pale blond, straw-like hair. Behind his back, we call him 'Sludge', a distorted version of his name, or 'The Bad Commander'.

I ask to see Sludge at the company command post in Zvanivka one morning in November 2022. 'Command post' sounds impressive; it's really just another dilapidated house, similar to the one where I live with members of my platoon.

'Sir, it's about position number fifteen, in the birch trees opposite the Russian infantry unit,' I say. 'It's too exposed and I think it has been compromised. I am requesting permission to relocate it.'

The map behind Sludge's desk is stuck with colour-coded push pins indicating various positions. He throws a symbolic glance over his shoulder at the map, not long enough to focus on any single location. I jump to my feet to show him where position number fifteen is.

'Permission denied, Lieutenant.'

'But sir, it's dangerous for my drone pilots. The Russians can see it. We must get away from there.'

'It's none of your business, Lieutenant. Go back to your video games.'

I dismiss the insult equating drone operations with video games as the reaction of an old codger who doesn't understand technology. 'With all due respect, sir, it *is* my business. This is *my* platoon, and these are *my* men. If anything happens to them, it will be my responsibility.'

'They belong to the Ukrainian armed forces and they are there to observe Russian troop movements.'

There is no point insisting further, though I will try several times before the end of the year. Each time, the Bad Commander responds with callous indifference. On another occasion, we argue about leave for front-line soldiers.

'Sir, my men have been sitting for months in trenches. It is cold and dirty, and the trenches are infested with rodents. They need a few days away from the front line, if only to let them have a bath and get some proper sleep.'

'Permission denied. We need everyone we've got in the front-line positions.'

'But sir, they are only human. I don't think they can take it much longer.'

Sludge glares at me over the top of his wire-rimmed glasses. I click my heels and salute, not to show respect but to mock him. Arguing with an obtuse and uncaring commander in a failed attempt to defend the interests of my men is a low point of my military career.

Sludge is responsible for ordering deliveries of food and

water to base camp in Zvanivka, but we begin to run short. When I confront him with the problem, he shrugs. I contact brigade headquarters behind his back to order more supplies. He doesn't notice.

I feel protective of Vlad, the drone pilot who participated in the failed assault mission in September, when his best friend was killed alongside Captain Dmytro. As a commander, I must know everything about everyone in my platoon. Vlad remains a dedicated soldier, but I can tell he is grieving. I never forget how distraught he was at having to leave Oleksandr's body under attack in that village. I try to encourage him and keep him cheerful. Perhaps it is maternal instinct, but I do that with all my boys. I believe women commanders show more empathy to subordinates.

Vlad's call sign is Ayid, the Ukrainian word for Hades. He is from Zaporizhzhia, and he lives in the same house as me, Sergeant Andriy and the others. Vlad did not want to be a soldier, but when he received his call-up papers, he didn't argue or try to avoid service. He's a hard-working young man who follows orders. He goes to very dangerous places to retrieve drones that lose their signal. I value him a great deal as a drone pilot.

Zvanivka. 28 December 2022

'Looks like I've drawn the short straw,' Vlad says. 'I knew I would spend New Year's Eve in the trenches. I'm replacing Oleksii in position fifteen. Raise a glass to me at midnight.'

The rest of us are still eating breakfast. Vlad is wearing body armour and a helmet. He carries a heavy backpack with rations for several days in the dugout, and his AK-74 is slung across his chest. He reminds me of a boy decked out in uniform and equipped for his first day at school. A few days earlier, I gave Harry Potter-themed key chains to all my men for Christmas. On his way out into the frozen morning, Vlad smiles and dangles the key chain between thumb and index finger. 'Maybe it will bring me luck,' he says.

But there is melancholy in his eyes and later I remember his smile, a fated smile if ever there was one. Peaceful but not happy. The sort of smile you see often in combat zones, a sign, perhaps, of acceptance or resignation. Resignation, because you know that sooner or later you will probably die.

Zvanivka. 1 January 2023

My telephone rings before dawn. It's the Bad Commander.

'There's been a Russian airstrike with a 500-kilo glide bomb on position fifteen. Your drone pilot was killed. Another pilot from the other platoon is also dead. A third soldier is wounded.'

I want to scream at the commander. *This is your fault,* I think. *I told you to move that position. I told you how dangerous it was.* But I remain silent. My thoughts turn instead to the dead soldier. *Vlad. Honest, reliable Vlad. My best pilot. I wanted him to live. Why is it always the best ones who die?*

'Are you there, Lieutenant?'

'Yes. I'm here.'

'I'm sorry.'

Too little, too late. Since that New Year's Day phone call, I feel a sense of dread every time the phone rings.

In the hours that follow, the rest of the squad abandon the front-line position. They carry the bodies of the dead soldiers and their wounded comrade 15 kilometres to base camp. As platoon commander, it is my job to identify Vlad's remains. His face has been obliterated by the explosion, but we recognize him from the photograph of his father tattooed on his chest.

I have asked every soldier in my platoon for a list of next of kin, in descending order of closeness, with phone numbers. It is my responsibility to ring Vlad's mother in Zaporizhzhia.

'Did he suffer?' is her only question.

'Honestly, no. It was an aerial bombardment and a piece of shrapnel crushed his skull. It killed him instantly. He never knew he'd been hit.'

I hold the Bad Commander responsible not only for what happened to Vlad, but for the deaths of ten other soldiers who died under his command. Now he faces a mutiny. Every soldier in the company refuses to follow his orders and he is transferred out. It is sad that people had to die to prove his incompetence. We had complained that he was unprofessional, and we asked to have him replaced, but the higher-ups didn't listen until soldiers were wounded and died and the rest of us revolted. With such major failures, you usually get promoted, rather than punished. Our former commander works in brigade headquarters now, in a higher position. We still have to talk to him, but he is no longer our direct commander on the front line.

IV

War Without End

It is simply a matter of chance whether I am hit or whether I go on living. I can be squashed flat in a bomb-proof dugout, and I can survive ten hours in the open under heavy barrage without a scratch. Every soldier owes the fact that he is still alive to a thousand lucky chances and nothing else. And every soldier believes in and trusts to chance.

Erich Maria Remarque, *All Quiet*
on the Western Front, 1929

Zvanivka and Zakytne, Donbas. January 2023

It's a good thing we got rid of the Bad Commander, because we are in for a hard time with Wagner. Yevgeny Prigozhin's convicts and mercenaries have a different style of fighting from the regular Russian troops we have fought until now. In January 2023, Wagner seizes Soledar, 19 kilometres south of our base in Zvanivka. Social media is filled with images of Prigozhin and his soldiers relishing their triumph in Soledar's cavernous salt mines. They pound our base camp with artillery, forcing us to relocate to our present position at Zakytne, a hamlet on the Siverskyi Donets river where my comrades and I live in an unfinished, abandoned brick house, between the cities of Slovyansk and Lyman. The mountainous terrain means that the Russians cannot shell our position as easily as other areas of the front line, but we often hear outgoing Ukrainian fire. When I hear incoming artillery fire, it is usually exploding near Lyman, a railway junction town set amid once beautiful forests, about 10 to 15 kilometres from Russian front lines. The Russians held Lyman from the end of May until early October 2022, when Ukrainian forces reconquered it. It is very badly damaged, and no one is rebuilding because the government will not give reconstruction funds for any town within 30 kilometres of Russian lines. The Russians might retake it, and money is too scarce to be squandered.

My platoon comprises me and twenty-five men. Ten are based in Slovyansk, from where they fly Ukrainian-made Leleka-100 Unmanned Aerial Vehicles. Leleka means stork, and these birds have a two-metre wingspan. They look like model aeroplanes. We use them only for reconnaissance.

The other fifteen of us are based in several houses in Zakytne. We are about 15 kilometres from the trenches, which are constantly being shelled, and about 20 kilometres from Russian positions, within reach of their artillery but out of range of small-arms fire. We rotate back and forth to three dugouts on the front line.

Our lifestyle reminds me of the post-apocalyptic stories I composed in creative writing class at university. We use water from a well for washing and toilets, and generators for electricity. The generators are noisy, and you must change the oil and fill them with petrol. The only heat we have in winter is from a wood-stove. We chop the wood ourselves, which works up a sweat. I tell myself that one sleeps better in the cold anyway. Carrying water, chopping wood and servicing the generator are all part of our daily routine. I boast that I don't need creature comforts. I never complain in front of the men, but I'm a city-dweller at heart and this is a hardship for me. I have adapted because I have no choice. Fighting a war would be so much easier if one had the basic necessities.

In the late autumn and winter we are invaded by rodents. I imagine it was like this in the Middle Ages. Rats pullulate in the grey zone, where they feed on the bodies of hapless soldiers. One of our dugouts is home to two cats. The gentle cat keeps the mice under control. The fierce Tom attacks the rats. The other two dugouts use rat poison and smear a gooey, petroleum-like grease called Solidol on wires and cables to keep the rodents from chewing through them.

We are two platoons in Zakytne, spread out in about ten houses. Every house has at least one cat by necessity. My black and white moggy, Villi, patrols our house, where mice are legion. They chew everything, including the wires to the generator and the Starlink satellite dish, which we rely on for communications. We find mice sleeping in the battery cavities of drones. I take a video of dozens of mice jumping out of the generator when I turn it on, and I post it on my Facebook page. Someone steals it, posts it on TikTok and gets three million hits. I am furious.

One night, I am reading on my camp bed on the top floor when Villi prances up with a reddish-brown creature with a fluffy tail in his maw. The cat drops it like a present on the floor beside me, then starts to bat it with his paw. I rescue the little animal and put it in an empty jar. It trembles with fear but eagerly eats the cheese I give it. I look it up online in the Ukrainian Red Book, a compendium of rare and extinct animals, and discover that an exotic species of dormouse had taken refuge in our attic. I set it free outside the following morning.

The houses of Zakytne are staggered up the hillside, not unlike photographs I've seen of villages in southern France or Italy, except that buildings are more spread out and it is not picturesque. Trees overhang the narrow streets. There's a quarry nearby, at a place the locals call the chalk hill. Before the war, perhaps 500 people lived here. There are scarcely 100 left now, without gas, electricity or an internet connection. I'm not sure why they stay; perhaps because it is home, or maybe they are 'waiters', hoping for a Russian victory. Most of the remaining civilians are elderly. They are outnumbered by soldiers in the streets. Some locals grow food in their gardens and plant tidy flowerbeds around their houses, which strikes me as absurd in a combat zone. A few keep cows and sell us dairy products.

I am the only woman in a house filled with men. I eat, sleep, wash and live alongside my brothers-in-arms. They know when I need privacy. I have never received unwanted sexual advances. I am the commanding officer and I have a gun.

February 2023

Wagner launches a week of non-stop human wave attacks against our trenches. They use no tanks or armoured vehicles, only cannon fodder. I watch the battle as it is relayed live by reconnaissance drones, and report back to headquarters.

Ukrainian infantrymen are mowing down Russians with machine guns. It is worse than killing. It is slaughter, elimination, annihilation, death on the assembly line. The Russians are shredded by our machine guns, but they just keep coming. Arms, legs, heads and torsos fly into the air, scatter across the frozen grey zone. It is beyond anything one could imagine. I try to count the numbers of Russians in the assault, identify their weapons, watch for weak links in our defences. I wonder what it is like for our men, how they do not go mad from killing so many people. They are being assaulted by a horde of zombies. The Russians don't seem to care if they die. In a sense they are already dead.

One afternoon I am studying videos with our military intelligence unit when infantrymen bring in a Russian soldier for interrogation. He is twenty-two years old. He wears handcuffs and his uniform is stained and torn.

'How did you come to join the army?'

'I'm in Wagner, not the regular army. Prigozhin came to the prison where I was in Novgorod and offered us freedom if we would fight for six months in Ukraine.'

'Why were you in prison?'

'A man tried to rape my sister, so I killed him. I was tried and found guilty of murder and sentenced to fifteen years.'

'What are your orders?'

'I didn't want to fight,' the young man says. My colleagues tell me prisoners always say that, but this soldier seems intelligent. In his case it may be true.

'I am the head of a militia unit. It's my job to lead men through the grey zone to Ukrainian lines.'

'You've seen how they are mowed down by machine guns. It's surprising you weren't killed,' the interrogator says.

'The number of our casualties is staggering. Whole units are wiped out. They just send in another.'

'How do you motivate your men to go forward?'

'I just ran ahead of them with my assault rifle. I was praying I could make it to your lines. I had a plan to throw myself on the ground and wave the white T-shirt I'd hidden inside my uniform. I never shot any of my fellow fighters, but there are "punishers" with machine guns whose job it is to kill anyone who tries to turn back, escape or surrender. Prigozhin got the idea from Stalin's famous "Not a step back" order during the Second World War. "Blocking detachments" are deployed at the rear to shoot cowards. I'm lucky they didn't shoot me. Sometimes men are sodomized with gun barrels, bottles or broom handles if they refuse to go into battle. Once you are humiliated that way, you will always be treated as sub-human. We are caught between two fires, and either way we will die.'

'Is there anything else you want to tell us?'

'Give me a map.' The prisoner picks up a red pen from the tabletop and begins marking Russian paths and positions. He asks for a map of Soledar town which he studies eagerly before digging the pen in like a knife, tracing a circle over and over. 'This is for your artillery gunner,' he says, writing down the exact map coordinates. 'It is Wagner headquarters in Soledar, where Prigozhin sleeps when he visits. You must hit the basement.'

I don't know what our intelligence and security service did with the prisoner. I have no idea what happened to him. He may have become part of the exchange fund, or perhaps they offered him other options. It doesn't really matter.

When you live in the combat zone, you cling to every beam of light, to the tiniest happy moment. Petro, a soldier in my platoon, comes to see me in base camp. He is a shy man and seems slightly embarrassed.

'Lieutenant, my wife is expecting a baby.'

Petro's wife has scheduled a Caesarean section for 8 March, so he knows the birth date already. He doesn't want to arrive home too early, in order to have as much time as possible with the baby. He asks to earn more leave by doing extra time in the dugout beforehand, departing just in time for the birth.

I tell him that this is a clever idea. We both know that we are always short-handed. I can give him only a week off and wish I could give him more.

'That's fine, Lieutenant. I was afraid it would be less, or not at all. I'm grateful.'

I pray that nothing will happen to Petro before he sees his first child. While he is on duty in the dugout, we organize a whip-round at base camp. We don't know the baby's sex, so I choose a white onesie and an air purifier for its bedroom and order them online. Before Petro departs, I give him the address of the parcel hub in Zaporizhzhia where he can pick up our gift.

On the night of Petro's return, I summon him to the house on the walkie-talkie. He blushes when he sees us sitting in a circle on the floor of the main room, with a home-made sign saying, 'Congratulations'. I have stoked up the wood-stove so it is warm. We celebrate the birth of his baby boy by sharing a bottle of wine and smoking a hookah pipe.

I think of the scene in *All Quiet on the Western Front* where the narrator and Kat roast a stolen goose in a shed on the edge of the battlefield: 'We don't talk much, but we have a greater and more gentle consideration for each other than I should think even lovers do,' Remarque writes. 'The brightnesses and shadows of our emotions come and go in the flickering light of a gentle fire. What does he know about me? What do I know about him? Before the war we wouldn't have had a single thought in common – and now here we are, sitting with a goose roasting in front of us, aware of our existence and so close to each other that we can't even talk about it.'

*

'Thank you, all of you, for the presents. My wife was really touched. And baby Dmytro likes the onesie,' Petro says.

'Dmytro, like our late commander?' a soldier asks.

'Yes. Maybe he will be a warrior… But actually, I'd prefer he grew up in peace.'

'We all would,' I say.

Studying the circle of faces by the light of the candles and the wood-stove, I sense that the others share my emotion. Tonight, it is enough to be together and share Petro's happiness, despite the dull sound of artillery in the background. It helps us to think about new life amid so much death. *This is a natural process. Some must die so that others may live. People die and others replace them, and this is the way it must be*, I tell myself. But my philosophizing flounders on the deaths of Dmytro, Yehor, Vlad, my husband and my father. It is impossible to see their violent deaths as natural, or for that matter, the Wagner prisoners throwing themselves into our machine-gun fire. I block out such thoughts because I do not want to spoil the moment.

I have seen the last of the Russian meat grinder, at least for the time being. The war settles into an uneasy calm along our part of the thousand-kilometre front line. Sometimes we receive orders to go on the offensive. We seize 50 metres here, 50 metres there, but mostly our attempts are unsuccessful, and we turn back. It has become impossible to take territory without unacceptable numbers of casualties.

We are on edge throughout the spring of 2023, waiting for the Ukrainian army to launch its much-trumpeted counter-offensive. Headquarters and the government are very secretive and we have no idea what is going to happen or what our involvement will be. The offensives of 2022, which liberated so much territory in Kharkiv and Kherson oblasts, set a high standard that will prove impossible to replicate.

When the Ukrainian offensive finally starts on 4 June 2023, it concentrates on Russian lines in Zaporizhzhia oblast, more than 300 kilometres to the south-west of us. The goal is to punch through the occupied zone, all the way to the Sea of Azov, taking the cities of Tokmak and Melitopol and severing the land bridge from Russia to Crimea. Ukrainian forces capture only a few small villages in Zaporizhzhia oblast. By the end of the year, the goal of breaking through Russian lines to the Sea of Azov has become an impossible dream.

At every stage of the war, our Western allies limit the range or firing power of the weapons they give us, out of fear of pre-cipitating a war between NATO and Russia. While we wait and wait for the artillery shells, tanks and fighter aircraft we need to liberate the south-east, Russian General Sergei Surovikin – who earned the sobriquet 'General Armageddon' in Chechnya and Syria – is building an impenetrable, three-layer, 120-kilometre line of defence in Zaporizhzhia oblast, comprising tank traps, concrete pyramids known as dragon's teeth, and up to five land-mines per square metre. Surovikin's foresight, combined with NATO's dithering, makes our goal unattainable.

In August 2023, high-ranking American officials let it be

known that they are disappointed with the slow progress of the Ukrainian offensive. They say we have too many soldiers along the front line in Donbas, and that we should divert troops to the southern front even if that means higher casualties. Because my brigade is helping to hold the line in Donbas, it feels almost like a personal rebuke.

These remarks by unnamed officials, published in an American newspaper, rankle with Ukrainian officers. If we divert resources from defending our sector in Donbas, the Russians will certainly seize the opportunity to move forward. Do the Americans expect us to hand Donbas to Putin on a platter, in the hope of an illusory breakthrough in the south? Complete control of the Luhansk and Donetsk oblasts has been Putin's minimal objective since the war started in 2014. In September 2022, he declares the arc of four eastern and southern regions comprising Luhansk, Donetsk, Zaporizhzhia and Kherson to be part of Russia. But he does not control a single region entirely. We are determined to keep it that way.

If you are sitting in an office in Washington, projected casualty figures are simply numbers in a strategy paper. If you are a Ukrainian officer risking your life and the lives of your soldiers in the combat zone, every number has a human face and story. When I hear that Washington expects us to sacrifice more soldiers, I think about the way the Islamic Republic of Iran used boys as kamikaze minesweepers in the 1980–88 Gulf War. Children ran across Iraqi minefields with keys to paradise pinned to their uniforms. Each time we clear a minefield, the Russians resow it within hours by spraying the area with cluster munitions.

After the clashes with Wagner in January and February, little changes for our brigade in 2023. There are skirmishes and local assaults, but nothing on the scale of earlier battles. There is nothing restful about this period, though, because you know you can be attacked, or asked to go on the offensive, at any moment. The line may be static, but holding it requires immense effort. A kind of numbness sets in. The only comfort is that you are losing fewer people.

While we wait tensely in northern Donetsk oblast, the longest battle of the war unfolds in Bakhmut, 60 kilometres south-east of our position. Tens of thousands of Ukrainians and Russians die there between August 2022 and May 2023. The casualty rate is so high, and the strategic value of Bakhmut so negligible, that the absurd standoff is compared to the Battle of Verdun in the First World War. Behind the scenes, a debate rages between Ukraine's military and political leadership, and between President Zelenskiy and his Western allies, over the utility of sacrificing huge numbers of men to hold Bakhmut. The commander-in-chief of Ukraine's armed forces, General Valerii Zaluzhnyi, who is popular with the troops, agrees with Ukraine's Western partners that Bakhmut should be evacuated. Zelenskiy says it must be held whatever the cost.

Politicians care about symbols. Soldiers reason in terms of utility and human lives. When Prigozhin announces on 20 May that Bakhmut has fallen to his forces, Putin calls the Wagner leader the same night to congratulate him for conquering a field of ruins. Our defence ministry is reluctant to admit the city has fallen. Ukrainian troops on the outskirts of Bakhmut continue to harass the Russians encamped in the flattened city.

Prigozhin is like a strutting cockerel after he takes Bakhmut, so puffed up with his own importance that he harbours delusions of leading Russia. For the few hours of his mutiny on

24 June, we think that Putin's power is crumbling and the war may be entering a new phase. When the Kremlin shoots down Prigozhin's private jet two months to the day later, I remember having seen waves of Wagner mercenaries dying in front of our trenches and I feel a grim satisfaction that evil has killed evil.

I have learned to be cautious about my own government's statements. On 17 November 2023, our defence ministry announces that several hundred Ukrainian soldiers control a strip of land 50 kilometres long and up to eight kilometres deep along the eastern, left bank of the Dnipro river, from just west of the Nova Kakhovka dam which the Russians destroyed in June. The Dnipro is the main front line in south-central Ukraine. Small units of Ukrainian naval and special forces are reported to have used inflatable boats to cross at night over a period of months. Russian drones and artillery have allegedly been pushed back from the riverbank opposite Kherson city, which they had continued to attack since it was liberated in 2022.

The reported seizure of the eastern bank raises wild hopes of a Ukrainian assault on the isthmus of Crimea, 70 kilometres to the south-east. But as weeks pass, it becomes apparent that Ukrainian forces have at best a precarious foothold on that bank of the Dnipro. Soldiers say the area is all mud and bomb craters filled with water. The bridges over the Dnipro have been blown up, and it is impossible to ferry sufficient reinforcements and materiel across the river. Attempts to conquer the east bank are a suicide mission. Soldiers recount having to walk on the bodies of comrades in the mud, and being forced to leave wounded men behind because there are not enough boats to bring them back.

The conflict heats up for my battalion in late 2023, when Russia again set its sights on nearby Lyman. It will be a propaganda coup for Russia and a big setback for us if they recapture the city. We wait for them to complete the assault they have started. We know we are next because ours is the only brigade in the area they have not attacked yet. We prepare as best we can, deploying FPV drones and anti-tank weapons in the hope of preventing them from breaking through our lines.

*

On the morning of 1 December 2023, I receive a call on the walkie-talkie from one of our front-line positions.

'Student has been killed by an enemy FPV armed with a rocket-propelled grenade,' a soldier whose call sign is Shorty tells me.

'How did it happen?'

'We were all in the dugout. It was quiet. Student climbed out. I think he needed to go to the toilet. An FPV armed with a rocket-propelled grenade crashed into him and exploded and that was it. Now they are lobbing mortars at us.'

'Abandon the dugout as soon as the shelling subsides. Bring Student's remains if you can. If you can't, we'll go back for him this evening.'

Student was twenty years old. He had volunteered to serve with the Lviv Territorial Defence Forces and was given that call sign because of his youth. He was assigned to the next brigade down the line from us. He sometimes shared a dugout with my platoon, and I had worked with him.

My soldiers go back in the evening but find only pieces of the young man. The mood is gloomy, but these things happen all the time, so the men treat it almost routinely. They retrieve the body and we move on. That's it. Student died in the morning; we gather up his remains in the evening. When something like this happens, we usually try to move the dugout because it has been compromised. We can't find a new position at night, so we wait until the following morning, using rain and fog as cover, to look for a new spot. Then we move equipment from the old dugout to the new one.

We notice movement on the Russian lines in the aftermath of Student's death: more anti-tank weapons, mines and assaults on our left flank. On the drone screen I watch two tanks approach our front line, doing reconnaissance by fire. We think it's not a real assault, more a test to see if we'll fight back. We are mistaken. Russian infantrymen get out of the tanks and come forward, while the tanks move back and keep firing. Our artillery platoon aims shells at the tank, but it is just out of range.

This is typical of how a Russian assault is made. Infantrymen are carried in tanks or BMP fighting vehicles. The armour drives as far forward as possible and deposits the infantrymen, who advance on foot while the armour retreats to a safe distance from which it continues to fire.

The Russians are attacking the nearest brigade, which overlaps ours. The separation between brigades is fluid, so it affects us as well. Unfortunately, the Russian assault is successful. They take the neighbouring brigade's position and several others. I don't know how many Ukrainians they kill because it was the other brigade's line, but it is very close to us. We help a little with fire support, but we do not intervene because it is not our sector. We are just observing the assaults.

Attention focuses on General Zaluzhnyi. The commander-in-chief owes his popularity to the successful defence of Kyiv at the beginning of the war and the reconquest of nearly 75,000 square kilometres of territory in the offensives of September and November 2022. He is loved by the military because he prioritizes preserving the lives of his soldiers. But tension mounts between General Zaluzhnyi and President Zelenskiy following the failure of the counter-offensive.

On 1 November 2023, the British magazine *The Economist* publishes an interview with Zaluzhnyi which sends shock waves through Ukraine's defence and political establishment. 'Just like in the First World War, we have reached the level of technology that puts us into a stalemate,' our top commander says. 'The simple fact is that we see everything the enemy is doing and they see everything we are doing. In order for us to break this deadlock, we need something new, like the gunpowder which the Chinese invented and which we are still using to kill each other.'

The impasse favours Russia, with a population triple the size of Ukraine's and an economy ten times larger. If Ukraine is to win, Zaluzhnyi says, we must gain superiority in air power, including drones, in artillery fire, electronic warfare and the ability to breach minefields. I and my fellow front-line officers hear that Ukraine has inventions underway which will make a difference. Small steps will be possible, but it won't be as fast as our allies would like.

General Zaluzhnyi says we must draft half a million troops and train them better. That too is a challenge. Everyone who was going to volunteer has done so already, and Zelenskiy fears the political consequences of extending the draft. We are short on time and facilities for training. In March 2022, Russia rained cruise missiles on the Yavoriv base, where I attended officers' training in 2017 and which was used by Zelenskiy's International Legion, 10 kilometres from the Polish border and 30 kilometres from Lviv. Thirty-five people were killed. The lesson was clear: Russia will attack any place where Ukraine attempts to train large numbers of troops.

To an army officer like me, the truth of General Zaluzhnyi's essay is self-evident. As the commander of a drone platoon, I have seen how technology freezes the front line and makes mechanized assaults all but impossible. But the article infuriates our political leaders, who believe some truths are better left unsaid. A spokesman for President Zelenskiy accuses the general of giving comfort to the enemy and scaring Western allies. People are tired, Zelenskiy admits in a press conference. 'But this is not a stalemate.' I think of the surrealist René Magritte's painting of a pipe, entitled *The Treachery of Images*, on which he has written, 'This is not a pipe.'

Two days after the publication of General Zaluzhnyi's article, Zelenskiy sacks General Viktor Khorenko, the commander of Ukraine's special operations forces, in further evidence of a rift between our political and military leadership. The move is surprising because special operations have been so successful against Russia's Black Sea Fleet and in drone attacks on targets deep inside Russia. Zelenskiy also fires the head of the medical forces, without explanation.

On 8 February 2024, Zelenskiy finally sacks Zaluzhnyi and replaces him with Colonel General Oleksandr Syrskyi. The army love Zaluzhnyi, a warm, friendly father figure who is close to the US and UK, and who is known to have a deep aversion to all things Soviet and Russian. We have expected Zelenskiy's move for months, but nonetheless hoped that Zaluzhnyi might keep his position. I post a photograph on my Facebook page of me with Zaluzhnyi, from my medal ceremony in December 2022, saying, 'Thank you, Mr General.'

'Zaluzhnyi's sin was to be more popular than Zelenskiy,' says Ruslan, a soldier in my platoon, expressing a widespread perception. Several of us are sharing a pot of *lecsó*, a Hungarian stew made of peppers, sausage and tomatoes, one evening soon after Zaluzhnyi's replacement by Syrskyi.

'Zaluzhnyi was willing to admit it when he made a mistake,' I say. In his interview with *The Economist*, Zaluzhnyi said he'd been wrong to think that huge casualties would discourage the Russians. He said that losing 150,000 dead, as Russia had in Ukraine, would stop a war in any normal country.

Zaluzhnyi had abolished Zelenskiy's rule requiring front-line troops in Donbas to seek written permission to retaliate for Russian fire; a rule that enraged many in the military. Soldiers believe Zaluzhnyi told Zelenskiy the truth – that it was impossible to take back territory with inadequate weapons and ammunition. We suspect that Syrskyi told Zelenskiy what he wanted to hear.

There were other disagreements. At the end of the summer of 2022, Zaluzhnyi wanted to attack the Russians in the southeast, to break the land bridge between Russia and Crimea. But Zelenskiy said no, he wanted to take back Izium in Kharkiv oblast, which was less strategically important. Zaluzhnyi obeyed orders and Syrskyi carried out the plan, but it gave the Russians nine months to fortify their positions in the south-east. By the time Ukraine launched the counter-offensive, it was too late and Zelenskiy blamed Zaluzhnyi for its failure.

I draw a historical parallel between Zaluzhnyi and Colonel Petro Bolbochan, who in 1918 led Ukrainian forces against the Bolsheviks in Crimea. Bolbochan did a good job, but he was arrested and executed for criticizing the irrational policies of the government of the Ukrainian People's Republic.

Shorty brings up the fact that Syrskyi was born in Russia, where his parents reportedly still live. There are thousands, perhaps millions, of Ukrainians in similar situations, but we wonder if Syrskyi's family background could give the enemy a hold over him.

'Syrskyi is eight years older than Zaluzhnyi. He was a Soviet artillery officer, but the Russians hate him,' Andriy says. 'They call him a traitor in the service of "Nazis".'

Syrskyi's reputation for coldness contrasts with Zaluzhnyi's famed humanity. In March 2023, Zaluzhnyi kneeled before the mother and partner of Dmytro Kotsiubailo, who was known by his call sign, Da Vinci, because he had wanted to be an artist. At twenty-seven, Da Vinci was the youngest battalion commander in the history of the Ukrainian army. He was killed near Bakhmut.

Zaluzhnyi thought it wasn't worth sacrificing Ukrainian lives for Bakhmut, and kneeling at Da Vinci's funeral was his way of apologizing. Syrskyi was the commander at Bakhmut, and his attitude was 'Victory or death!' He had been equally determined at the Battle of Debaltseve in 2015, where Ukraine lost 260 men. Syrskyi's willingness to sacrifice soldiers in the 'meat grinder' earned him the unenviable nickname of 'butcher'.

I tell my men we are not in Donbas to judge our commanders, that our mission is to hold ground. Wood crackles in the stove. An owl hoots outside. Silence falls over the group, interrupted only by the sound of spoons in our tin bowls.

One month after his dismissal, General Zaluzhnyi was appointed Ukraine's ambassador to London. In November 2023, a joint investigation by Der Spiegel *and the* Washington Post *had alleged that Ukrainian saboteurs trained by Britain and acting on orders from Zaluzhnyi had blown up the Nord Stream pipelines two months earlier. Zaluzhnyi denied involvement in the operation.*

Early in the war, with few exceptions, the Russian and Ukrainian air forces stopped using aircraft because there was too great a risk of being shot down by air defence missiles. In October 2023, Russia began using glide bombs to wipe out the bunkers and buildings of Avdiivka, an industrial suburb fifteen kilometres north-west of Donetsk city and 150 kilometres from our position. Pro-Russian separatists had briefly held Avdiivka at the beginning of the war in 2014, but we took it back and spent nine years fortifying Ukrainian positions there.

Glide bombs are traditional gravity bombs with payloads of between 250 kilos and 1.5 tonnes, retrofitted with wings and satellite guidance systems. They glide for up to 60 kilometres to their target, keeping the aircraft that launched them out of reach of air defence missiles. The weight of glide bombs explains their immense destructive power. By comparison, a Russian 152-millimetre artillery shell weighs about 40 kilos. Russian defence minister Sergei Shoigu claimed in March 2024 that Russia has a new, three-tonne glide bomb at its disposal.

The deployment of glide bombs is an important factor in Russia's slow but continuous advance in Donbas. They obliterate everything in the path of Russian troops, enabling infantry to move forward. The Ukrainian defence ministry says Russia dropped more than 3,500 glide bombs during the first four months of 2024.

Because Ukraine has received only a handful of Patriot missile batteries, Russia's use of glide bombs forces commanders to choose between defending Ukrainian front lines or defending cities. More air defence missiles and/or more fighter bombers would enable Ukraine to intercept glide bombs or shoot down the aircraft that launch them.

But the first of sixty F-16 fighters promised by Belgium, Denmark, the Netherlands and Norway did not begin to arrive until August 2024. There is also talk of Sweden, which joined NATO on 11 March 2024, donating dozens of JAS 39 Gripen fighters, comparable to the F-16.

The Russian meat grinder resumed at Avdiivka, where the Ukrainian military says more than 17,000 Russian soldiers were killed in four months of battle. I watched footage posted by combatants from both sides with a sense of horror tinged with envy and relief. By definition, a soldier wants to be where the action is and contribute his or her utmost to the defence of the country. At the same time, it is only human to dread hardship and extreme danger.

Unlike Bakhmut, Avdiivka has real strategic value. The Russians have controlled Donetsk city, the capital of the region, since the war started in 2014. The Ukrainian presence in nearby Avdiivka was a constant threat, and they wanted to create a buffer zone around Donetsk. Avdiivka also lies on the road to Pokrovsk, 40 kilometres to the west and the link between Ukrainian forces in the northern and southern parts of Donetsk oblast.

Russia had claimed no military successes since Bakhmut in

May 2023. Putin wanted a victory before his sham re-election on 17 March 2024. At the beginning of the year, only a few hundred people from a pre-war population of 30,000 remained in Avdiivka. Winter in Donbas is particularly brutal. Sub-zero temperatures burn your skin and cut through you like a knife. The first blizzard struck in late November, but residents of Avdiivka could not light stoves or campfires out of fear that Russian drones would detect smoke and transmit coordinates to artillery gunners. Food distribution points were also targeted. Even 'waiters' who hoped for a Russian victory began fleeing the battered city. The Russians closed in with a pincer movement on the 22 kilometre-long, shell-cratered supply corridor linking the town to the Ukrainian-held west of the oblast. The Russians fired on everything that moved in the corridor. Previously called the Road of Life, it was rechristened the Road of Death. We attempted to stave off the Russian assault with FPV kamikaze drones which destroyed large quantities of Russian armour.

By the second week of February 2024, Russian bombardment had made the Road of Death impassable. Our troops in Avdiivka risked being cut off entirely from Ukrainian-held territory. On 17 February, eight days after he replaced Zaluzhnyi as commander-in-chief, General Syrskyi ordered Ukrainian forces to withdraw from Avdiivka. Syrskyi stressed his desire to preserve the lives of Ukrainian soldiers when announcing his decision.

Avdiivka fell because of shell hunger. Joe Biden blamed Republicans in Congress who were still blocking military aid for Ukraine. The effect on our morale was devastating. On bad days, we wondered if there was any point in getting up in the morning, when we were out-numbered and out-gunned and our allies appeared to have abandoned us. The US House of

Representatives finally passed the bill on 21 April. Biden signed it three days later. It will take time for the weapons to arrive.

Our government tried to put a brave face on the loss of Avdiivka, noting that the city was entirely destroyed and that Russia had paid a huge price in casualties to take it. General Oleksandr Tarnavsky, the commander of Ukrainian forces in the area, said we had no choice 'in a situation where the enemy advances by marching over the corpses of its own soldiers and has ten times more artillery shells'. My comrades in Avdiivka described a disorderly rout, with no time to evacuate weapons and equipment, much less destroy documents and lay mines for the Russians. A mission to rescue wounded Ukrainian soldiers was aborted, and General Tarnavsky admitted that they would be captured by the Russian army.

After retreating from Avdiivka, Ukrainian forces fell back to a series of small villages several kilometres to the west. That line was overrun by Russian forces in April, putting Pokrovsk at risk. 'The situation at the front has worsened,' General Syrskyi admitted on 28 April. Ukraine had faced acute shortages of men, weapons and ammunition for months. Putin intended to exploit his advantage to the maximum while we waited for new conscripts and weapons.

The small hilltop town of Chasiv Yar, whose pre-war population of 13,500 had dwindled to 682 by May, was expected to fall next. Twenty-five thousand Russian soldiers were reportedly converging from Avdiivka, 83 kilometres to the south, and Bakhmut, 17 kilometres to the east, to seize Chasiv Yar, which had been Ukraine's fallback position when Wagner conquered Bakhmut one year earlier.

Russia pounded Chasiv Yar with up to two dozen one-tonne bombs daily, and Zelenskiy said Putin wanted to seize the town before the 9 May holiday celebrating the Soviet victory over

Nazi Germany. If Russia took Chasiv Yar, it could threaten Kramatorsk, a city of 150,000 and home to Ukraine's eastern command, and Kostiantynivka, the main supply point for Ukrainian forces on the eastern front.

Farther north, Kharkiv and Kupyansk were also in danger. Russia had tried and failed to seize Kharkiv, Ukraine's second city, only 30 kilometres from the Russian border, at the beginning of the war in 2022. By the spring of 2024, only a third of Kharkiv's three million inhabitants remained. After a period of relative calm, Russia stepped up aerial attacks on the city, destroying the power plant which supplied half of Kharkiv's electricity at the end of March. Kharkiv's mayor, Ihor Terekhov, appealed to Ukraine's western allies to send air defence missiles.

In Kharkiv and Kupyansk, an important railway junction 118 kilometres south-east of Kharkiv, the army planted dragon's teeth and dug new trenches in the hope of stopping a Russian assault. Ukraine had liberated Kupyansk along with most of Kharkiv oblast in September 2022. Russia has attempted to retake it since the summer of 2023.

While the Ukrainian army struggled on the eastern front, we took heart from the small victories of the air force and naval service. Russia's use of glide bombs led Ukraine to quietly move some air defence systems towards the front lines, enabling us to shoot down more aircraft. Based on photographic and video evidence, the Oryx website says Ukraine has shot down 105 aircraft since the beginning of the war, while Russia has downed 75 Ukrainian combat aircraft. Since the beginning of 2024, the Ukrainian air force has downed two of nine Russian Beriev A-50 radar early warning planes and an Ilyushin Il-22 airborne command plane. Our air force also claims to have destroyed about a dozen Su-34 fighter-bombers and at least one Su-35 fighter.

Ukraine does not own a single warship, yet it is turning the Black Sea into the graveyard of the Russian navy. In the first two years of the war, Ukraine's military intelligence service HUR says it sank nearly thirty Russian vessels – close to one-third of Putin's Black Sea Fleet – using a combination of Ukrainian-made Neptune anti-ship missiles and Magura sea drones, as well as Franco-British Storm Shadow/SCALP cruise missiles, which we received in the summer of 2023. The sinking of the flagship *Moskva* in April 2022 was followed by the destruction of the *Novocherkassk* landing ship in December 2023, the *Ivanovets* guided missile ship and *Tsezar Kunikov* landing ship in February 2024 and the *Sergei Kotov* patrol ship in March. We have done considerable damage to naval installations at Sevastopol and Feodosia in Crimea, and Novorossiysk on the Russian mainland at the eastern end of the Black Sea. On 10 March, Russian publications reported the sacking of Admiral Nikolai Yevmenov, the head of the Russian navy. Though it is not officially confirmed, Yevmenov appears to have been punished for Russia's humiliating retreat from the western Black Sea.

Ukrainian exploits have ensured that no Black Sea port is safe for Russian vessels. We have forced Putin to abandon his blockade of Ukrainian ports, enabling us to resume grain exports from Odesa. Russian missile carriers have been forced to launch their missiles from a greater distance, giving our air defences more time to react. Ukraine has twice attacked the Kerch Bridge linking Crimea to Russia.

Zelenskiy prompted a government crisis in Germany by pleading for Taurus cruise missiles to destroy the bridge once and for all. Russia intercepted and later leaked a videoconference call between four German officials, recorded on 19 February 2024, in which they discussed the possibility of providing Taurus missiles to Ukraine. Chancellor Olaf Scholz formally refused to do so on 26 February.

In apparent retaliation for Ukraine's success in the Black Sea, Russia launched a series of attacks on Odesa. Twelve people, including five children, were killed in a 2 March drone strike on an apartment block. Four days later, a missile exploded a few hundred metres from Zelenskiy and the visiting prime minister of Greece, killing five people. On 15 March, at least twenty people were killed, including two first responders, in Russia's first 'double tap' missile attack on Odesa, in which a second salvo is fired after rescue workers and medics arrive on the scene of the first strike. On 31 March, Kyrylo Budanov, the head of the HUR, warned that Russia had replenished its stock of Kalibr cruise missiles and could resume firing them from ships and submarines in the Black Sea.

My comrades tell me that war is a marathon, not a sprint. I returned to Donbas in June 2022 ready to run a sprint. I got tired and almost burned out. Then I pulled myself together and set out on a marathon of unknown duration and destination. I am not so much demoralized as tired. Fatigue has burrowed into me, and I know I am not as effective as I once was. Our war of attrition has turned into a war of exhaustion, not just for me but for the country and for our Western partners.

I see exhaustion in my men, who are less motivated than before. A soldier who understands what the war is about, who wants to live and wants to win, learns quickly. But the new conscripts we receive do not want to learn. They cannot accept the fact that they have been drafted and they often end up dying. They are not capable of replacing those who flocked to recruitment centres on 24 February 2022.

Most of our troops have been fighting for more than two years. They have 'attended' family events – births, weddings and funerals – on their smartphones. It's a lot to ask of anyone, especially when the burden is not evenly shared. They need to be rotated out, but we know that fresh conscripts cannot replace veteran fighters. Dedicated soldiers understand that rotation will not be effective, so there is no remedy for their exhaustion.

I miss the beautiful unity we felt in the first months of the war, and I feel increasingly alienated from civilians. In May 2023, fourteen months after I rejoined the army on the day of the invasion, I am given ten days' leave. I travel with a friend to Zakarpattia, in the foothills of the Carpathian Mountains in the far west of Ukraine. One evening in a restaurant, we get into a discussion with men working in the local tourism industry. I wear civilian clothing, so they do not know that I'm a soldier.

'The war is about politics,' says one of the men, a driver for tourists. 'I say let the oligarchs slug it out. They created this whole mess so they could make more money.'

'I don't see what's political about it,' I say. 'Don't you think it's about land, about Ukraine's territorial integrity, which Putin violated?'

The driver gives me a strange look and continues. 'I hear people in Crimea and Donbas don't really want us there anyway. In that case, I say let them go. Our leaders have been rabbiting on for years about joining Europe and NATO. It's like waving a red flag in front of a bull. Don't get me wrong; I don't like Putin. But I think NATO and our politicians provoked him.'

'Nothing can excuse what the Russians are doing,' I say. It

irritates me when civilians more than a thousand kilometres from the combat zone try to explain the war to me.

'How do you know so much about it?' the driver asks.

'I'm a front-line officer in Donetsk oblast. I lead a reconnaissance platoon.'

'Wow, I'm impressed. Aren't you afraid?'

That is always the first question everyone asks me.

'No.'

'Have you seen anybody get killed?'

'Yes. A lot.'

'For example?'

'I don't want to talk about it.'

'Well hats off. Good for you, sister. You're a brave woman. Keep safe. I'm glad there are people like you, but fighting's not for me. I have health issues.'

One often hears this sort of thing from civilians. I am tired of the driver's whining, and I end the conversation abruptly. I am enjoying my holiday, so I don't let it bother me at the time, but I remember the conversation. In Kyiv on the same trip, things seem almost normal, compared to the devastation of Donbas. I am happy to go the cinema and theatre, to experience something other than war.

But when I take a short break in October 2023 to visit my mother, I feel annoyed. Maybe I am just tired. Maybe it is because civilians are becoming more and more detached from the war. I can't help looking at young men in the streets, imagining them as infantrymen or assault troops and resenting the fact they have not joined up.

Zelenskiy has been reluctant to extend conscription because he fears damaging social cohesion. He waits nearly a year after our parliament, the Verkhovna Rada, passes a bill lowering the conscription age from twenty-seven to twenty-five, to sign the bill into law in April 2024. Zelenskiy says Russia is preparing to mobilize another 300,000 soldiers on 1 June. But he denies what Zaluzhnyi said five months earlier, asserting that we need fewer than 500,000 new soldiers.

At the beginning of the invasion, the draft age was set high because the army wanted men with military experience who require less training. Zelenskiy also said he wanted to preserve the young so they can rebuild the country after the war. As a result, forty is the average age of our million-strong armed forces. There are far more forty-year-olds in Ukraine than men in their twenties, because the birth rate dropped dramatically during the terrible 1990s.

The Verkhovna Rada passed a separate law, also in April, intended to increase incentives to join the military and punish those who evade service. Men who fail to register for the draft may have their drivers' licences suspended. An extra bonus is offered to front-line soldiers. Death benefits are officially raised to fifteen million hryvnia (about €355,000), which the army has been paying for some time.

Ukrainian soldiers are currently required to serve until the end of the war, whenever that may be. The bill originally foresaw a thirty-six-month limit on mandatory service, to encourage more to join up, so that volunteering would not be an open-ended commitment. The provision was scrapped at the request of General Syrskyi, who says rotation and demobilization should be addressed in a separate bill later.

While I was on leave in October 2023, I met Viktoria, a friend from university, for coffee. Our conversation turned to the shortage of manpower in the army and the debate about conscription.

'You've heard they are talking about drafting women?' I say. 'Ukraine needs all citizens eighteen and older.'

'You don't think they're going to do it, do you?'

'They *should* do it. I see no justification for exempting women. Didn't we campaign for equality when we were students? Being in the army doesn't mean you have to carry a gun. There's plenty of administrative work. If you get drafted, you can join my platoon in Donbas. It will be just like old times!'

Viktoria is not amused. She tosses her long, shiny hair over her shoulder and her eyes dart down the busy street in front of the café. 'Not on your life! No way. I have a good job and I love my boyfriend. If they try to draft me, I'll run away and apply for citizenship in another country.'

'But Ukraine doesn't allow dual citizenship. You'll have to give up Ukrainian nationality!'

'Who cares?'

'Viktoria, I can't believe you're saying that! What did we demonstrate for at Maidan? Why did we protest if we're not ready to defend ourselves, our families and our country with weapons? Your attitude doesn't make sense.'

'That was then. This is now. Do you think the politicians' kids fight in the trenches? In today's world it's every man for himself. I don't see why I should die for a lost cause. We're going to lose anyway, Yulia.'

I feel as if I've been hit with a sledgehammer. Viktoria and I no longer have anything in common. Was our decade-long friendship a lie?

'Oh. I've upset you,' Viktoria says. 'I'm sorry, Yulia. I'm being honest. Maybe you should be honest with yourself. Ask yourself what the hell you are doing in Donbas.'

I look at my watch and feign surprise, say I am late for a non-existent appointment. I put a few hundred hryvnia on the table to pay for the coffee, and rush away. My friendship with Viktoria is over.

'I'm beginning to think I have a problem with civilians,' I tell Sergeant Andriy on returning to base camp in Donbas.

'What do you mean?'

I tell him about my conversation with Viktoria, and the resentment I felt towards young men in the streets of Kyiv.

'Unfortunately, society is not ready for mobilization,' Andriy says. 'That's why they cannot replace soldiers like us who have been fighting for two years. That's why we had the scandal about the recruitment centres.'

In the summer of 2023, Zelenskiy sacked all heads of regional recruitment offices because many were taking bribes not to draft men. Other over-zealous recruitment officers have begun rounding up men in public places and shipping them directly to the front, without even allowing them to go home. Such practices create panic.

*

'Do you think it's worth fighting for a society that is not willing to participate in the defence of the country?' I ask Andriy.

'I think we shouldn't dwell on it, because thinking about it just makes it harder,' he replies.

'What bothers me most are civilians who have never seen the war and declare they are tired of war; you must have seen the memes about neurasthenic couch potatoes. We're all tired of the war, but the difference between us on the front line and civilians is growing. The mood is changing. Look how support for the army is dwindling.'

I tell Andriy that when I joined up on the first day of the invasion, the recruitment centre was packed, that I saw a middle-aged man and a young woman with painted fingernails fighting over a machine gun. They were signing volunteers up in school notebooks and had to turn a lot of people away. There were hundreds, perhaps thousands, of private charitable funds supporting the armed forces. For a while, private funds gave the army more money and equipment than the government did. We need 400,000 hryvnia (close to €10,000) to buy two drones at present. A year ago, we would have got that in a week. It's been two months, and we cannot get the money. When the Russians stage missile attacks on cities, people remember us briefly and the donations go up. But when it's quiet, there is nothing. I suppose that is human psychology.

'The mood has changed,' Andriy says. 'People are starting to talk about signing for peace. As soon as they hear the words "total mobilization", they say "Let's sign for peace".'

The outlook is unremittingly bleak in late 2023 and early 2024. Russia sends New Year's greetings in the form of an eighteen-hour barrage of drones and missiles that kills forty-one civilians – a record – across Ukraine. Until now, Kyiv has been largely spared because it is protected by Western air defence missiles. But the Russians have learned to saturate our air defence systems with swarms of drones. Most Ukrainian cities have little or no protection from aerial bombardment.

The failure of Ukraine's counter-offensive is the most salient fact of the preceding year. We learn that sanctions on Russian petroleum have not worked, that our enemy is earning more petrodollars than ever. In fact, the Russian economy is growing, stoked up on military spending. In February, Putin gloats over his victory at Avdiivka and the death in prison of the Russian dissident Alexei Navalny.

Interest in Ukraine has plummeted since Hamas attacked Israel on 7 October. The US diverted to Israel tens of thousands of US-made 155-millimetre artillery shells which are desperately needed in Ukraine. When I read posts by Ukrainian citizens on social media saying, 'Let's support Israel', I think: *What about supporting Ukraine? Our country is on the European landmass and it's nearly thirty times the size of Israel. Surely that means something.*

On 1 April 2024, Israel provokes Iran by bombing its embassy in Damascus, killing sixteen people, including eight officers from the Islamic Revolutionary Guard Corps. Iran retaliates overnight on 13/14 April, launching at Israel 330 cruise missiles, attack drones and ballistic missiles.

Russia has been firing a near identical mix of drones and missiles at Ukraine for months, killing civilians and destroying 80 per cent of our electricity network. Israel and Ukraine are in theory both allies of the West. But Ukraine has been left almost defenceless, while US, British, French and Jordanian fighter jets help Israel shoot down 99 per cent of the Iranian projectiles. A seven-year-old Bedouin girl is severely wounded by falling shrapnel from a missile intercept over Israel. No one in Israel dies and there is no significant damage.

Ukraine reacts to the blatant double standard with hurt incredulity. If the West can protect Israel, surely it could protect Ukraine? Are Israeli lives really worth more than Ukrainian lives? Why are we considered second-class partners?

The European Union promised to give us one million 155-millimetre shells by March 2024. In November they told us it will be more like 420,000. On 1 February 2024, Europe finally votes to give us €50 billion over four years, after months of delay by Putin's useful idiot, Hungarian Prime Minister Viktor Orbán. As our ammunition hunger grows, Republicans in Congress block $61 billion in military aid for Ukraine for six months, on orders from Donald Trump. We are fighting with our hands tied. The possibility that Trump could win the US presidential election on 5 November 2024 hangs over us like doomsday.

Most nights, I collapse onto my camp bed in exhaustion and sleep the sleep of the just. The rare dreams I have are filled with anxiety.

One night in late 2023 or early 2024, I find myself with my brother, Bohdan, at a checkpoint manned by a Russian soldier. It is dark and freezing. Bohdan and I have somehow wandered into Russia, and I am panic-stricken. I carry only a Ukrainian passport.

'Your documents!' the soldier says in Russian.

'I am from the Donetsk People's Republic,' I tell the soldier, using the Russian name for the occupied and annexed territory. I can think of no other explanation as to why I should carry a Ukrainian passport.

'You should have a Russian passport by now!' the soldier says.

I mumble something about having been very busy, followed by protestations of love for Russia. *How can I escape? I must get out of here.* In the darkness, I see only the soldier's face framed in his shapka hat, the assault rifle strapped across his chest and the snowbanks that surround us. Bohdan is silent. I can see no way out. They will find out that I am a Ukrainian officer. They will throw me in prison.

I wake up with a tremendous sense of relief. I am not in Russia but in a derelict house with my brothers-in-arms in the Ukrainian-held part of Donetsk. It's at least 10 kilometres to the nearest Russian soldier.

V

A Ukrainian Childhood

The night is so moonlit, so starry, so bright
There's so much light you could gather needles
Come, my love, weary with toil
If just for one minute to the grove

Don't be afraid that you'll get your feet wet in the cold dew
I will carry you home, my dear one, I will carry you home.
I will carry you home, my dear one, I will carry you home.

'The Night Is So Moonlit', one of Ukraine's best-
loved folk songs, from a nineteenth-century poem by
Mykhailo Starytsky, set to music by Mykola Lysenko

Independent Ukraine was four years old when I was born on
18 July 1995. At every stage, my life has mirrored the changing
fortunes of my country. You might say we grew up together.

The lives of my parents and my early childhood were
marked by the poverty and chaos of the 1990s. Like millions
of Ukrainians, I experienced a political awakening and found
a sense of national identity in the early years of this century.
I participated in the Euromaidan Revolution of Dignity as a

university student in 2013/14 and watched horrified as Russia retaliated by invading Crimea and Donbas. In 2016, and again in 2022, I took up arms to defend my country.

After independence in 1991, Tamara worked as a cashier in a currency exchange outlet in Kyiv. The Ukrainian economy had collapsed with the Soviet Union, and there were scarcely any jobs to be found. Criminal gangs frequently robbed exchange shops at gunpoint, so my mother's work was dangerous. My father, Mykola, was a security guard at the same exchange shop. That is how my parents met.

Tamara is from a poor family in the Kyiv region. She does not remember her father. Her mother worked for the railways. As a child in the late 1960s and 1970s, Tamara lived with her sister and their mother in a dormitory reserved for railway workers, which the Soviet state provided to them free of charge. They had a very rough time. My maternal grandmother was an alcoholic who died of cancer in her forties. That left only my mother and her older sister, Svitlana, who acted as a kind of surrogate mother to Tamara. Svitlana eventually found a good job at a telephone call centre.

My father, Mykola, was born and raised in Lazarivka, a village in Zhytomyr oblast, 90 kilometres west of Kyiv. When he finally moved to the capital, he found it incredibly exciting and never tired of wandering around the city. He was intelligent but unstable. Extravagant is the word that comes to mind when I try to describe my father. He was fascinated by history and all things military. Over the years he worked as a tour guide and in the tax office. He tried to open a shop but seemed incapable of staying in one place and concentrating on a single subject. He never found steady, long-term employment. Making model aeroplanes and military vehicles was one of his favourite hobbies.

Mykola's family were rich farmers in Zhytomyr until the Soviets seized their land as part of Stalin's policy of collectivization in the 1930s. His grandparents were sent to a collectivized farm and could no longer support their four children. Mykola's mother, Lyuba, ended up in an orphanage. The family were later reunited and regained some of their land. They grew fruit and vegetables and raised livestock. But Lyuba was haunted for the rest of her life by the trauma of abandonment and the orphanage. She distrusted anyone outside our immediate family, a trait I called her Soviet memory. She suffered from psychosomatic illnesses and when she died in 2019, I suspected it was because of the negative emotions bottled up inside her.

Lyuba's suspicious nature may have come from her day job at the forensic police department, where she was responsible for janitors and cleaning services. When we were small, my brother and I went there often with her. We were aware that the director relied on Lyuba, but she never talked about her employment. When she was working, she stayed in her apartment in Vyshneve, the dormitory town south-west of Kyiv where Tamara and I live. But her real home, where she grew old and died, was the two-storey red-brick dacha or country house she built on her portion of her parents' land in Lazarivka. Her property has a deep well with clear water, the best in the village.

We called my paternal grandmother Baba Lyuba, using the familiar Ukrainian term for grandma. She rose at four o'clock every morning, worked all day, cooked in the evening and went to bed at eleven o'clock at night. We told her to pay someone to do the gardening, but she always replied, 'No. This is my land. I will cultivate it myself.' She grew fruit and vegetables and, close to the house, she planted flowers, especially violets. On the day of my birth, my father planted a walnut tree in Lyuba's garden.

I spent many of the happiest days of my childhood in Lazarivka, though I also remember it as a place of toil, because we were made to work with Lyuba in the garden. Like most children, I loved to hear my parents and grandmother recount events I could not remember, in which I was the central character. 'Tell me about when I was little,' I said often. One particular incident entered family lore.

Lyuba was petite, with sun-leathered skin. She loved me and my brother more than anything or anyone. She told me this story countless times.

'I am working in the garden one day when you disappear. You are two or three years old, and I search everywhere for you. Your parents have gone to run an errand and I am in a state of panic by the time they return. "Yulia is missing!" I tell your father.'

'What! How can that be? When did you last see her?' he asks.

'She was playing in the grass. I was on my knees in the flowerbed and when I turned around, she was gone.'

'You stupid, stupid woman! How could you let her out of your sight? What if she's been kidnapped? Or carried off by an animal?' It is the only time my father speaks harshly to his mother.

'She would have made a noise!' Lyuba says. She is crying. My mother is crying. They search every corner of the house and comb the garden, shouting 'Yulia! Yulia!'

'She must have fallen in the well,' Lyuba says through tears. 'I will jump into the well and fetch her. You can lower me down with the pulley.'

Just then they notice the family cat sprawled in the sun in front of the garden shed.

'What are you purring for?' Lyuba shouts at the cat. 'Don't you know this is a terrible sorrow?'

My father pushes open the shed door to find me sleeping on a sack of grain inside. No one ever figures out how, as a toddler, I managed to pull the door shut behind me. Perhaps my regard for felines as creatures with almost mystical powers comes from this story.

My first memory dates from a year or two later, when I am around four years old. I call Mykola Tato or Daddy. He and I are digging potatoes in the garden. It is hot and I grow sleepy. He carries me into the dacha to lay me down on Baba Lyuba's bed for a nap. He cradles me in his arms and croons an old Ukrainian folk song, 'The Night is So Moonlit'. It is really a love song, but Mykola sings it like a lullaby.

I will carry you home, my dear one, I will carry you home.
I will carry you home, my dear one, I will carry you home.

Another early memory is of picking peas in the garden with Baba Lyuba. She teaches me to pull the bright green pod apart between my thumbs and index fingers and push the pearl-like peas into a burlap sack. I eat so many raw peas that I end up with a terrible tummy ache. Mykola runs with me through fields of sunflowers to the doctor's clinic. I am his princess in distress; he is my knight in shining armour.

My parents are poor, but the first five years of my life in Bucha are happy. I am enchanted by Viktoria, the nanny I stay with while my parents are working. I play with a neighbour boy called Vova. Our life revolves around the Good News Baptist Church. Mama dresses me up every Sunday morning and I stand between my parents, my tiny hands in theirs, while they sing hymns and recite the Lord's Prayer. Baptist missionaries from America organize summer camps for children where we roast marshmallows and hot dogs on bent coat hangers over campfires and cook potatoes wrapped in aluminium foil in the coals. The missionaries speak only a few words of Ukrainian, but Tamara manages to communicate with them by using hand gestures and a dictionary.

Incongruous as it may seem, given my later calling as a soldier, I am a feminine little girl who loves pretty clothes. Once, Tamara takes me to a department store in Kyiv, where I see a velvet dress with a lace collar. I know we cannot afford it, so I don't even ask. But silent tears run down my cheeks in the car on the way home. I see my mother's reflection in the rear-view mirror, watching me cry in the back seat, and I feel guilty because I know I have hurt her.

McDonald's sets up shop in Ukraine when I am a small child. For us, it is not a fast-food chain but a real restaurant, a special treat which we indulge in on the occasional weekend. My parents order me the 'Happy Meal' for children, which includes a burger, fries and a free toy. I always wait for the toy.

My father purchases half of a crumbling house that has no running water in the suburbs west of Kyiv. The other half is occupied by American Baptist missionaries. Our living conditions must be shocking for them, or perhaps they think it is exotic, like camping or going on safari in Africa to spread the word of God.

My little brother Bohdan is born while my mother, father and I still live in the bad house. Soon after Bohdan's birth in 2000, Mykola leaves Tamara for a neighbour called Larysa, whom he later marries. She is the mother of Vova, the little boy I play with. Mykola's departure is very hard for Tamara. She has stopped working to have Bohdan, because Mykola was earning money at the time. She finds herself in her mid-thirties with no husband, no job and no prospects for the future. I have never forgotten seeing my mother sobbing.

Larysa must feel guilty, because she finds a job for Tamara in the call centre at the Kyivstar phone company. Or perhaps it is out of self-interest, so that Mykola will not have to give us so much money. Everything is difficult. After my parents' divorce, Baba Lyuba takes us into her apartment in Vyshneve, to get us out of the bad house. She helps us financially for a while.

When Tamara goes back to work, I have to look after Bohdan. I resent it because I can't go out to play with other children. Our relationship is terrible. We fight a lot, until Bohdan grows big enough to defend himself and I can no longer hit him. He matures very fast and by the age of eighteen he takes up with a girlfriend and finds his own apartment. They marry but his wife turns out to have an addiction to gambling in casinos. We try to help her, but she can't change, so they separate. I'm not sure when and how Bohdan and I go from beating each other up to loving each other, but my little brother is my best friend in the world now.

It is Christmastime in the early 2000s, not long before we move to Baba Lyuba's apartment. Tamara has done her best to decorate our home with tinsel and flashing lights. The doorbell rings one evening and she opens the door to missionaries from the Good News Baptist Church. I am fascinated by 'Big Jack', a giant of a man who wears white socks and huge sneakers that remind me of boats. His wife, Margie, is an energetic, sparrow-like woman.

They stand grinning in the doorway, wearing pointed red Santa hats with white pom-poms and holding red cloth bags filled with presents.

'Merry Christmas! Ho, ho, ho!' Big Jack says. Bohdan and I know the Americans bring presents, and we run to them in our pyjamas. Margie drops to her knees and hugs us. Tamara proposes tea or coffee, but the Americans decline.

'We can't stay long. Santa has asked us to deliver a lot of presents,' Big Jack says.

Bohdan and I stand in front of the couple, shifting with impatience from foot to foot.

'Were you a good girl this year, Yulia?'

I look at Tamara who answers for me. 'Yes, except when she fights with her brother.' Bohdan is transfixed by the gifts spilling out of the bags. We tear off the wrapping paper. My present is a Barbie doll in a swimsuit with impossibly long legs that bend to a sitting position and back to standing. I have never seen anything like her.

'Be careful not to bend Barbie's knees in the wrong direction or her legs will break. They bend only one way, like your knees in real life,' Margie says. She hands me a second package, which contains a tailored suit, high-heeled shoes and a hat for Barbie.

Bohdan receives a red sports car operated by a hand-held remote control with stop, go and speed buttons. Big Jack puts the batteries in the zapper and the car zooms across the living-room floor. It is even more wondrous than the bendable Barbie.

'Can I try? Can I try?' I beg Big Jack.

'It's your brother's present. Let him try first.'

Bohdan runs to the car, turns it back to face in our direction, pushes the go button and laughs with glee when it races back. In an unusual show of brotherly love, he hands the zapper to me, so I can play with it. Tamara nudges us to say thank you to our friends. Years later, when I pilot a drone for the first time in Donbas, I remember the joy of remotely controlling Bohdan's toy car.

'Merry Christmas!' Big Jack repeats as they go out the door. 'Jesus loves you!'

*

Tamara has always liked talking to people. Once my brother and I are grown up and can provide for ourselves, she decides to go to college. She jokes that she is old enough to be a grandmother and that she is studying with people who are the age of her children. Tamara is persistent and gets her degree. She is now a successful psychotherapist, working for the military and for people displaced by the war. For the first time in her life, she finds her work satisfying. She has become more loving and understanding as a mother.

When we were attending church, we were poor but happy, because the Baptists made us feel accepted. After we leave Bucha, we stop going to church. I am separated from my beloved Viktoria. I blame myself for my father's departure. I think it is my fault: that I have done something wrong which made him go away. With time I mature, and I realize that Mykola is a womanizer; that it is his fault our family fell apart. I am angry with him, and we don't talk to each other for a long time. He tries, but I refuse all contact.

I wouldn't say my childhood was unhappy, because you don't think in those terms when you are a child. There were happy moments. It was just difficult. That was the fate of a child born in the 1990s, a terrible decade in Ukraine.

We move three times in three years while my parents are

splitting up. The first time is to the bad house, and I attend the local elementary school. Each time I switch schools, it is hard for me. I am not naturally sociable, and I find it difficult to make new friends. Things finally settle down when we move to the apartment in Vyshneve where my mother still lives, and which I consider my home.

Then Mykola insists that Bohdan and I enrol at the Leader Lyceum in an elite district of Kyiv called Pechersk. My father's former history professor has become the principal at the Leader, and he says we can attend free of charge. But the school demands so-called charity donations from parents. They are, in fact, disguised bribes that my mother has to pay.

Our classmates are the children of sports stars, deputies in the Verkhovna Rada and high-ranking officials. It is a good school, but for a child from a poor family with a turbulent past it is difficult to adapt. My clothes look shabby compared to my classmates'. Their parents' drivers pick them up after school, while Bohdan and I wait for Tamara to collect us when she finishes work in the evening. The school is in downtown Kyiv, and we live outside the city limits. Mama won't let me make my own way home until I am 12 or 13 years old.

When I am nine years old, I read the Harry Potter books and I want to go to Hogwarts. As a teenager, I see a thriller in which Nicole Kidman plays an interpreter caught up in assassination plots at the UN headquarters in New York. After that, I want to be an interpreter. English is my favourite subject at the Leader Lyceum. I especially like area studies, where we learn about the culture of the US and United Kingdom. The school divides students into four streams and I choose humanities, so my classes focus on history, language and literature.

We speak Russian at home. As a child, I watch Russian cartoons and learn Russian legends about Prince Ivan. I remember the one where the magical grey wolf helps Ivan to capture the firebird, which was the basis for Igor Stravinsky's ballet. I love Leo Tolstoy's *War and Peace*. I also like Dostoevsky, though he is confusing for me. I read the poetry of Pushkin and Lermontov, and find the great classics of Russian literature more interesting than Ukrainian literature, which is poorly taught, with texts assigned to children too young to understand them. I have the impression that my Ukrainian literature teacher looks down on me because I am poor.

In those days, my father still believed in the fairy tale about Ukrainians and Russians being one people, which is surprising given what happened to his family in the 1930s, and for someone who knows history. Mykola enjoys going to MAKS, the annual international air and space show outside Moscow. He takes me and Bohdan one year, when I am thirteen or fourteen. I find Moscow dingy, hostile and depressing. He also takes me to St Petersburg, which is more to my liking, with its canals and neoclassical architecture painted in pastel colours. A distant cousin of ours has married an officer in the Russian intelligence service, the FSB. We go to see them in Moscow. I believe they still live there, though we are no longer in contact.

For more than a decade after independence, Ukrainians are not really concerned with their cultural and national identity. We are thinking about how to eat, how to survive. Everyone is struggling. I assume Russia is a friendly country and that we are one people, because that is the message Mykola conveys to me.

The Orange Revolution in late 2004 and early 2005 introduces me to the concept of national identity. I am only nine at the time. Mykola takes me to Maidan Nezalezhnosti, Independence Square, during the two months of demonstrations. (Ukrainians usually shorten the name to 'the Maidan', a word of Persian origin meaning 'square'.) My father hoists me onto his shoulders so I can see the throng of people assembled in the centre of the capital. We are more tourists than demonstrators.

Nine years later, I will run into Mykola by chance in similar demonstrations. By then we better understand what is at stake. The pro-Russian president, Viktor Yanukovych, is unseated twice, by both revolutions. In November 2004, he rigged the presidential election. The defeated candidate, Viktor Yushchenko, was disfigured by poisoning with dioxin during the campaign, presumably by Russian agents.

The Orange Revolution is the first time I hear words like national dignity and consciousness. I don't understand it fully, but I know it is about freedom of speech and being allowed to decide for one's own country. The protests result in a repeat of the election, which Yanukovych loses. Yushchenko serves for five years as president. He is an intellectual who is willing to spend government funds on culture and national identity. He creates the memorial to the Holodomor, the famine created by Stalin's forced collectivization of agriculture in 1932/33 which killed close to four million Ukrainians. But Yushchenko, who was previously a banker, is criticized for being indecisive and for appointing friends and family members rather than professionals to key positions. The 2008 world financial crisis hits Ukraine particularly hard. In 2010, disappointment with Yushchenko leads to victory for the dreadful Yanukovych in a fair election.

I perform well in the general education assessment examinations at the end of secondary school. In history class I have learned about the Kyiv-Mohyla Academy, which was founded in 1615 and was an important seat of learning until the early nineteenth century. The most famous alumnus is Hetman Ivan Mazepa, the Cossack leader who allied himself with Sweden and

Poland to fight the Russian czar Peter I and was immortalized by Voltaire and Byron. By coincidence, the 54th mechanized brigade, which Illia and I later fought in, was given the honorary title 'Hetman Ivan Mazepa' in 2020.

When it reopens as a national university at the time of independence in 1991, Kyiv-Mohyla embraces the promotion of the Ukrainian language, culture and identity. Armed with high test scores, I am accepted. Tamara, Bohdan and I celebrate with tea and cake, which is all we can afford. I start my university studies there at the age of seventeen.

I fail to obtain a government scholarship, so Tamara pays my tuition fees at Kyiv-Mohyla. It costs 19,000 hryvnia annually, the equivalent of about €2,800 at the time. It is a substantial sum for our family and means scrimping on food and other necessities. But Mama never complains. 'Your education is the one thing that no one can take from you,' she often tells me.

Ninety-five per cent of students spoke Russian at the Leader Lyceum where I completed my secondary studies. At school in those days, speaking Ukrainian was regarded as uncouth and reactionary. To be fair, I must note that the Leader has become more patriotic in the intervening years, and I am now on good terms with a school I resented when I was growing up. We decorate our front-line position with drawings sent by children from the Leader. There's one with a heart that is blue on top and yellow on the bottom, like the Ukrainian flag. There's a very good pastel of a tank battle, in ochre and khaki. The Leader bought a drone for my platoon. They painted the empty shell casings I sent them and auctioned them on behalf of the Hellish Hornets.

I arrive at Kyiv-Mohyla having always spoken and studied in Russian. Suddenly I am plunged into an environment where everyone speaks Ukrainian. It is not about persecuting Russian-speakers, but about affirming Ukrainian identity. The university is a centre of Ukrainian ideas and thinking, and this is very exciting to me.

I still dream of becoming an interpreter and I want to study English philology, but it isn't on offer, so I enrol in the Ukrainian philology department instead, to study the Ukrainian language and the country's history and culture. A new world opens up to me, a world that had always surrounded me, but which I had ignored. Russian and Ukrainian are as similar as Dutch and German, or Spanish and Portuguese. Most Ukrainians speak Russian. A Russian who has not learned Ukrainian could probably pick up about 50 per cent of a conversation. Then there is Surzhyk, the Russian–Ukrainian pidgin that is spoken – but not written – by many Ukrainians, especially in central and eastern parts of the country.

Russian and Ukrainian are both Slavonic languages, with the same cases and freely structured sentences; in other words, the noun does not have to precede the verb, as in English. The main difference is in vocabulary. And they also have different accents. Ukrainians replace the hard G with a soft H, the Russian I with a Y.

As a philologist, I do not believe there are ugly or beautiful languages. My preference for Ukrainian is more political than linguistic, because Russia has often used language as a weapon. Just as Hitler considered any German-speaker to be German, Putin thinks any Russian-speaker is Russian. He attacked Ukraine on the pretext of defending the Russian language. But his scheme has backfired. Instead of defending Russian, Putin has made it the language of the enemy. I know many

Russian-speaking Ukrainians who have switched languages since the full-scale invasion.

In much the same way that Britain tried to stamp out the Irish language, Russia tried for centuries to eliminate Ukrainian. The Valuev Circular of 1863 banned the publication of textbooks in 'Little Russian', as it refers to Ukrainian. 'A separate Little Russian language never existed, does not exist and shall not exist, and the tongue used by commoners [Ukrainians] is nothing but Russian corrupted by Polish,' the decree says. Tchaikovsky's joyful Symphony No. 2 is called the 'Little Russian' because it includes three Ukrainian folk songs.

More than 150 years after the Valuev Circular, Putin says that Ukraine does not exist and there is no such language as Ukrainian, only a dialect of Russian.

In 1876, Czar Alexander II forbade all printing in the Ukrainian language, except for reprints of old documents. The same decree banned lectures, the staging of plays and the import of publications in Ukrainian. In the 1930s, Stalin brutally suppressed the 'Executed Renaissance' by killing or deporting to the Gulag teachers of the Ukrainian language and prose writers, poets and playwrights working in Ukrainian.

Since the 2022 invasion of Ukraine, there has been a heated debate about the 'de-Russification' of Ukrainian society. Russia's most vocal opponents knock down statues of Pushkin and call for bans on the performance of Tchaikovsky's music. I have thought a lot about it, and I believe that after you have read Shevchenko, Lesya Ukrainka, Ivan Franko, Hrushevsky and Vynnychenko, then you can read Russian literature. But I think it would be better to take Russian literature off Ukrainian school curricula, because attitudes form at an early age.

I made no friends at secondary school because my affluent classmates considered me socially inferior. At Kyiv-Mohyla my family's poverty does not seem to matter, and I blossom. Olena, the daughter of a professor of medieval literature, becomes one of my closest friends. Like all my friends at Kyiv-Mohyla, she has grown up in an intellectual environment. It's a competitive milieu, and I feel a little intimidated by it. I work hard to catch up, to measure up to them.

Thanks to Kyiv-Mohyla, I learn that Ukraine has authentic medieval literature, which Russia does not have. I am able to read texts in old Ukrainian and I become fascinated by the richness of Ukraine's European heritage. At some points, I dare say Ukrainian culture surpassed that of the rest of Europe.

I learn that ancient Greece founded colonies along what is today Ukraine's Black Sea coast in the first millennium BC. In the eighth and ninth centuries AD, Viking conquerors known as Varangians, hailing from present-day Sweden, settled in lands that are now Belarusian, Russian and Ukrainian. A group of Varangians led by Rurik and known as the Rus' settled in Novgorod in AD 862. Twenty years later, Rurik's relative Oleh established the Kyivan Rus' state farther south, in present-day Kyiv. It was ruled by Rurik's descendants, the Rurikid dynasty.

Rurik's great-grandson, Volodymyr – Vladimir to the Russians – abandoned Slavonic paganism for Christianity in AD 988, a condition for his marriage to Anna Porphyrogenita, the daughter of Byzantine Emperor Romanos II and sister to emperors Basil II and Constantine VIII. Volodymyr ordered that all pagan idols be thrown into the Dnipro river, and that the Rus' people be baptized en masse in the same river, by representatives of the patriarchate in Constantinople. (The Constantinople patriarchate would separate from Rome and become the Orthodox Church in 1054.)

Some historians regret that Kyiv embraced Eastern Christianity, because ultimately it distanced us from the European mainstream. Before he died in a Soviet labour camp in 1985, the poet Vasyl Stus wrote in *Tvory*, published posthumously in Kyiv, that Constantinople 'brought us, the easternmost part of the West, into the East. Our individualistic Western spirit' was 'stamped by despotic Byzantine Orthodoxy'.

About three-quarters of Ukrainians remain Orthodox to this day. Putin claims that shared faith in Orthodox Christianity is evidence that Ukraine and Russia are 'one people', but the Russian Orthodox Church has been an instrument of colonization for centuries. Some of its clergy sided with Russian separatists in Donbas when the war started in 2014/15. They refused to bless or baptize Ukrainian soldiers loyal to Kyiv, and stored weapons in church buildings.

The Russian Orthodox Patriarch Kirill is an ideologue of Putinism who supported the 2022 invasion of Ukraine. Kirill wrote that 'The peoples of Russia and Ukraine came from one baptismal font' and said the invasion was the result of confrontation between the West and Russia. Russia claims to be protecting Orthodox Christians in Ukraine, even as it kills them in their thousands. Russia has attacked Orthodox holy places in Ukraine, including the Sviatohirsk Lavra monastery on the right bank of the Siverskyi Donets river, one of the three most sacred sites in Ukraine for Orthodox believers.

Both Ukraine and Russia claim lineage back to the Kyivan Rus'. But the Kyivan Rus' were not Russian. They were a distinct medieval European dynasty that was destroyed by the Mongol horde in the thirteenth century.

Today's Russians are descendants of the Principality of Muscovy, which was founded in the second half of the thirteenth century, about 400 years after the Kyivan Rus' dynasty was established. The Mongol Golden Horde sacked Kyiv in 1240. The Mongols also took Muscovy, but the Muscovites were good collaborators and transformed themselves into vassals of the Mongols. It wasn't until 1721 that Peter I – Peter the Great to Russians – renamed Muscovy the Russian empire. He took the name Russian from Kyivan Rus'. That is why Ukrainians say that Russia stole our history.

Our Viking origins and the early-eighteenth-century alliance between Cossacks and Swedes created a lasting affinity. It is not a coincidence that Scandinavian countries are among our strongest supporters in the war with Russia. Peter I defeated the Swedish King Charles XII and his Cossack ally, Hetman Ivan Mazepa, at the Battle of Poltava in 1709. The shared blue and yellow colours of the Swedish and Ukrainian flags may be a vestige of that alliance. Peter I seized large parts of present-day Ukraine and took artefacts from Kyiv to Russia.

Our ties to Europe continued long after the Viking Oleh founded the Kyivan Rus' in AD 882. Under the rule of Yaroslav the Wise, Grand Prince of Kyiv in the first half of the eleventh century, Kyiv was considered second only to Constantinople in beauty. Built on hilltops, the city was surrounded by two walls and boasted hundreds of golden onion domes topped with crosses. It is difficult to imagine such opulence today. Trade roads from western Europe, Arabia, Asia and Asia minor converged in Kyiv. The Rus' dynasty controlled the Dnipro, the mainstay of the network of rivers from the Baltic to the Black and Caspian seas.

Yaroslav married Ingegerd, the daughter of the king of Sweden, who is known to Ukrainians as Iryna. He built Saint Sophia Cathedral, where they were buried together. When Yaroslav's tomb was opened nearly 900 years after his death, the remains of a tall woman with Nordic features were found beside him. Elizabeth, Anna and Anastasia, daughters of Yaroslav and Iryna, married the kings of Norway, France and Hungary respectively. A fourth daughter, Agatha, is believed to have married into the English royal family. This is why we call Yaroslav the father-in-law of Europe.

Anna Yaroslavna, the royal couple's youngest child, is better known by her French name, Anne de Kiev. King Henri I of France was widowed in 1044. A pontifical order banned marriage to blood relatives and Henri searched far and wide for a new wife before deciding he must have Anna. The court in Kyiv was a place of great culture, known for literary and musical evenings where poets and musicians performed. Yaroslav believed strongly in education and Anna probably spoke her mother's Swedish tongue, Old East Slavic, Ancient Latin, Greek and French.

Henri twice sent ambassadors to Yaroslav's court, the first time in 1048 to persuade the grand prince to give his daughter in marriage, the second time in 1050 to bring the bride back to France, which was then a lesser power than the Kyivan Rus'. In the hope of convincing Yaroslav, Henri sent brocade from Flanders, leather doublets from Étampes, linen from Reims and lace from Orléans. Anna made the long journey up the Dnipro river, across Lake Ladoga and the Baltic and along the coast of Frisia. In her dowry she brought bearskins and sable furs, Persian silks, perfume from Armenia, caviar and vodka. The couple married in Reims, where Anna was crowned Queen of France.

Though Henri was considerably older than Anna, their marriage was happy. She reigned over his household in Senlis and bore four children, giving the Greek name Philip to the eldest, who would become King Philippe I on Henri's death in 1060. Anna was co-regent to the young king. She took as a second husband the Comte de Valois, Raoul de Crépy, who boasted of being the young king's adviser and stepfather.

The Mongol conquest ended the period of Kyiv's greatest influence, but it did not end relations between European powers and what is today Ukraine. Prince Danylo Romanovych, the founder of the city of Lviv, tried to defend Kyiv against the Mongol invasions of 1240/41. He later pleaded with Pope Innocent IV to send a crusade against the Mongols. Danylo kept his part of the bargain and converted to Catholicism, but Innocent never sent the promised army.

When Russia assaulted Ukraine on 24 February 2022, Ukrainians referred to the invaders as 'the horde from the east'. Some see the failure of Europe and NATO to defend Ukraine as a repetition of the West's betrayal of Danylo nearly eight centuries earlier.

The Republic of Genoa dominated the Black Sea coast, which thrived as a centre of commerce, until the middle of the fourteenth century. The 1569–1795 Polish–Lithuanian Commonwealth ruled much of Ukraine, especially the western part, until the end of the eighteenth century, when the Austro-Hungarian Empire took over Galicia, which included much of western Ukraine, until the First World War.

The Mongols could not cut Ukraine off from Europe. Every European current in art, literature, philosophy and science permeated what would become Ukraine. Russia was different. The Mongols isolated Russia for 240 years and infused it with their aggressive and bellicose habits. The princes of Muscovy acquired a taste for territorial expansion, which they called 'the gathering of the Russian lands'.

Eastern Ukraine was industrialized by European investment in the nineteenth and early twentieth centuries, when Belgium, France, Britain, Germany and Switzerland invested heavily in the development of Donbas, which was still part of the Russian empire. Belgium provided two-thirds of all investment in coal. There was a direct train from Brussels to Donbas. In Belgium, which comprised nine provinces at the time, Donbas was known as 'the tenth province'.

France invested most heavily in iron and steelworks. The British transformed the village of Yuzivka into the industrial city of Donetsk, built around a metallurgy plant, which was constructed by John Hughes, a mining engineer from South Wales. Three-quarters of the iron in the entire Russian empire was produced there. The German industrialist Gustav Hartmann built a steam locomotive plant in Luhansk.

This substantial European investment was nationalized by the Bolsheviks in the 1917 Revolution. Donbas, along with the rest of Ukraine, became part of the Soviet Union for most of the twentieth century. Industrial equipment installed there by Europeans more than a century ago has been poorly maintained, but much of it still functions.

So we Ukrainians have Greek, Swedish, Genoese, Polish–Lithuanian, Austrian, Belgian, British, French and German antecedents. We are Europeans, though our history is also Mongol, Cossack, Russian, Slavic and Turkish. We have been pulled back and forth between East and West for a thousand years.

Under the influence of Olena's father, the professor of medieval literature, she and I decide to write research papers on aspects

of Ukrainian apocryphal literature, stories that were never recognized by the Christian church or accepted into the Bible, and
which were thought to be heretical. Folk legends and traditions
have grown up around these apocrypha. They contradict the
teachings of the Church and have had a profound influence
on Ukrainian literature. My research paper is about walks to
hell in the apocrypha – the actual experience of travelling to
hell – which is not in the standard Bible. While I am writing
about walks to hell, Olena writes about walks to heaven. I am
only half-joking when I tell her a decade later that our choices
were premonitory. I have walked to hell in Donbas, while she
has walked to heaven in the prosperity and safety of Germany,
where she is a post-doctoral student.

When Olena defends her thesis via video link with Germany
late in the summer of 2023, I attend on Zoom from my platoon's
base camp in the combat zone in Donbas. It is important for me
to be there, because I dream of continuing my own research and
completing a master's thesis on walks to hell in the apocrypha.
Half the professors at Olena's viva voce examination had been
my teachers at Kyiv-Mohyla.

Contrary to the impression given by the esoteric nature of
Olena's and my research, Kyiv-Mohyla has been a hotbed of
political activism since the 2004 Orange Revolution. In 2010,
some of my classmates founded an informal group of like-
minded people called Vidsich, which means Rebuff, signifying
their intention to oppose the pro-Russian policies of President
Viktor Yanukovych. The group proclaims its dedication to the
promotion of human rights and Ukrainian identity. I participate
in my first street demonstration with Vidsich in December 2012,
a few months after starting university. We picket Yanukovych's
office to protest against indications that he may take Ukraine
into Putin's Eurasian Customs Union, which the leaders of

Russia, Belarus and Kazakhstan founded in 2010. It would in 2014/15 evolve into an imitation of the European Union for post-Soviet states, christened the EEU (Eurasian Economic Union) by Putin.

I am drawn to Vidsich's philosophy of non-violence, inspired by the teachings of Mahatma Gandhi. We stage many marches, sit-ins and round tables. In 2014 we will form one of the leading *sotni* or self-defence groups at Euromaidan. Unlike other demonstrators, we never throw Molotov cocktails or engage in any form of violence.

I dislike Yanukovych instinctively and intensely. It is not because he is from Donetsk, but because he is visibly uneducated, stupid and corrupt. He has been convicted and imprisoned twice for assault and robbery. He is incapable of communicating or holding a dialogue and of representing Ukraine abroad. His first lady, Lyudmyla, is an equally shady character.

Already in 2012, the choice is between Russia and Europe. I want us to be part of the European Union, not Putin's Eurasian Economic Union. It is obvious to me that a peaceful economic agreement with Russia would open the door to Russia meddling in Ukrainian politics. I believe that Ukraine will benefit more from cooperation with Europe than from closer relations with Russia.

I have become convinced that Ukraine is historically a European nation with European values, which was hijacked by the Russian empire, the Soviet Union and the Russian Federation. I see the European Union as a beacon of civilization in a savage world. We want to free ourselves from Putin's bullying and join a union that enjoys democracy, free and fair elections, freedom of speech, prosperity, and the rule of law. We want to come home to Europe.

VI

Get Away from Moscow!

Aren't you thrilled today by the very idea of the revival of your nation?

Mykola Khvylovy, *Woodcocks*, 1927

9 Kultury Street, Kharkiv, eastern Ukraine. April 2013

I and my classmates Olena and Viktoria use our spring break from Kyiv-Mohyla Academy to make a literary pilgrimage. We go directly from Kharkiv railway station to the Slovo building, a grey five-storey apartment block which was purpose-built to be an artists' colony in the late 1920s.

We stand in front of the granite plaque in the shape of an open book to read the 122 names of the building's first inhabitants. Many are familiar to me from *The Executed Renaissance, An Anthology, 1917–1933, Poetry, Prose, Drama and the Essay*, which is required reading in our Ukrainian literature class, and which I carry in my backpack. The Ukrainian writers' works were destroyed under Stalin or banned until the dying days of the Soviet Union. Other texts were smuggled out.

Some of the writers' names are followed by the annotation 'shot at Sandarmokh', the forest and mass grave site in Karelia, on Russia's border with Finland, where nearly 300 representatives of the Ukrainian Renaissance were executed in the Great Purge of Stalin's perceived enemies in 1937/38. Numerous Ukrainians were among the 1,111 prisoners shot at Sandarmokh between 27 October and 4 November 1937 to mark the twentieth anniversary of the October revolution.

'So many of them murdered,' Olena says, shaking her head as she scans the list. Olena is the gentlest member of our band of friends, more at ease in the Middle Ages than in the savage twentieth and twenty-first centuries. 'And to think they all lived here...'

There is one name I want to see more than the others. My eyes run down the columns until they settle on: Mykola Khvylovy (1893–1933, committed suicide).

'Look!' I say to my travelling companions, tracing the engraved letters with my index finger. 'Here's Khvylovy.'

In the black and white photograph one usually sees of him, Khvylovy has thick black hair and eyebrows, large, soft eyes, a pale face and a sensitive expression. He would have been a heart-throb in any generation, and I'm not surprised that his first marriage ended because of his infidelity.

Khvylovy's prose can be almost as difficult as James Joyce's. I am struggling through the Ukrainian translation of *Ulysses* for another class at Kyiv-Mohyla. Joyce was a contemporary of Khvylovy, though they came from different worlds. Each in his own way blew his language apart. Khvylovy's novella *I (Romance)*, was an attempt to see inside the mind of a Soviet secret policeman, and it is disturbing. The Cheka agent sentences his own mother to death out of an obsession with revolutionary purity.

Khvylovy's most famous quotation, 'Get away from Moscow! Onward to Europe!', has caught the attention of our civil disobedience group Vidsich, which aims to loosen the grip of our former Russian colonizers over Ukraine. Among other measures, we advocate a boycott of Russian goods.

I find Khvylovy's political pamphlets more accessible than his poetry and fiction. He was fascinated by the relationship between art and politics and accused Russia of using language and culture to colonize Ukraine. He said nineteenth-century novels were infected with 'Dostoyevskism' which made heroes of 'little grey people'. Khvylovy criticized many of the writers we were taught to admire for 'epigonism', meaning that they merely imitated the works of previous generations. He wanted modern writers to be strong-willed, intellectually curious revolutionaries who would look westwards to Europe for inspiration.

A woman with auburn hair stands a few metres away, listening to the tail end of my impromptu exposé on Khvylovy. 'You must be the girls from Kyiv-Mohyla? Madam Onyschchenko is obviously a good teacher. I am your guide, Tetiana. Welcome to Slovo House.'

'We are not *girls*. We are *women*,' Viktoria corrects her. She says it with humour and the three of us laugh with Tetiana. She is an academic, a museum curator and a friend of our literature professor, who has set up the appointment. Tetiana holds the keys to the Slovo building, literally and figuratively.

'Shall we, ladies?' Tetiana says, gesturing for us to enter. We climb the stairs as she tells us the building's history.

Ukrainian writers flocked to Kharkiv when it became the capital of the Ukrainian Soviet Socialist Republic in 1919, Tetiana tells us. Lenin wanted to encourage minority and heritage languages. Imperial Russia had suppressed Ukrainian culture for generations, and writers were excited by the idea of

Ukrainization. But they were poor. Some slept in their offices. Others relied on charity for food and lodging. In the mid-1920s, a writer called Ostap Vyshnya went to the local authorities on behalf of the writers' union, asking the Soviet government to provide housing for intellectuals. The officials seized the opportunity to house potential troublemakers in a single building. It made it easier to keep them under surveillance. The secret police could tap the telephones and bribe neighbours to spy on one another.

We wonder how the writers could be stupid enough to accept the government's offer. Tetiana notes that they had nowhere to sleep and they stored manuscripts in jars to prevent mice eating the paper. In such circumstances, it was impossible to refuse. The secret police were active, but the Soviet Union had not yet shown its ugliest face. The architect Mytrophan Dashkevych was commissioned to design the building. When the money ran out in mid-construction, Ostap Vyshnya travelled to Moscow and appealed all the way up to Stalin, who approved the budget immediately.

Dashkevych designed the building in the form of a giant C, the Cyrillic letter for S, the first letter of Slovo, meaning 'Word'. Tetiana shows us an aerial photograph of the building which reveals its unusual shape. It is one of many fine examples in Kharkiv of constructivism, which grew out of the Russian Futurist movement and was associated with Bolshevism. In painting, constructivism was abstract and cubist. In architecture, it relied on technology and engineering and avoided all forms of decoration.

The writers and artists who lived in Slovo House were considered an elite, but that did not stop the Soviets from arresting, deporting and killing them. The sixty-six apartments were luxurious for their time, with high ceilings, separate baths and toilets, spacious kitchens, central heating and telephones. There was a solarium for sun-tanning and showers on the roof.

Tetiana leads us to the third-floor apartment which was occupied by Khvylovy, his second wife, Yulia Umantseva, and her daughter Lyubov.

Khvylovy was born in Trostianets, about 150 kilometres to the north-west of Kharkiv, in Sumy oblast. His mother was a Ukrainian schoolteacher, and his father was a Russian labourer whom Khvylovy described as a drunkard and 'a highly careless person'.

I am an impressionable eighteen-year-old and I feel a sense of kinship with Khvylovy. I too have an unreliable father, whose first name, Mykola, is the same as Khvylovy's. The writer's wife was called Yulia, like me. Khvylovy used Yulia as a pseudonym.

While Tetiana is speaking, I study the apartment. It is spacious and airy, but at the same time the heavy concrete walls make it feel oppressive. The sparse, modern furniture must resemble the furniture that Khvylovy and Yulia had at the time. *He must have seen the trees budding outside the window just as we see them today.*

Before the Bolshevik revolution, Khvylovy was expelled from two separate secondary schools for left-wing activism. He was drafted in 1914 to fight in the First World War. From 1915, he wrote, he endured 'three years of marches, hunger, terrible horror that I would not dare to describe'. When the war ended, he organized a volunteer unit of Free Cossacks to fight the Germans and the White Russians. It was a time of great upheaval, and he fought other Ukrainian groups as well.

In 1921, when things began to settle down after the war and the revolution, Khvylovy headed for the capital, Kharkiv, vowing to 'conquer' it, like many an ambitious young man. He met other writers, signed literary manifestos and published poetry with such titles as *In the Electrical Age*. He fervently believed in the Ukrainian Renaissance and founded literary circles with modernist names such as Vaplite and Prolitfront. An artists' group called Urbino convened in his apartment.

Khvylovy kept insisting that Ukraine must have a separate identity from Russia. Stalin had replaced Lenin's multiculturalism with demands for centralization, socialist realism and Russification. Stalin complained about Khvylovy to the head of the Communist Party of Ukraine. At a time when Communist parties in Europe followed Moscow with something approaching adoration, Stalin wrote, 'the Ukrainian Communist Khvylovy... calls on the Ukrainian leaders to get away from Moscow as fast as possible.'

Khvylovy was widely read in Russia, and, like all dictators, Stalin was paranoid. After he singled out Khvylovy for criticism, his henchmen in Kharkiv made Khvylovy's life unbearable. He tried to write pro-Soviet literature, but somehow could not refrain from denouncing Ukraine's dependence on Russia. He published a pamphlet entitled *Is Ukraine a Colony or Is It Not ?*

The arrests began in Slovo House in 1931. First, the actress Halyna Mnevska was imprisoned and sent into permanent exile because she refused to denounce her husband, Klym Polishchuk, who would later be shot at Sandarmokh. More arrests followed, against the backdrop of the Holodomor, when famine victims lay dying in the streets of Kharkiv.

Khvylovy's best friend, Mykhailo Yalovy, with whom he co-founded the Vaplite literary movement, was arrested by secret police on charges of espionage and plotting to assassinate a Communist official. Khvylovy and two other writers, Mykola Kulish and Oles Dosvitniy, met in Khvylovy's apartment to try to find a way forward. In utter despair, Khvylovy went into the bedroom to write his last words: 'Arrest of Yalovy – this

is the murder of an entire generation... For what? ... Today
is a beautiful sunny day. I love life – you cannot imagine how
much...'

Khvylovy's fellow writers heard the gunshot and rushed into
the bedroom to find him dead. 'He may have pulled the trigger
on the revolver,' the Ukrainian nationalist Dmytro Dontsov
wrote later, 'but Moscow put the weapon in his hand.'

Khvylovy considered himself a Bolshevik and a Communist
until the end, but those beliefs clashed with his Ukrainian patriotism and distrust of Russia. Representatives of the Executed
Renaissance had six options. They could parrot Soviet propaganda, remain silent, go into exile, be executed by a firing squad,
waste away in the Gulag or take their own life, as Khvylovy did.
In Slovo House, the Executed Renaissance flourished briefly
before it was extinguished by Stalin.

Almost nine years after our visit, Slovo House was damaged
by Russian shellfire in the first days of the full-scale invasion. The
author Viktoria Amelina spent a one-week writer's residency in
Slovo House in the summer of 2022. She subsequently dug up
a diary penned by her fellow author Volodymr Vakulenko, who
was murdered by the Russians during their occupation of Izium
from April to September 2022. Vakulenko had buried his diary
under cherry trees in his garden. Amelina published it, writing
in the preface, 'My worst fear is coming true: I'm inside a new
Executed Renaissance. As in the 1930s, Ukrainian artists are
killed, their manuscripts disappear, and their memory is erased.'
Amelina herself was killed in the 27 June 2023 Russian missile
strike that took the lives of thirteen people in the popular Ria
pizza restaurant in Kramatorsk.

In October 2023, PEN Ukraine reported that at least sixty-five
Ukrainian cultural figures had died as a result of the invasion.

The wheel of history has returned to the point of departure. Like Stalin before him, Putin gives his opponents the choice of silence or collaboration, imprisonment or exile, suicide or execution. Putin's opponents, like Stalin's, are murdered or arrested on bogus charges of conspiracy, espionage and extremism.

*

Motivated by the desire to 'get away from Moscow', hundreds of thousands of Ukrainians descended into the streets of Kyiv from 21 November 2013 until 22 February 2014. President Viktor Yanukovych's refusal to sign the Association Agreement, which Ukraine had been negotiating with the European Union for six years, was the spark that ignited the Maidan revolution.

Many Ukrainians were convinced by the anti-EU propaganda peddled by the Ukrainiskiy Vybor organization, founded by the pro-Russian oligarch Viktor Medvedchuk. The name means 'Ukrainian Choice', but it was in fact Russia's choice. The group broadcast silly television advertisements in heavily accented French and English, against backdrops featuring the Eiffel Tower or Big Ben. Actors warned that the EU Association Agreement would drive up prices and unemployment and bring same-sex marriage to Ukraine.

At the end of each advert, a deep voice intoned in Russian, 'Didn't understand a word? It's a foreign language and a foreign union! We [Putin's Eurasian Economic Union] speak the same language [Russian].' It was a silly argument, since Armenia, Kazakhstan and Kyrgyzstan are members of the union but speak totally different languages.

I considered the adverts to be grotesque anti-Ukrainian propaganda, but some of my relatives and acquaintances bought into their ideology. I heard things like, 'Why do we need Europe? We need Russia because we are brotherly nations. Europe will not understand us.'

The anti-LGBT argument was especially effective in the early 2010s. Ukraine has since become more tolerant on gender issues, while Russia has grown more extreme. Putin passed a law against 'gay propaganda' in 2013. In November 2023, the Russian Supreme Court banned what it called 'the international LGBTQ movement', which does not even exist as an organization. Every time Putin does something like this, it strengthens my impression that he is dragging Russia backwards, that he will end up ruling over the ignorant population of a country in economic decline. The Russian people choose not to protest about such nonsense. I say let them suffer. We protested against Yanukovych and drove him out. They accept rule by Putin, so they are responsible for what happens to them.

Medvedchuk, the founder of Ukrainiskiy Vybor, was a deputy in the Verkhovna Rada when he and his wife, the television presenter Oksana Marchenko, were put under house arrest in May 2021, accused of treason and of looting publicly owned resources in Russian-occupied Crimea.

Medvedchuk's reputation for treachery is long established in Ukraine. He was the court-appointed public defender for the dissident poet Vasyl Stus at Stus's trial in 1980. Instead of defending Stus, Medvedchuk listed his alleged crimes against the Soviet Union and declared that he deserved to be punished. It is not clear whether Stus's death in a Soviet labour camp was caused by starvation due to his hunger strike, or if he was murdered. Twenty years later, Stus was posthumously awarded the Hero of Ukraine medal. His legacy will come to mean a great deal to me, through my father.

When the Russian opposition leader Alexei Navalny dies at

a penal colony in the Arctic Circle on 16 February 2024, I think of Stus. It is usually impossible to determine the exact cause of death in a Russian prison, but I consider Russia's rulers to be guilty of murdering political prisoners regardless.

As head of Leonid Kuchma's presidential administration from 2002 until 2005, Medvedchuk issued secret memoranda known as *temniki* to Ukrainian television editors, dictating what they could and could not say. Putin is godfather to Medvedchuk and Marchenko's daughter Daryna. When the 2022 invasion started, Ukrainian intelligence suspected that Medvedchuk was funnelling money from Putin to Russia's collaborators in Ukraine. Had the invasion succeeded, Putin would probably have installed Medvedchuk as his puppet ruler.

Ukraine imprisoned Medvedchuk and Marchenko from April to September 2022, when they were traded for the defenders of the Azovstal steel plant in Mariupol. They went to live in Russia, where Medvedchuk tried to set up a Ukrainian government in exile. This is Putin's standard method, which he practised in Crimea, Donetsk, Luhansk and occupied parts of the Kherson and Zaporizhzhia oblasts, and earlier in the Chechen and Georgian territories he seized. He creates a fake government, then goes through the charade of concluding agreements with it. After the invasion, Medvedchuk's 180-million-euro yacht, the *Royal Romance*, was seized in the Croatian port of Rijeka. His private helicopter and business jet were also confiscated and given to the Ukrainian military.

Medvedchuk doesn't change. On 27 March 2024, the Czech government froze his assets, along with those of Artem Marchevskyi, a Ukrainian-Israeli dual national who ran a news website for Medvedchuk called Voice of Europe. The Czech foreign minister Jan Lipavský said Medvedchuk oversaw the operation from Russia with the goal of spreading 'pro-Russian narratives undermining Ukraine's sovereignty while infiltrating the European Parliament'.

The Vidsich movement isn't big, only ten or fifteen students, but we are in the forefront of the protest movement against Russian influence in Ukraine. In the weeks leading up to the Euromaidan protests, we are alert to indications that Yanukovych may pull out of the EU Association Agreement and instead join Putin's Eurasian Economic Union. We print hundreds of thousands of leaflets and distribute them widely. The message of the leaflets is that Ukraine is in danger of being dominated by Russia for decades to come. We ask why the puppet Yanukovych is selling Ukraine to Russia. We do not ask Ukrainians to vote for a specific party or politician. We cannot be accused of protesting on behalf of anyone. We simply argue the pros and cons of being in Europe versus being in a customs union with Russia.

I get up at five o'clock in the morning to hand out leaflets at the entrance to the Khreshchatyk and Maidan metro stations during rush hour. I return there each evening. We distribute leaflets door to door and entrust large quantities to people from other districts. I encounter a great deal of hostility. 'Who pays you to do this?' a middle-aged, middle-class man asks me one morning. He grabs the pamphlet, glances at it, crumples it up and throws it to the ground. 'I'll bet you're on Soros's payroll!' he shouts as he heads down the stairs. The Hungarian-American billionaire George Soros set up an organization in Ukraine before independence. Soros admits that it played a role in the Maidan revolution. His pro-democracy Open Society Foundations will be banned in Russia in 2015.

Other commuters accuse me of working for Western liberals,

for the United States or for Ukrainian opposition parties. 'Why are you protesting when there is nothing wrong with the country?' an ageing woman challenges me another morning. 'Everything is fine. The roads are being repaired. The subway is being built. You young people don't know how good you have it.'

Most of the time I don't reply because people are hurrying to or from work. They just want to say something unpleasant and rush off. There's no time for a rational discussion.

The police crack down. One afternoon we are gluing leaflets to a public hoarding in a pedestrian area when Katya, a leader of Vidsich, shouts: 'Look out! Police coming! Disperse!'

Olena and I stuff leaflets into our rucksacks and hastily put the lids on our glue pots. We drop our glue-covered brushes and run as fast as we can, pausing at the end of the street to turn back and see several comrades being led away by police.

Another time we don't hear the police come up behind us. 'Give me those leaflets!' one of them shouts. My eyes dart around in search of an escape route, but the rush-hour crowd is dense and there are at least two cops blocking our path. I give the officer a big, innocent smile.

'What's the matter, officer?' I ask.

'You are distributing subversive material.'

'It's not subversive at all! I love Ukraine and I want a better future for my country. Don't you?'

The cop is relatively young and looks almost amused. 'All right,' he says. 'But hand over the papers.'

'Please, officer, I spent my own money to print them. It's very hard for me to earn money! Don't you have children? They may be standing where I am one day.'

To my relief, the policeman rolls his eyes, throws up his hands and walks away with his colleagues. Some of my comrades are not so lucky and end up in the police commissariat. The secret, I tell them, is to be sweet and polite, not confrontational.

On a third occasion, we stack more than a thousand leaflets on a folding table in a shopping centre. Two policemen are about to confiscate them when a few metres away a man shouts, 'Stop, thief! Thief! Help! Police!'

The cops rush to him. He pats his empty pockets and points at an escalator. 'It was a youngster in a hoodie. I saw him. He stole my wallet. A blue hoodie. Please, officer, can you catch him?' As the policemen head up the escalator in pursuit of the non-existent pickpocket, the good Samaritan says to us: 'Hurry up. Get out of here!' We pack up the table and our leaflets and run.

*

I often wonder how people can swallow Medvedchuk's ridiculous pro-Russian propaganda. In my experience, it is usually people who watch television and do not read books who buy into that sort of rubbish. In the beginning, my father does not support Ukraine joining the EU, but he changes his mind during Euromaidan. My mother respects my decision to join the pro-Europe protests, but I wouldn't say she supports me. The strongest opposition in my family circle comes from my maternal aunt, Svitlana, and from my paternal uncle, Dima.

'Why do you go into the street? Why do you hand out leaflets?' Aunt Svitlana asks me one night when she is staying over with me and Tamara.

'Titka, I'm protesting because I want a better future, for myself and for Ukraine,' I say. Tamara senses an argument brewing and gets up to fuss in the kitchen.

'If you want a better future, you should concentrate on your studies,' Svitlana says.

'Please understand, Titka. Ukraine belongs with Europe, not with Russia. You remember what it was like being part of the Soviet Union. You can't say the Russians ever treated us well. In Europe, they believe in human rights, democracy, freedom and prosperity. I want Ukraine to have those things too.'

'But we have them already! You're only eighteen years old. Who are you to judge? Why don't you keep quiet and mind your own business? If you get arrested, it will be a blot on your record. You're going to wreck your future, not make it better.'

I am clearly not going to change Svitlana's mind. I thank her for her advice and tell her I'll think about it, knowing full well that my mind is made up. The following evening, when Svitlana has returned to Chernihiv, I ask Tamara if she can explain why, twelve years after independence, people like my aunt have not changed their attitudes.

'Mama, do you remember how you and Tato got annoyed with advertising in the Ukrainian language? When I was growing up, I heard you say that things were easier when Ukraine was part of the Soviet Union.'

'I thought that for a long time. I don't think so any longer. I don't like Yanukovych either, but they say Putin is offering Ukraine fifteen billion dollars. It seems to me the European Union is just pie in the sky. Maybe Russia understands us better.'

'Mama, do you really think you'll ever see any of the fifteen billion? It will go straight into Yanukovych's pocket! I remember you telling me about long queues to buy necessities in Soviet times, how you saved and saved for boots and a coat but there were none to buy, so you wore an old jacket with holes in it and rubber boots all winter. Not only was the economy terrible, you had no freedom of speech, or any other kind of freedom. How can people be nostalgic for that?'

'Perhaps it's more sentimental than economic or political,' Tamara says. 'It is a kind of nostalgia, not unlike the Germans' *ostalgie*. Yes, things were bad then. I don't think people are nostalgic for the Soviet Union per se, but for their lost youth. Everything seems better to them because they were young then.'

'Thank you for being so calm and rational. Thank you for being you, Mama,' I say and give her a hug.

My most vehement argument is with my father's younger brother Dima, who was a member of the Berkut riot police during the 2004 Orange Revolution, when his commanders ordered him to beat up protestors. Dima has retired by 2013, but as the Maidan protests get underway in November and December, he grows angry.

'You're provoking the police. It's your fault if the police are violent!' Dima tells me when I run into him at Baba Lyuba's apartment one evening.

'This is a democracy and the police aren't supposed to beat up protestors. We were told that was a thing of the past.'

'Young people are never satisfied,' Dima says. 'Why do you always want to change things? You're going to make a bad situation worse.'

'But Yanukovych is Putin's puppet. He's taking us backwards, to the Soviet Union.'

'Maybe we're better off with the Russians we know than the Europeans we don't know. The Europeans will probably let us down in the long run anyway. It's a dangerous game you students are playing, Yulia. People are going to get hurt and it will be your fault.'

I must be tired, because I start to lose my temper. 'You're not that old, Uncle Dima. Why do you have such an outdated, Soviet mentality? For you, the individual has no rights. The individual is a tiny pixel who counts for nothing.'

'It's not about rights or individuals; it's about law and order. Anarchy is the worst thing of all. You and your lot are making chaos and disorder for no good reason. Yanukovych won the last election fair and square. People like you overthrew him nine years ago and—'

I interrupt my uncle. 'Nine years ago, Yanukovych *stole* the election. People like you were beating up protestors to protect him!'

'I didn't protect Yanukovych. I was doing my duty as a policeman and protecting the rule of law.'

'The rule of law? You mean the law of the jungle! You *know* he stole that election.'

'Maybe. But replacing him with Yushchenko didn't solve anything. The economy just got worse.'

'Stop it. Enough. I won't have you arguing in my house,' Baba Lyuba says. I remember that she worked for the forensic section of the police department for decades, and I suspect she agrees with Dima, although I've always been her favourite grandchild.

My uncle and I say good-night politely, for Lyuba's sake, but our relations remain frosty for years to come.

On 21 November 2013, the government announces that Yanukovych will not sign the Association Agreement with the EU after all. He says he will instead join Putin's Eurasian

Economic Union, which Putin conceives of as a rival organization to the EU. Two months earlier, Putin had bullied Armenia into the same decision. At some point over the next three months, probably when the Berkut riot police start shooting protestors with live ammunition, Euromaidan transforms itself into our Revolution of Dignity. The movement is no longer about Yanukovych's failure to sign a trade agreement, but about the most fundamental rights to life and freedom, which are incompatible with domination by Russia.

Berkut means 'golden eagle' and the special police, who act on the orders of the interior minister, have established a sinister reputation for terrorizing Yanukovych's political opponents. They are held responsible for most of the 108 civilian deaths at Euromaidan. Thirteen police officers are also killed in the violence. Soon after the protests end on 22 February 2014, the Berkut are dissolved and replaced with the National Guard.

I and my comrades from Vidsich are on the Maidan on 21 November when the government announces it is 'suspending' preparations to sign the Association Agreement. It is raining and we gather to discuss strategy.

'What a bastard Yanukovych is!' says Katya. 'I wonder if Putin bought him with money or threatened to kill him.'

'Probably both,' says Viktoria.

'So what do we do now?' I ask.

'Look. The Vilnius summit, where Yanukovych was supposed to sign the agreement, is not until 28/29 November. Maybe he can still be persuaded to sign it.'

That evening, the Ukrainian journalist Mustafa Nayyem posts an invitation on Facebook for people to come to the

Maidan for a cup of tea. (Nayyem became a deputy in the Verkhovna Rada from 2014 until 2019 and headed Ukraine's reconstruction agency from January 2023 until he resigned on 10 June 2024, apparently due to political infighting.)

Hundreds of people gravitate to the central square, many of them wearing blue and yellow Ukrainian flags like shawls over their shoulders. For three months, the Maidan alternates between a sort of permanent fair, with people laughing and talking, eating from field kitchens and warming their hands over barrel fires, and a war zone complete with barbed wire, barricades, tear gas and snipers. Smaller, spin-off demonstrations occur in other Ukrainian cities. The protests bring together men and women of all ages, professions and social classes, from left- and right-wing parties, united in their determination to overthrow the corrupt and violent Yanukovych. Polls show that the highest percentage of protestors are from western Ukraine, reflecting its more European, anti-Russian history, followed by central Ukraine. Just over a fifth come from the east.

*

We hand out leaflets from our tent near the centre of the square. The broader protest movement organizes itself loosely in a system of *sotni*, a term used for its combat troops by the UPA, the Second World War Ukrainian Insurgent Army which fought the Soviets and the Nazis. The Cossacks had used the same term long before that, for hundred-strong units. Our *sotnya* has nowhere near that number, but it doesn't matter. We want to establish a historical link to the warriors of the UPA.

We are women activists from Vidsich and we declare ourselves the female squad of the sixteenth regiment of the Euromaidan self-defence force. Katya, from Vidsich, is the head of the squad and her husband Mykhailo is the regiment commander. We wear cyclists' helmets and carry plywood shields, no other weapons. Our *sotnya* is assigned to protect a specific area around Lyadski Gate, a monument built in 2001 to commemorate the medieval gates of Kyiv. A sculpture of the archangel Michael, the symbol of the city, perches atop the archway.

Just before the protests start, several far-right movements unite under the banner of Praviy Sektor or Right Sector. They and the far-right party Svoboda have their own *sotni*. They too claim to represent the heritage of the UPA. In 2013/14 and to this day, the Russians harp on the fact that a small portion of the UPA briefly allied itself with the Germans, in the hope of driving the Soviets out of Ukraine, in order to portray all Ukrainians as Nazis.

I resent the nationalist groups exploiting history to legitimize themselves, and I fear the Russians will exaggerate the presence of extreme right-wing groups to give the anti-Russian movement a bad name. There are parliamentary deputies from Svoboda who played an important role in the Communist Party and who worked for the KGB. There are shady characters in Praviy Sektor too.

Praviy Sektor will be incorporated into the Ukrainian army after the full-scale invasion in 2022. They are a fierce military formation, and they contribute a lot to the war effort, proving their worth through deeds. Not all of them are bad. I respect the Praviy Sektor soldiers who fight in the army. But on the Maidan in 2013, it is more about politics than defence. I fear the nationalists risk hurting Ukraine's interests because they are so radical.

Students from Kyiv-Mohyla Academy are known as *Mohyliantsi*. At the beginning of the Maidan protests, I visit other universities with Vidsich leaders to recruit students to join the demonstrations. Around 21 November, we lead a big column of protestors to the Maidan. I am one of five young women marching in the front line with a drummer. The singer Ruslana marches with us, and she climbs the fence of the medical school and talks to the dean, to convince him to let his students join the protests. Ruslana had won the 2004 Eurovision Song Contest, and she is famous not only in Ukraine but throughout eastern Europe. She stays on the Maidan through three months of protests, and sings our national anthem, 'Ukraine Has Not Yet Perished', every day. The crowd sings along and Ruslana asks them to hold up the torches on their smartphones, to show our numbers. It is exhilarating to see the vast square dotted with thousands of tiny lights while the chorus rises in one voice. We feel our unity and strength then.

> The glory of Ukraine has not yet perished, nor the will.
> Still upon us, young brothers, fate shall smile.
> Our enemies shall vanish, like dew in the sun.
> We too shall rule, brothers, in our country.
> Soul and body shall we lay down for our freedom,
> And we will show, brothers, that we are of the Cossack
>   nation!

This music can still bring tears to my eyes. The lyrics were written by the poet and ethnographer Pavlo Chubynskyi in 1862. Mykhailo Verbytskyi, a Greek Catholic priest, composed the music the following year and it was performed for the first time in Lviv in 1864. It became our official anthem after independence in 1991. When you hear it sung by thousands of people in a big open space, it has incredible power, like a huge choir singing Hallelujahs. I feel proud when we sing it on the

Maidan. It means even more to me when I hear it now, because I have a deeper understanding of the price we have paid to sing it. The first line about Ukraine's glory probably inspired the slogan *Slava Ukraini*, glory to Ukraine, which was the greeting used by members of the UPA and which has become a rallying cry since Russia's 2014 invasion of Ukraine.

One night in December when the Berkut are advancing towards the Maidan, Ruslana talks to them from the stage, repeating over and over, 'Calm. No violence. Calm. No violence.' There are more than 2,000 riot police spoiling for a fight, and it is as if she hypnotizes them. They abandon their assault on the demonstrators. It reminds me of my own encounters with the police and reaffirms my belief in non-violence.

I go to the Maidan after classes every afternoon and return home to sleep, because I'm a second-year student at Kyiv-Mohyla Academy and a home girl who isn't accustomed to sleeping outdoors, especially in freezing weather. On the night of 29/30 November, I take the last train home to Vyshneve. At four o'clock in the morning, the Berkut stage their first violent attack on the Maidan encampment. It is a turning point in the Revolution of Dignity and galvanizes public support. My father is there with his friends, who are veterans of the 1979–89 Afghan war. Because he knows Kyiv's downtown well, Mykola is able to show trapped students a secret passageway so they can escape.

One day protestors are throwing Molotov cocktails on Hrushevskyi Street near the stadium. Mykola tells me how the protestors capture one of the Berkut guys and start beating him. My father intervenes and says, 'Don't beat him, because you may end up in the same trench one day.' He means that the Berkut man might switch sides. The protestors give the riot policeman to my father who takes him back to his unit. He probably would have been lynched otherwise. When they meet months later in the trenches of Donbas, the former Berkut man greets my father like a brother.

On 8 December, I and my sisters from Vidsich are crossing Bessarabska Square, a few blocks south of the Maidan, when we come across several hundred young men confronting three lines of army special forces. Most of the protestors seem to be from Svoboda. The special forces are guarding the pink granite statue of Lenin. I think it strange that the army is deployed to protect a statue, but this is the mentality of Yanukovych. I snap a photograph with my smartphone. There are conscripts among the special forces, so they are not as violent as the Berkut. The guys from Svoboda advance unopposed, sling a cable around Lenin's neck and attach it to a crane mounted on a truck. If the special forces don't stop them, they look set to pull the statue down, the classic symbol of the downfall of a dictator.

The ambience is tense. We don't want to get caught in a battle between special forces and Svoboda, so we work our way through the crowd, towards the Maidan. As we reach the far side of the square, we hear a loud crash, cheering and singing. Lenin lies on the ground in pieces. The young men attack his head with sledgehammers. Protestors collect pieces of granite for souvenirs. The ritual of *Leninopads* or Lenin downfalls will be imitated across the country.

The Maidan protests become more and more violent, but my *sotnya* remains true to our ideal of peaceful resistance. This may sound foolish, because it becomes clear from the moment the first Molotov cocktail is thrown that peaceful resistance will not be enough to make Yanukovych leave office.

We make our first attempt at mediation in early December, as the violence worsens. Katya, Viktoria and I prepare kitchen trays with a samovar of tea, plastic cups and sandwiches. One of us brandishes a white flag as we approach a column of fierce-looking Berkut in black uniforms and helmets. We probably ought to be afraid, but we are not.

'What have we here?' an officer says as we approach the column. His nose and mouth twitch, which I interpret as a sign of disdain.

'Don't beat us. We don't have weapons,' Katya says.

'We don't beat ladies bearing gifts.'

'Can we talk to you?' Katya asks.

'Sure.'

Viktoria and I distribute tea and sandwiches, which the riot policemen consume greedily.

'Things are getting out of control here. Please stop attacking protestors,' Katya says. 'We are all Ukrainians. Our president is a corrupt man. It will be better for the country if he steps down.'

The officer's nose twitches again. He declines the refreshments and barely listens. While Katya is talking, he looks over her shoulder, surveying the lines of protestors armed with paving stones, sticks and Molotov cocktails. Both sides want to fight.

'Please, will you stop the violence?' Katya insists a last time.

The Berkut officer grunts. We walk back across no man's land to rejoin our *sotnya*, still waving our white flag.

The Trade Unions Building has become headquarters for the various Maidan protest groups. Praviy Sektor occupies the fifth floor of the building.

A few minutes after returning from our failed peace mission to the Berkut to our tent at Lyadski Gate, we receive a visitor: a tall, wiry man carrying a revolver in the waistband of his trousers. We stare disapprovingly at the revolver.

'I watched you ladies going over to the Berkut lines,' he says. 'What do you think you're doing?'

'What do *you* think you are doing, telling us what to do? Who are you anyway?' Katya says.

'Sorry, I forgot to tell you. My name is Viktor.'

'I'll bet you're from Praviy Sektor,' Katya says. Viktor nods. 'We are trying to make peace,' she adds.

Viktor snorts with laughter.

'Listen, sweetheart, this is a revolution and revolutions are violent. You girls are silly. You are going to get caught in the middle.'

Katya sticks to her guns. 'We *know* revolutions are violent. We studied the Bolshevik revolution, like you did. Remember, it killed ten million people in two years. Is that what you want for Ukraine?'

'Yanukovych and the Berkut are scum,' Viktor says. 'Be careful.' He is not the only one to express displeasure with our failed mediation. We make one or two further attempts, without the samovar and sandwiches, but with equal futility.

The weeks draw into months. I lose all sense of time. The Maidan is the centre of my life now. I can barely remember what life was like before. On the afternoon of 18 February, my *sotnya* joins a large column that is marching to Mariinskyi Park. Protestors attack police lines and the Berkut fire tear gas. We do not participate in the assault and decide to retreat to the Maidan. We have replaced our original tent with a sort of hut on the square, near the monument with the angel. I look up the hill towards Zhovtneviy Palace and the flowerbed clock, where the Alley of the Heavenly Hundred now commemorates civilians killed in the uprising. I see people running down the hill, fleeing the Berkut. The riot police are lined up like legionnaires in a movie, with the sun reflecting from their shields. We realize that it is going to get ugly.

'You have a choice. Soon you will not be able to leave the Maidan. Either you go or you stay, but if you stay you must be ready to die,' says Katya. No one leaves. Wearing our cyclists' helmets as a derisory means of self-protection, we begin dragging everything we can find – rubbish bins, pieces of fencing, plywood, sandbags filled with snow, burning car tyres – to build a barricade around our area of Lyadski Gate.

It is dark and our eyes and throats sting from the smoke and tear gas. There is a steady crackle of gunfire. A man walks past me pushing a shopping trolley filled with Molotov cocktails. Suddenly he jerks violently, unnaturally, and grabs his upper arm. Blood drips from the hand he uses to hold his wound. He has been shot by a sniper. People rush to help him. It is the first time I have seen someone shot close to me. I assume the sniper targeted him and not me because he had the Molotov cocktails. I think to myself: *Ukrainians are shooting Ukrainians because of Yanukovych and Putin.*

The Berkut climb from adjacent buildings to set fire to the upper floors of the Trade Unions Building. Smoke and flames pour out of the windows.

'Bring blankets and tarpaulins, mattresses, sofas; anything soft for our comrades to jump on!' a leader shouts from the stage at the centre of the Maidan. Our hut faces the Trade Unions Building and I see people trying to slide down ropes or jumping out of windows, lit up by flames. Memories of that night are like a slide show where one image flashes after another. I cannot remember it chronologically.

I am not paralysed by fear, but I feel shock and a rush of adrenaline. I know that I am witnessing history and would not forgive myself in the future if I hadn't been here. If one day I have children, they will ask me what I did during the Maidan protests.

My mobile phone rings. Tamara is as close to hysteria as I have ever heard her.

'Yulia, I know what is happening. I've driven into town and I am waiting in the car for you, two blocks away. You must not stay there. It's too dangerous. Let me take you home. I will not go home without you.'

I am tempted to argue, but part of me is relieved. I haven't got over the shock of the Molotov cocktail man being shot beside me. It could be me next time. I say a sheepish goodbye to my comrades, but they are too focused on the burning Trade Unions Building to notice my departure. I run to Tamara's car and sleep the whole next day. On 20 February I return to the Maidan.

Putin says the fact that US Assistant Secretary of State Victoria Nuland distributed cookies to the Maidan protestors while she was in Kyiv to see Yanukovych in December proves that the revolution was a coup fomented by the Americans. The phrase 'cookies from the State Department' becomes a synonym for US aid to Ukraine. I don't rule out the possibility that some people received Western funding, but no one I know was ever offered money. Putin calls it a coup because he refuses to acknowledge that it was a popular, national uprising which brought people together from all over Ukraine.

The Russo-Ukrainian war starts when Russian armed forces – the famous 'little green men' – seize the building of the Crimean parliament on 27 February 2014. Maidan protestors are the first to volunteer for the army. If they had been paid demonstrators, like those who were bussed in to carry pro-Yanukovych placards at the beginning of the protests, I don't think they would have risked their lives to go to war.

I don't really understand the enormity of what is happening in Crimea and what is about to happen in Donbas, because I am focused on Kyiv and who will form our new government. Nearly a decade later, when I am on duty in the combat zone, I read Anastasia Levkova's novel *There Is Land Behind Perekop*, set in Crimea in 2014. (Perekop was an ancient city on the isthmus of the Crimean peninsula, which the Red Army destroyed in 1920.) The main character is a pro-Ukrainian woman who says that when Russia invaded Crimea, Kyiv forgot about the Black Sea peninsula and didn't care. This hurts me and makes me ashamed, because it is true. We didn't pay enough attention to the initial Russian invasion of Crimea and Donbas.

The Maidan revolution may have precipitated the outbreak of war, but I am convinced it would have happened regardless. I think Putin was planning the war for a long time before Maidan, and the immediate aftermath of the protests was the optimal time to attack because the country was at its weakest. Had it not been for Maidan, had Yanukovych remained in office, Putin might have occupied Ukraine without military force, culturally, politically and economically, as he occupies Belarus. Maidan made him realize that force was the only way to control our country.

Though I did not share the belief of Praviy Sektor and Svoboda in the necessity of violence, they were probably right when they said Yanukovych would not have given up without it. Our revolution found a balance by using limited violence; just enough to scare Yanukovych and convince him that he was in physical danger, but without destroying everything or imposing long-term terror.

I do not know what would have happened if Yanukovych had stayed and repressed protestors the way Putin does in Russia, by killing them and throwing large numbers into prison. But I think that, unlike the Russians, we would not have dispersed. We would not have left the Maidan. We were never going to give up.

Maidan Nezalezhnosti. The morning of 22 February 2014

'He's gone! Yanukovych took as much loot as he could and flew away on a helicopter!'

Yanukovych has fled to Moscow via Crimea. The news ripples across the Maidan. We have won! It is a huge relief, and we ought to feel victorious, but there are corpses on the ground covered with blankets. Most of the 108 civilian deaths occurred on 18–20 February. Church bells toll for them, and the crowd sings a sad song, '*Plyve Kacha*'. The title means 'the duckling swims', but it is about a mother saying farewell to her son who is going off to war.

My dear mother, what will happen to me if I die in a
foreign land?
Well, my dearest, you will be buried by other people.

The mass funeral, bells and singing offer a brief respite, a moment for grief and reflection after battle. It is not euphoria. Yes, we won, but so many died. Russian troops have already started sneaking into Crimea, so we do not celebrate our victory for long.

Protestors flock to Mezhyhirya, the lavish, 343-acre estate that Yanukovych built 23 kilometres north of Kyiv. We want to see what he did with the Ukrainian people's money. The main residence, called Honka, is an absurd amalgamation of log cabin and palace, with faux classical ruins on the grounds, a zoo populated by exotic animals, greenhouses to grow tropical fruit, a collection of expensive sports cars and a fake Spanish galleon. It has statues in the bathrooms, a gold sculpture of a loaf of bread and a grotesque nude portrait of Yanukovych. The whole thing is in such incredibly bad taste that it gives new meaning to the word kitsch. A gilded chapel separates the bedrooms of Yanukovych and his mistress. I wonder: *Did they have sex and then pray for forgiveness before going to sleep?* I had thought of Yanukovych as weak, corrupt and disgusting, but living for a week in his palace – yes, *living* in his palace – adds a new layer of weirdness.

Andriy Parubiy, a deputy in the Verkhovna Rada who has been a coordinator of the *sotni*, and who will head the security council of the next president, Petro Poroshenko, convenes a meeting to discuss what to do with the palace. The entire cabinet has fled, including the minister of the interior. The legal system, prosecutor's office and police have ceased to function. There is no one to take charge of the palace and Ukraine's nascent government fear that it will be pillaged and destroyed if nothing is done to protect it.

Parubiy says the female squad of the sixteenth regiment of the Euromaidan self-defence force, our *sotnya*, is the youngest, most ideological and honest group of protestors. When we hear that we have been chosen to protect Mezhyhirya, Katya asks: 'Why didn't he just say, "because they are virgins"?' We laugh hard for the first time in months. Parubiy wants us and one other *sotnya* to inhabit Yanukovych's garish palace until the government can seal it off and conserve it as a museum of corruption. Because we are honest students who do not steal, we are invited to spend a week patrolling the complex, lounging on Yanukovych's furniture and bathing and sleeping in his embroidered linen. We send packing another *sotnya* when it starts looting.

I am eighteen and a half years old at the end of the Euromaidan revolution. I have grown up during those three months. Perhaps they planted the seed of my vocation to be a soldier. My teenage years are nearly over, and Ukraine too is maturing. I feel fortunate to have participated in such a fundamental moment of Ukraine's modern history, but I look back on it with mixed feelings because I realize now that it was the opening battle of the Russo-Ukrainian war, the first act in a decade of pain, sorrow, death and destruction.

VII

The Love of a Soldier

Vouchsafe to me, O God, upon this earth,
The gift of love, that pleasant paradise,
And nothing else besides!

Taras Shevchenko, 'Prayer', 1860

12 March 2015

I am in the metro, on my way home from the library at Kyiv-Mohyla Academy, when my phone beeps.

'Thought you should know your father has sent us another soldier. Love, Mum.'

Tamara is a good sport. She believes in supporting the army. I know she is right, but I cannot help being annoyed. 'Oh God, another soldier!' I groan. I don't want visitors. I just want to rest.

This is at least the fifth time that my father has asked us to lodge one of the soldiers he seems to pick up like stray animals. He cannot resist the temptation to talk to people, especially soldiers from the eastern front. In his manic way, he wants to help everyone. The soldiers are recovering from war wounds, or merely passing through Kyiv on leave. They need a bed for a night or two and it costs my father nothing to offer the apartment of his former wife and daughter.

As I turn my key in the front door, Mykola's latest stray rises from the living-room sofa and walks towards me with hand outstretched, ready to shake mine.

'Illia,' he says.

'Yulia,' I reply, scowling.

But the young man is handsome. He clasps my right hand warmly in his. I do a quick inventory. Blond hair, blue eyes, and a red beard like a Viking. He is half a head taller than me, with broad shoulders and, I can tell from the outline of his long-sleeved khaki T-shirt, a well-toned body. *Humph*, I think, *this time Mykola sent a polite one.*

It is late evening, and I am tired and anxious about a seminar I have not adequately prepared for the next morning. I barely speak to the smiling soldier. Bohdan is staying with Baba Lyuba, so Tamara has put the soldier in his room, which had recently become mine. I will have to sleep in the twin bed beside my mother's.

I am careful not to make any noise when I go out early the next morning. The door to Bohdan's room is ajar and I glance at the sleeping soldier. I watch his bare chest rise and fall for a few seconds, cursing myself for having been so unsociable the previous evening. I think of myself as an introvert and often feel awkward with people.

I return home early that Friday afternoon. I've checked my Facebook page on the train and I see that Illia Serbin wants to be friends, which makes me smile. I wonder if he will be there when I get home.

Tamara is at work at the Kyivstar call centre. I sense Illia's presence behind the closed door to Bohdan's room. I sit down and accept his Facebook invitation on my smartphone.

I text him: 'Would you like to meet in the kitchen, to chat, drink tea and play chess?'

Illia walks in a few minutes later.

'How long are you staying?' I ask bluntly.

'Are you that eager for me to leave?' he says, feigning offence.

'I'm sorry. That's not what I meant.'

I silently weigh the prospect of Illia's companionship against the need to catch up on homework over the weekend.

'I have to rejoin my unit in Mariupol on Sunday night,' he says. 'I'm a volunteer scout with the 131st special reconnaissance battalion. I'd like to stay tonight and again tomorrow night if that's okay with you and your mother.'

'Of course. We don't mind. Stay as long as you like,' I stammer.

I bring the chess board from the living room and place it at the end of the kitchen table. We sit across from one another, cradling steaming mugs of tea in our hands.

'Where did you meet my father?' I ask. I don't really care, but I am trying to make conversation.

'In the neurology department at Kyiv Central Hospital. We compared notes on our back injuries.' My father joined the National Guard right after Maidan. He fell head first from the top of an armoured vehicle near Slovyansk three months later and is still in rehabilitation.

'What happened to you?' I ask.

'Oh, nothing really. The terrorists were shelling our base, and I cracked a vertebra practising my double back flip.' He laughs as if it were funny.

Almost everyone refers to the Russian-backed separatists from Luhansk and Donetsk as terrorists. The secessionist parts of Donbas are called the ATO, for Anti-Terrorist Operation zone.

'Are you in pain?' I ask.

'It's improving, slowly but surely.'

'What's it like, being stationed in Mariupol? Have you seen much fighting?'

Illia evades questions about combat. He prefers to talk about daily life in his unit, often with dark humour, and seems to treat being in the front line in Donbas as an ordinary job rather than some kind of exalted experience. He doesn't use words like heroism or courage.

'I'm with a great bunch of guys. When we're not fighting terrorists, we joke a lot. My best friend is a medic. His call sign is Javier. We sleep on bunk beds in the barracks. Javier uses the bed like gym equipment, to do pull-ups and acrobatics. One day he swings down from the top onto the bottom bunk, but he doesn't see that our platoon's pet cat is curled up sleeping. Javier lands on the animal and crushes it. The cat is still alive, but it is suffering. We've lost men in battle, but this is the only time I've seen Javier cry. He gives the cat a lethal injection, with tears streaming down his face. We are all sad, so we try to turn the incident into something funny. If you can laugh at something, it takes the sting out of the sadness. We bury the cat on the training ground, with full military honours. And we rename Javier "the-medic-who-kills-cats".'

'That's not funny at all,' I say. 'I love cats.' But I too am laughing.

Illia shrugs apologetically. 'There's not a lot to laugh about these days. At least we try.'

'How long have you been a soldier?'

'I joined up a year ago, right after the Russians seized Crimea.'

'And before that?'

'Before that I was a farmer. My mother and I grew strawberries and raspberries on family land just outside Kyiv. We have an orchard with apple and fruit trees, and we sell fruit in the market. I liked driving the tractor. My parents also run a small business, renovating apartments. They wanted me to work with them, but I was desperate to leave. I...' He pauses to search for the right expression, neither too harsh nor too flippant. '...don't get along with my father.'

'Why not?'

'He gambles, and I hate that. My parents are poor, despite having a successful business. Their house is falling apart. I don't see why I should earn money so my dad can throw it away in the casino. I am closer to my maternal grandmother and uncle in America. Before the war, I talked about joining them there, but my parents wanted me to stay close and earn money. They live on the outskirts of Kyiv, and they didn't want me to be a soldier. I lied to them when I joined up. I said I was going to work in construction in Germany. That's why I needed a place to stay when I was discharged from hospital.'

'My father is difficult too,' I say, commiserating. 'But we have a lot more in common than you and your dad, it seems. We agree on most things when he is sober. I just can't stand it when he drinks.'

'My dad is never nice,' Illia replies with a steely tone. 'We have nothing in common.'

'My dad and I were both in self-defence *sotni* during the Maidan protests. I almost joined the military with him, but I wanted to finish my degree first. If all goes well, I'll graduate fifteen months from now.'

'You did the right thing,' Illia says. 'What are you studying?'

'Philology.'

'What's that?'

'The development of the Ukrainian language.'

'My family have always been Ukrainian-speakers.'

'I grew up speaking Russian, until I was accepted at

At my father's grave.

My brother Bohdan, in oversized cadet's uniform, General Serhii Kulchytski and my father Mykola at his National Guard swearing-in ceremony in early April 2014.

Illia and me on duty in Donbas.

A selfie of Illia and me in November 2017.

Illia and me soon after
our marriage on
30 May 2015.

In mourning for my husband, Illia, near the wall of St Michael's Golden-Domed Monastery in Kyiv, where portraits of fallen soldiers are displayed.

My father Mykola holding me as an infant in the garden of my grandmother's home in Lazarivka, Zhytomyr oblast, around 1996.

My father, mother, little brother and I outside the Good News Baptist Church, around 2000.

As a woman, I had to fight for the right to stand guard duty like other soldiers. I am shown here in Klynove in 2016.

On duty near Soledar, Donbas, in 2023. The badge on my flak jacket shows a Ukrainian woman in traditional dress holding a Javelin anti-tank missile.

Target practice with an AKM rifle.

Me with a Russian T-64 tank in a village we liberated in Donbas.

Me at the family dacha in Lazarivka during the 2020 Covid lockdown.

With my friend Mila, a medic who serves with me in the 25th Kyivan Rus' battalion of the 54th mechanized brigade of the Ukrainian army.

We call our drones birds and give each one a name. I am shown here with a new arrival at our front line position in Donbas.

General Valerii Zaluzhnyi, then Commander-in-Chief of the Ukrainian Armed Forces, congratulated me when I was awarded the Medal of Courage on 6 December 2022. He is now Ukraine's ambassador to London.

Me in traditional dress. (Photo by Anastasia Olijnyk for the *Ultimate Ukrainian Magazine* 2021. Courtesy of Spilna Mova, LLC.)

My father, mother, little brother and I in the cockpit of a plane at Zhuliany airport near Kyiv, around 2003.

I graduated from Kyiv-Mohyla Academy, the oldest university in Ukraine, with a degree in philology in June 2016.

I hold a Mavic quadcopter in a field in Donbas. No previous war has seen drones deployed so extensively in battle.

With my paternal uncle, Dima.

My little brother Bohdan and I outside Leader Lyceum in Kyiv around 2006.

My childhood nanny Viktoria with her husband Oleh, who was shot dead by Russian troops during their 2022 occupation of Bucha.

Kyiv-Mohyla. In the past three years, I've learned to love the Ukrainian language. You might say Ukrainian is my mother tongue and I learned it at the age of seventeen... Why did you want to be a soldier?'

'I've wanted to be a warrior since I was a child. It's a calling. I want to defend defenceless people, civilians, women and children. I want to fight for justice. If there wasn't a war in Ukraine, I would find one somewhere else.'

'When I saw you last night, I thought you looked like a Viking.'

Illia laughs. 'My call sign is Viking.'

'How old are you?' I ask him.

'I'll be twenty-two next month. And you?'

'I'll be twenty in July.'

We talk all weekend. On Sunday, Tamara makes a packed lunch for Illia. I offer to go with him to the main railway station in Kyiv. We emerge from the metro and walk a few hundred metres into the bustling terminal. Illia thrusts his khaki rucksack into my hands. 'Hold this for a second,' he says, disappearing, only to reappear a few seconds later. He holds out a small bouquet of daisies, their stems wrapped in tinfoil, purchased from a station vendor. He looks like a schoolboy offering a present to his teacher.

We descend several flights of stairs to the station platform where soldiers are saying goodbye to their loved ones. We continue talking until the railway company, Ukrzaliznytsia, announces that the night train to Mariupol is departing. Illia grazes my cheek with the back of his hand, gives me a bear hug and clambers up the steep iron steps, turning to smile and wave as he heads into the corridor.

Watching him disappear, I feel an almost physical pain, as if an invisible string is pulling my heart after the departing soldier. I look down at Illia's little bouquet and think, *dear God, don't let anything happen to him.* A teardrop falls on the yellow centre of one daisy.

'Bye-bye Symirochka,' Illia texts me a few minutes later. Symirochka is the name of my and Tamara's pet cat, whom Illia played with in our apartment. It is also the name of a girl in the *Fyksyky* cartoon who spends her time rescuing a naughty boy from trouble.

'Thank you for being my friend in Kyiv,' Illia writes. 'I will not forget you.'

'Have a safe and happy journey, warrior,' I text back. We continue to message each other almost constantly. There is nothing profound about our exchanges. Most of them are silly. Our friendship slides effortlessly into romance. Neither of us says, 'Let's be boyfriend and girlfriend.' It just happens.

'I want to see you, Symirochka,' Illia writes a week later. 'When can I see you?'

'How about Easter weekend?'

'Can you come to Mariupol?'

'Yes!' I book the train ticket. 'Arriving Good Friday 10 April!' I message.

'Hooray!' Illia says. 'We can celebrate Easter, and my birthday two weeks early! I'll book us an apartment and I'll demand two days' leave. They've been nice to me since I was injured.'

The Minsk II Accord, which was supposed to lead to a cease-fire, disarmament and local elections, was signed two months before my Easter 2015 trip to Mariupol. But fighting continues on the coast to the east of the city, where the Azov regiment, the National Guard and the Ukrainian armed forces are trying to dislodge the 'terrorists' who have massed tanks and artillery at Shryokyne, just 11 kilometres from Mariupol. Azov had driven the separatists out the previous summer, and the city is scarred from the fighting, with many boarded-up windows and gutted buildings. Half the residents of the nondescript high-rise where Illia has rented an apartment for the weekend are refugees.

I hadn't realized that the Kyiv to Mariupol train goes only as far as Berdyansk, because of the risk of shelling and skirmishes on the railway line. Illia has told me to take a taxi for the last stretch of the journey. The Zaporizhzhia and Donetsk oblasts, which I must travel through, are unknown territory to me. One year into the war, I have a civilian's exaggerated image of the troubled region. Like most inhabitants of the west and centre of the country, I assume that every resident of the east is a Russian-backed separatist, traitor and terrorist. Later I will learn this is not the case, but on the night of 10 April 2015 I am a naïve nineteen-year-old bound for a romantic rendezvous in a war zone, and I am petrified.

The hour-and-a-half taxi ride from Berdyansk station to Azovstal station in Mariupol seems interminable.

'Why are you going to Mariupol?' the chatty, middle-aged driver asks me. I see his eyes watching me in the rear-view mirror and I think he looks shifty.

'To see friends,' I reply curtly.

'What friends?'

'Friends.'

'How long are you staying?'

'Not long.'

'What will you do there?'

'Tourism.'

'Funny time to do tourism in Mariupol,' the driver says. I remain silent. *What if he is a Russian agent? What if he abducts me? Would Illia know how to find me? Would Illia save me?* Until now, I have thought of the war in terms of bombing, shooting and shelling, as an engine of physical destruction. I hadn't realized how it poisons everyday relations among people, sowing distrust and suspicion.

I am infinitely relieved to see Illia waiting for me at the taxi stand at Azovstal station. The driver takes my rucksack from the boot of the taxi, gives Illia a disapproving once-over and drives off. I fall into Illia's arms.

'What a terrible man! I thought he was going to kidnap me!'

'He's just a taxi driver.'

'He asked too many questions.'

Illia enfolds me in a bear hug like the one he gave me when we parted. Then he holds me at arm's length and stares at me, grinning. His face changes. 'Symirochka,' he whispers. Our first kiss happens at the taxi stand, slowly, clumsily, as if we are hesitant and a little afraid.

The war has been going on for more than a year now, but I haven't really felt it in Kyiv. The air is different in Mariupol, charged with tension, salty and corrosive from the Azov Sea. Three months earlier, in January 2015, a rocket attack by the rebels killed thirty civilians in the city. The railway station teems with soldiers carrying weapons. The first times I hear explosions, even faint ones, I jump.

'What's that?' I ask nervously.

'It's nothing,' Illia replies. 'Terrorist artillery to the east.'

I follow his example and ignore the distant explosions, consider them part of the city's natural soundscape.

Mariupol wants to live. It is a city of culture, proud of its white, neoclassical theatre and Soviet-era mosaics and in denial about the danger. Illia shows me the landmark water tower with its white mullioned windows. We wander through parks and sit in cafés. Areas damaged in the previous year's fighting are under renovation and there is talk of a Disneyland-style theme park dubbed Mariland. The white-sand beach softens the brutalism of the Illich and Azovstal iron- and steelworks, surrounded by slag heaps and spewing smoke into the sky.

We linger in bed, happy in our self-contained, transitory world. The war, guns and explosions seem unreal to me, more theatrical décor than genuine threat. On Easter morning I stand on the balcony looking at the grey buildings across the street. Illia slips his arms around me and I turn to kiss him, the small of my back against the balcony railing. I pull my grandmother's ring off my finger and hold it up to tease my lover.

'What do you think would happen if you proposed to me?'

'What a great idea.' Illia says. 'Yes. Absolutely. Let's get married!' He takes the ring and slips it back on my finger, kisses me and carries me to the bedroom.

'Your skin is so soft,' Illia says, running his fingers over my body in a kind of wonderment. '*Pukhnastyk,*' he murmurs, using the Ukrainian word for fluffy. 'You are *pukhnastyk* like a kitten.' From now on, he has two pet names for me. I am Symirochka when we are with other people. The name of the cartoon character will later become my military call sign in Donbas. Illia loves all kinds of folklore and mythology. When he learns that, for Celts, a *pooka* is a mischievous creature which can bring good luck or bad, which can take the form of animals but also of humans, he shortens Pukhnastyk to Pooka.

We celebrate our engagement by decorating Ukrainian *Pysanky* Easter eggs with wax and dye I've brought from Kyiv.

'I want the simplest possible wedding,' I say. 'No guests, no friends, no family. Just you and me.'

'That suits me fine,' my fiancé replies.

'Let's have two children,' Illia says. He concentrates on the egg he is painting while discussing our future. 'A boy first, then a girl. Let's adopt foster children too. I want a foster family, because children are the future of the country, and they need to be educated. I'll build a big house and you can teach the children. You'll be a good teacher.'

Illia and I have spent just four days together in one month, but neither of us hesitates for a moment. Certainty is a rare thing in life, but I am absolutely certain of what I am doing. It is as if I were made for him, and he for me. We both feel that this was meant to be. Since I met Illia, I have started believing in fate. We choose our wedding date, Saturday 30 May 2015, before I catch a taxi to Berdyansk and the night train back to Kyiv.

Illia trusts me to do all the wedding planning. I buy our wedding rings and find an online flea market that sells antique *vyshyvanka*, traditional Ukrainian embroidered clothing. I purchase a shirt for Illia, a dress, a skirt and a *kiptar* sleeveless waistcoat for me. *Vyshyvanka* are yet another part of Ukraine's cultural heritage which the Soviets tried to wipe out, so wearing them has become a symbol of patriotism. My white wedding dress with red flowers embroidered on the sleeves is at least sixty years old. In the west of the country, families treasure generations of *vyshyvanka* as heirlooms, but the Bolsheviks were present in greater numbers in central Ukraine, where my family are from, so fewer survived. I have inherited no traditional clothing and decide to start a collection for our future children.

Illia requests four days' leave at the end of May. Tamara is a little hurt not to be included in the preparations, but she is used to letting her strong-willed daughter have her way, and she likes Illia. Mykola is also happy, because he can take credit for having introduced us, though I don't think he foresaw that this would happen.

I reserve a wooden cabin on a mountain top outside Yaremche, in the western region of Ivano-Frankivsk. The town is the headquarters of the Carpathian national park.

As soon as we arrive, we go to the registrar's office to apply for a wedding licence.

'Come back in a month,' the registrar says.

'But we want to get married tomorrow!' I say.

'I'm sorry, that's not possible,' she replies. 'There is a standard waiting period of one month.'

I am crestfallen. Illia squeezes my hand.

'My fiancé is a soldier on the eastern front,' I say. 'He has come all the way from Mariupol to marry me. He has only four days' leave before he goes back to fight terrorists. Please, madam. Please.'

The registrar's eyes dart from Illia's face to mine. She appears to like us, or perhaps we have touched a patriotic chord in her. She smiles weakly and shrugs. 'Well, it's against the rules, but this is wartime. All right. Come back tomorrow morning.'

The next morning, I put on my *vyshyvanka* dress and the red headband with a red and purple silk flower that Viktoria, my childhood nanny, has made for me as a wedding present. I give Illia the embroidered shirt I have chosen for him, which he wears over navy-blue trousers.

'You look so handsome!' I tell him.

Illia shrugs. 'When I'm dressed as a civilian, I usually wear technical clothing – cargo pants, jackets with lots of pockets,' he says. 'I always carry a knife, and for that you need pockets.' He produces a small package wrapped in brown paper for me. 'It's a Swiss army knife,' he says proudly. 'It's the most valuable tool you'll ever have. You should never be without it.'

'What a romantic wedding present!' I say teasingly.

Our landlady volunteers to drive us to the registrar's office in her old Soviet Lada. She serves as our witness and takes photographs with her smartphone. After the brief ceremony, Illia and I wander through the handicraft fair in the central market in Yaremche. There are all kinds of embroidered clothes, which are especially popular in the Carpathians. Farmers sell homemade bread, cheese, honey and sausages. Most of the food is expensive and we wander around tasting free samples. The vendors can see we're not buying, but they seem eager to share in our happiness and indulge us. An old man sells red wine from his vineyard in plastic bottles from the boot of his car. We buy a bottle to drink that evening in our cabin.

'Be careful,' the winemaker says jokingly. 'This wine tastes like nectar and goes down smoothly. Your head remains clear, but your legs get drunk fast.'

Our wedding dinner is a picnic of wine, bread and cheese. Despite coming from a plastic bottle, the red Carpathian wine is the most delicious I have ever tasted.

We play house, as newlyweds do. 'Where will we live?' Illia asks.

We talk about Lazarivka, the village in Zhytomyr oblast where Baba Lyuba has her dacha, or Vyshneve, the suburb on the south-west periphery of Kyiv where Tamara and Lyuba both have apartments. By chance, Illia has inherited a plot of land in Vyshneve.

'I am an urban dweller,' I say. 'I'd rather stay close to the city. In fact, I think I prefer living in an apartment. It's so much more convenient. You won't believe how much work there is to do in Baba Lyuba's garden.'

'But Pooka, we need a house for the children and foster children. We'll install solar panels on the roof, and make our own electricity with a wind turbine,' Illia says. It is 2015 and green energy is a theme only in Kherson, in the south, where there are a lot of solar farms. 'I want our house to be self-sufficient,' Illia continues. 'It will have a basement with a kitchen, bathroom and games room. We'll have a ping-pong table, computer games, a large television screen and a satellite dish for communications. It will be big enough for all of us to sleep there, so if the Russians ever use nuclear weapons, it can double as a bomb shelter.'

'That's a depressing thought.'

'After a year on the front line, every soldier knows you're safer underground,' Illia says. 'Haven't you ever played *Fallout*?'

'What's *Fallout*?'

Illia tells me about the series of post-apocalyptic computer games set in the United States in the twenty-first, twenty-second and twenty-third centuries. The games so far have taken place in various parts of California, Washington DC, Boston, the Midwest and the Mojave Desert. Everyone lives underground, to escape nuclear fallout. They're called vault-dwellers, and they must fight off hostile mutants and the remnants of the pre-war government. Sometimes they venture out into the Wasteland, wearing protective clothing. They survive famine and drought, and as currency they use bottle caps from a soft drink called Nuka-Cola Quantum. The hero is the Chosen One, the Lone Wanderer, the Sole Survivor. Sometimes he searches for friends or relatives who have disappeared. The earlier games had jazz music, including Louis Armstrong. The newer ones have heavy metal.

'It's all about life in the vault and fighting off threats, protecting your loved ones – survival,' Illia says. 'We'll play it some time. You'll enjoy it.'

Though we have only four days in the Carpathians, we quickly establish a routine. In the mornings we hike in the mountains, in the afternoons we go down into town. One morning we are walking in the forest when I almost step on a large, revolting lizard, a black salamander with yellow spots. It is ugly and primeval-looking and I think it's a bad omen. I have never seen one before and I believe the lizard is poisonous.

'Pooka,' Illia says. 'It's just a lizard.' The creature slithers away down the bank of the stream. I am embarrassed for having screamed. I know my fear is irrational. I was a feminist in Vidsich, at Kyiv-Mohyla and at Maidan, and here I am, reverting to stereotype, screaming at a lizard in a forest on my honeymoon in the Carpathians. Embarrassed as I am, I feel content and secure when my husband hugs me tightly.

The front line has stabilized since the Minsk II Accord on 12 February 2015. Illia is discharged from the army in the first wave of demobilization in July, after sixteen months' service. He moves in with me and Tamara in her apartment in Vyshneve. We live there together as a family for a year, one of the happiest of my life. I take contentment for granted, realizing only later how precious those months together were.

I have one more year of university to complete. Illia is developing a telephone app with his uncle, Oleksandr, in America, to help people renovate apartments. The app tells you how much paint or building materials to buy. In my third year, Kyiv-Mohyla gives me a scholarship, because other students have dropped out and professors praise my writing. We live sparingly on Illia's modest income and my scholarship. There are a lot of things we can't afford.

Illia supports me in my studies by organizing our daily routine. He cooks for me and Tamara and often phones to ask what time I'll arrive home, so that my dinner will be hot when I get there. His best dish is pork, potatoes and vegetables, cooked in clay pots in the oven.

Illia is enthusiastic about an assignment in my creative writing class to produce a fictional text set in the future. His military experience and fondness for the *Fallout* games help us invent a series of stories about teenagers struggling for survival in a post-apocalyptic Ukraine. Illia doesn't talk about combat in the east, but I know he has seen men die there. I believe the scenes we conjure up – of youths fighting amid ruins for food, territory and domination – are his way of working through what he has experienced. We try to include love, friendship and happy moments in the novellas, but the narrative keeps veering towards darkness. Illia wants us to publish the book as a sort of survival manual for our future children. We agree that it would be irresponsible to have children at this stage, because we don't have money or our own home.

Outside the hours I spend at university, Illia and I are inseparable. We are lovers, soulmates, best friends, brother and sister. We walk a lot. Sometimes we go to jazz or classical music concerts. We work out together at the gym. Illia knows I hate milk, but he makes me drink his concoction of milk, bananas and protein powder, 'to make you strong', he says.

June 2016

I wear a black gown and mortarboard for graduation from Kyiv-Mohyla Academy. Before the ceremony, I and my fellow graduates congregate in front of the pale-yellow rotunda building with its three-storey-high Corinthian columns. After independence in 1991, the Student Brotherhood started a tradition now observed by every graduating class. Buckets of soapy water, brooms and a ladder await us at the base of the five-metre-high statue of the eighteenth-century poet and philosopher Hryhorii Skovoroda, facing the academy on Kontraktova Square.

Skovoroda was educated at Kyiv-Mohyla and then became an itinerant philosopher-beggar whose work was published only after his death in 1794. In Ukraine, he is often compared to Socrates for renouncing the temptations of life in society. 'The world tried to ensnare me but failed,' is the epigraph he chose for his tombstone.

Graduates hold the hems of their black robes in one hand so as not to trip on the rungs as they ascend the ladder, while balancing a broom dipped in soapy water. Each student gives a cursory scrub to Skovoroda's head. Others stand on the ground, scrubbing the folds of Skovoroda's mantle or his bare feet. Most of us get soaked in the process, but we are laughing and happy and our gowns dry quickly in the summer heat.

Skovoroda was a bridge between the baroque period and the Enlightenment, whose ideals he espoused. He travelled throughout Ukraine, sharing his learning with common people. As graduates of Kyiv-Mohyla, we have been taught, it is our duty to do the same. Skovoroda wrote in Ukrainian, Church Slavic, Russian, Latin and Greek, and used many western European ideas and expressions. His embrace of the Enlightenment is often cited as evidence that Ukraine belongs to Europe. Though Skovoroda was born into a Ukrainian Cossack family near Kyiv, Russia claims that he was Russian. Their appropriation of our famous writers, painters and cultural figures is a common practice. Since the full-scale invasion, Russia has repeatedly targeted what it claims to be Russian culture. In May 2022, a Russian missile destroyed the eighteenth-century building in Kharkiv oblast where Skovoroda worked and died, and which held a museum dedicated to him.

After the ceremony, Illia and I walk around Podil, the oldest neighbourhood in Kyiv, where the academy is located, eating ice cream and talking. Podil burned down in 1811, so most of its pretty, brightly painted houses, long inhabited by artisans and merchants, date from the nineteenth century. Podil was first mentioned in chronicles in the middle of the tenth century, and nine centuries of artefacts lie beneath its streets. It spills down a hillside which ends on the bank of the Pochaina river. From the top of the hill, one enjoys a spectacular view over Kyiv.

Illia sometimes takes the metro in to the city to meet me after classes, and we walk in Podil often. We particularly like a little field which is an untouched piece of nature in the middle of the city. It is cradled between two hills, called Shchekavytsia and Khoryvytsia, where Shchek and Khoryv, two of the three brothers who founded Kyiv in AD 482, are said to have lived. The third brother, Kyi, for whom the city is named, lived elsewhere.

We lie on our backs in the field, staring at the stars as they appear in the twilight sky. I am still wearing my black gown. My mortarboard sits in the grass beside us.

'I love this city!' I exclaim. 'Lviv and Odesa are beautiful, but I don't ever need to live anywhere else. There is something about the vastness of the sky and the vistas, as if proportions in Kyiv were bigger than anywhere else. I am always happy to return here... Why don't we call our first child Khoryv?'

Illia laughs. 'From your favourite city to our son's name. You're all over the place, darling Yulia. It's a good idea. We'll call him Khoryv, and he will always remind us of your graduation. What about our daughter? What should we call her?'

'I want to call her Arianna, like Ariadne in Greek mythology, but without the "d" because Ukrainians can't pronounce the letter "d".'

Illia agrees. We will find names for the foster children later, unless they have names already.

'Do you ever mind that I haven't gone to university?' he asks.

'Not for one second,' I reply. 'You understand things by intuition, whereas I have to learn them. You are more intelligent than I am. You are the wisest person I know, and you teach me so much.'

I reverse the question. 'Does it ever bother you that your wife has a university degree and you don't?'

'No, Pooka,' Illia laughs. He pulls himself up on one elbow and leans over to kiss me passionately, lying in the grass under the stars in the meadow in Podil. 'I am so impressed with you, with your knowledge and intellect. With everything you do.'

After graduation, Illia and I go to Baba Lyuba's dacha in Lazarivka. I am restless and uncertain what to do now that I have finished my degree. I have not forgotten that when the war started, I thought seriously about becoming a soldier. Mykola and I have discussed it often.

France and Germany are still trying to revive the Minsk peace accords, but Putin toys with François Hollande and Angela Merkel like a cat with a mouse. He pretends there are no Russian forces in Donbas, that Russia is not a party to the conflict, that the separatist movement he created and controls remotely acts of its own volition. Putin negotiates not to make peace, but to buy time and strengthen his own forces while Europe holds back from arming Ukraine. He makes wild statements about a Ukrainian genocide against Russian-speakers, which is absurd, since most Ukrainians speak Russian, and respect for all languages is enshrined in the constitution.

The war sputters on. Casualties mount. Illia misses the camaraderie, adventure and excitement, the sense of purpose. He wants to return to Donbas.

'At Maidan, my friends and I admired Mahatma Gandhi,' I tell Illia one afternoon. We are lying on a blanket reading in the shade of the walnut tree in Baba Lyuba's garden. 'We advocated peaceful resistance, and we refused to use weapons. If you believe in non-violence, shouldn't you be against war?'

'Nearly everyone is against war. Especially the fighters. But I don't believe for a moment that Yanukovych would have given up power if our side had not used violence at Maidan. It was easy for you and your friends in Vidsich to be pure and leave the dirty work to the guys from Praviy Sektor and Svoboda. You could have handed out a billion leaflets and staged sit-ins for decades. Yanukovych would not have left office and Putin would control all Ukraine.'

Deep down, I know Illia is right, but the issue is important, and I want to provoke him. 'Don't we lower ourselves to Putin's level when we kill Russians? I'm not saying we should not fight, but I am trying to be consistent. If violence and killing are evil, is submission to dictatorship a lesser evil?'

'You've sat through too many philosophy seminars,' Illia says, mocking me gently. 'Civil disobedience may be a fine way to protest over domestic social issues and high taxes, but if I break into your house and kill your mother, steal your belongings and refuse to leave, you have a right to shoot me. Russia has colonized Ukraine since the eighteenth century. The Soviet Union starved millions of Ukrainians to death and deported millions more to Siberia. You know that, Pooka! When I kill a Russian soldier, it is not murder, but self-defence. If we want Ukraine to survive as an independent country, we must fight for it.'

'Hmmm. When the Russians seized Crimea, I wanted to be a soldier,' I say, 'but I think I was afraid to go to war alone. It would be easier to go with you.'

'Now that's more like it! Come to Donbas with me, Pooka! Let's join up together. I've seen how the army operates, and if we are strong, we can bend the bureaucracy to our will. We can start our own unit, do commando raids on the Russians. I'll teach you how to shoot and how to keep safe. We'll make a great team.'

I laugh at Illia's vision of a husband-and-wife commando. 'We'll be the Bonnie and Clyde of Donbas!' I tell him.

Illia does not react to my joke. He is focused on the idea and continues on his trajectory, thinking out loud. 'The regular army is full of career soldiers who are there for the wages, or, worse yet, old soldiers and officers who served in the Soviet army and harbour a weakness for Russia. You cannot trust them. I trust people who volunteer because they want to defend Ukraine. Their morale is better because they are motivated. Let's find a volunteer battalion to sign up with.'

Love, war and duty form a perfect circle for me. I cannot respect a man who refuses to fight for his country. I love Illia in part because he is a warrior. Without Illia, I doubt I would have joined the army.

VIII

Always

In every woman resides a soldier's heart.
Bound to tread darkness, alone and apart.
And all the help is unnecessary.
And no shoulder is worth crying on.
And all heavy things are carried by her own two hands.
And all loves have been lived and lost.
And all the loneliness is yours.
And one full night on earth is as bright as the whole life
   of the sun.

Ukrainian army private Yaryna
Chornohuz, 'A Stain Too Red', 2021

Lazarivka and Klynove. July 2016

Illia and I research volunteer units and settle on the 25th Kyivan
Rus' battalion of the 54th mechanized infantry brigade, which
is named after the dynasty founded by the Viking Oleh in the
ninth century. We remember Ukraine's history from grade
school, how medieval Scandinavians navigated Europe's great

rivers, the Danube and the Dnipro, and peopled colonies from the Baltic to the Black Sea.

We track down the officer who serves as secretary for the Kyivan Rus' battalion. He sends us pro forma invitations to join. We travel to the battalion's headquarters at Klynove, a village south-east of Bakhmut in Donbas. In a stuffy little office, on the corner of an old metal desk, we sign contracts with the Armed Forces of Ukraine. It is 17 July 2016, the day before my twenty-first birthday. It is almost like a second wedding.

I had expected no pay for volunteering and am surprised to learn that, as army privates, we receive a monthly salary of 7,000 hryvnia, about €165 at today's rates. We sleep in sleeping bags in the town's community centre, which serves as the battalion's headquarters, with other soldiers. We are careful not to show affection publicly, and at first our comrades do not even know we are married. When our commanders find out, they offer us a room. Illia declines, saying, 'We didn't come here to live together but to fight together.'

The battalion commander asks us to do administrative work until he finds separate units for us. 'If I wanted to be a bookkeeper, I could earn a lot more in Kyiv,' I grumble in private to Illia.

'Be patient,' he says. 'The officers like us. If we do a good job, it will pay off later.'

We live in the community centre headquarters for a couple of months, until Illia is transferred to an infantry unit. My request to join a reconnaissance unit is turned down. 'You are a woman and there is no place for you there,' an officer tells me. 'You've studied at university, so you will be more useful in administration. Besides, women are banned from combat units.'

That will change with the Law on Equal Rights and Opportunities for Women and Men during Military Service, which I campaign for vigorously with my sisters-in-arms from the women's veterans' association, Veteranka.

For my first year in the army, 2016/17, I am forced to work as a secretary and accountant. It infuriates me, but I have no choice. I realize now how useful it was because I know how the 'paper army' works. I get to know most members of the battalion very quickly.

Illia is pleased to be assigned to the Georgian Legion, a unit within the 25th Kyivan Rus' formed mainly by exiles from Georgia. Some Ukrainians and other foreigners also serve with them. The foreigners include Armenians, at least one Briton and a German. All, including my husband, wear the Georgian Legion's emblem: the head of a wolf with bared fangs and blood-red eyes. The wolf sports a red and white Georgian flag across its forehead like a bandana.

The Legion's commander is a bear of a man with the wonderful name Mamuka Mamulashvili, known across Ukraine simply as Mamuka. 'We were the first foreigners to join the Ukrainian army in 2014,' he boasts to me and Illia one night over a bottle of wine. We converse in Russian, the only language we have in common. Mamuka started fighting Russians at the age of fourteen, alongside his father Zurab, a former general in the Georgian army. 'We're a family business, like the two of you!' he tells us.

Mamuka says that Georgians and Ukrainians understand each other, despite the fact that Ukraine is nearly nine times the size of Georgia. Both countries were colonized by Russia, and declared independence just a few months apart. Now we are stuck in the same waiting room to join NATO and the European Union. Georgia fought Russian-backed separatists in 1992/93 and again in 2008. Their second war was the prelude to Ukraine's troubles.

Putin's *modus operandi* is always the same, Mamuka says. He lures Russian-speaking oligarchs and politicians with promises of money and power and incites them to declare independence so that Russia can recognize their phoney country. Georgia lost Abkhazia and South Ossetia – 20 per cent of its territory – this way, and the same thing is happening to the Ukrainian territories of Crimea and Donbas.

Putin negotiated with Georgia for years in bad faith and never concluded an agreement, Mamuka says. He did the same with Ukraine from 2014 until the 2022 invasion.

Ukraine became a candidate for accession to the European Union in June 2022. Georgia followed in December 2023. Five months later, in April 2024, riot police in Tbilisi clash nightly with pro-EU protestors. They oppose 'the Russian law', modelled on a law made in Moscow which would classify any organization receiving 20 per cent or more of its funding from abroad as 'foreign agents'. The law destroyed pro-democracy non-governmental organizations in Russia and is expected to do the same in Georgia.

I think of Illia's comrades in the Georgian Legion. Their country experienced Russian invasion and territorial losses before we did. Now they appear to be repeating our Maidan revolution. We are going in circles, but, for me, the lesson of Georgia is that Putin will not be satisfied with territorial gains. He is determined to control the politics of our countries. He uses the Georgian oligarch Bidzina Ivanishvili in the same way he used Medvedchuk and Yanukovych in Ukraine, to assert his influence and distance our countries from the West. If Putin is not defeated in Ukraine, I feel certain he will again try to impose his will over the entire country.

Klynove. 2016

The Ukrainian army gives me very little training. Everything I know about warfare I learn from Illia: how to clean and assemble a gun, how to choose appropriate equipment, how to protect myself. We go to the shooting range almost daily. Illia teaches me the nuances of military etiquette, how to behave in a male environment. 'Don't ever show weakness, Pooka. If you want to be treated as a professional soldier, as an equal, then you must be better than the men.'

The German tryptic of *Kinder, Küche und Kirche* is alien to Illia. He never says, 'You are a woman. Stay home. Cook. Have babies.' He may be my mentor in all things military, but ours remains a relationship between equals. It is important to both of us that we do this together.

Other soldiers are required to carry out guard duty at headquarters in Klynove. I ask why my name never appears on the roster. 'Because you're a woman,' my commanding officer tells me. I protest, to no avail, and begin appealing my way up the chain of command. 'I joined the army in good faith, as a loyal citizen of Ukraine,' I say to each officer. 'I deserve to be treated as an equal. I want to do guard duty.'

I do not know which officer relents, but one morning the name Private Yulia Mykytenko appears on the guard duty roster. It is a small triumph for me, though the women who come later are unaware that I paved the way for them. A journalist from Kyiv takes one of the first photographs of me in uniform, on guard duty. I wear a red headband and cradle a rifle. My long dark hair is in plaits.

In January 2024, a friend sends me a photograph of a commemorative set of six stamps issued by the postal system in the West African state of Liberia and entitled 'Women in the Russo-Ukrainian War'. I laugh when I see that eight-year-old photograph of me in the red headband on a Liberian stamp. The young woman in the photograph looks so innocent that I would like to grab her and shake her and tell her 'How stupid and naïve you are!' I came to the army with the idea that all warriors are honest and determined to defend the motherland. It didn't turn out as I thought, but I still believe in the warriors who serve with me on the front line.

I get my first taste of the reality of war at the end of 2016, while working in administration at battalion headquarters. The Russians and their separatist Ukrainian allies mount a fierce, five-day assault on our forces at Svitlodarsk, a town in the Bakhmut district. They use Grad missiles, heavy artillery and tank fire. Nearly 3,000 shells are fired on the first day. It is the biggest battle in five months. Nine soldiers from my brigade are killed and thirty-five others are wounded. The youngest fatality, a twenty-one-year-old squadron commander called Mykyta Yarovy, is killed by a sniper. His fiancée is expecting their baby. The eldest, Volodymyr Adreshkiv, is forty-seven years old and was an active participant in the Maidan revolution. He leaves three sons.

I process compensation for soldiers killed in battle, whose names and faces are familiar to me. One week I am helping Adreshkiv clear up a payroll problem. The following week

I prepare his death certificate. At the time, the state pays one million hryvnia in death benefits, about €24,000 at today's rates, divided equally among the dead soldier's immediate relatives.

Illia is not involved in the first battle of Svitlodarsk. When I tell him about the death benefits, he says, 'If anything happens to me, I want you to get all the money. Not a penny should go to my parents.'

In the spring of 2017, our battalion transfers to a training base near Kharkiv. My commander, the head of financial services for our battalion, is a drunkard who forgets to tell me that we are transferring out. A reconnaissance platoon is the last to leave Klynove. They walk through the village to make sure that no men or equipment have been forgotten.

'What are you doing here?' the platoon's lead sergeant asks me. He is a short, heavy-set Tatar from Crimea with slanted eyes, known by the call sign Mongol. I have been bored doing paperwork in Klynove, so I befriended soldiers from the reconnaissance unit who live in a nearby building. They sometimes take me on patrol with them.

'What do you mean?' I ask.

'Don't you know we've been redeployed? You're the last one here,' Mongol says.

'You mean our wretched commander left without me?'

'Guess so!' Mongol, his men and I have a good laugh.

'Here, help me with this equipment,' I say. We load a filing cabinet and desktop computer onto the back of their Soviet-made Gaz-66 army truck, which will later become mine. It is a cold, two-day road trip to Kharkiv. We are constantly together, scavenging for food, sleeping in abandoned houses in destroyed villages, telling one another stories.

I learn that, as a university graduate, I am entitled to officer training at the Hetman Petro Sahaidachnyi National Ground Forces Academy in Lviv.

'It's a great idea,' Illia says. 'Go, and we'll be able to start our own unit. We'll fight together.'

Illia and I talk every day while I am in training in Lviv and nearby Yavoriv. Things are relatively quiet in the east, so I don't worry about my husband. He takes an overnight train to spend a day with me in the western city.

I return to Kharkiv as a commissioned officer, a lieutenant, and I am assigned to command a motorized infantry platoon. In the meantime, Illia has become a master sergeant. I want him to be deputy commander of my platoon, not because he is my husband, but because he is a good sergeant. The higher-ups say no. Soldiers are not allowed to serve as subordinates to their spouses. I am disappointed but my spirits remain high. My company commander, Captain Latysh, treats me as an equal. I don't know how he got the call sign Latysh, which means 'Latvian', because he is Ukrainian. Sadly, he will later die of cardiac arrest.

On the training base, Illia lives with his platoon, and I live with mine, in the same large army tent with Captain Latysh and his subordinates. I am diligent and Latysh supports me. Illia and I take our meals together in the canteen. When our work is finished, we go to the forest together. It is almost as if we are dating.

In October 2017, Captain Latysh calls me into his office. 'Yulia, I need a commander for the reconnaissance platoon,' he says. 'The position is yours if you want it. It is a bigger responsibility because you will no longer be directly under my command. You will have more assets at your disposal, and you will have to take initiatives. The job will require a lot of walking, and there will be skirmishes with the enemy.'

I tell the captain I am honoured and ask for a few days to think about it. I am only twenty-two years old. Just sixteen months ago I was a university student. I am not certain that I am ready to bear responsibility for the lives of twenty men on the front line. The mere fact that Captain Latysh asks if I am ready makes me doubt myself. With hindsight, I wish I had ignored all the men who fuelled my uncertainty by telling me that I lacked experience. I would have achieved more. Looking back, I was doing a lot of things right.

The rumour spreads that I am about to be promoted to lead the reconnaissance platoon, the same unit I travelled with from Klynove to Kharkiv six months earlier. I want to believe that they will welcome my appointment, but I know how macho soldiers can be and I hear indications that they will resist being commanded by a young woman. Mongol is in his fifties and has quite a few children, some of whom are older than me. Other commanders are sceptical, even hostile. I know the mood in the unit, and I steel myself for opposition.

Illia and I discuss it and he assures me that he will help me, that I will make a fine reconnaissance platoon commander. He has a friend in an infantry platoon – a tall, strapping Ukrainian known by the call sign Sportik, meaning athlete – who agrees to transfer to my platoon, for moral support.

The Ukrainian army is not diplomatic. In fact, we sometimes say it is 'hot anarchist'. Fist fights are not unusual. Volunteer battalions like ours lack the rigid discipline of professionals who have known a lifetime of subordination. When I tell Captain Latysh that I would like the job, I know there will be challenges. The first is to break the news to my platoon. It would obviously undermine my authority if my husband went with me. Sportik volunteers to accompany me to their tent. I will say I want to introduce them to a new comrade.

One evening after mess, Sportik and I walk into the reconnaissance unit tent. Some of the soldiers are away on leave. About ten are present.

'Come in. Have a seat, Lieutenant,' Mongol says, gesturing towards a camp bed.

Sportik and I sit down. Mongol and two other soldiers, who go by the call signs Apostle and Fedot, sit on the bed opposite. The other men hang back, standing or sitting, but staring and listening intently.

'I have been appointed to lead the reconnaissance platoon,' I tell them. 'I want your full cooperation. I realize there are some things I don't know. I am ready to learn from you. I want to have a dialogue.'

'You? You don't know anything about reconnaissance!' Apostle scoffs. He is in his mid-thirties, with black hair. He has a certain moral authority over the others because he has served in the platoon since the beginning of the war three and a half years earlier.

'I did military research and analytics for the SBU in 2013 and 2014, when I was at university,' I say. I instantly regret attempting to justify myself; it shows weakness. I have descended to Apostle's level.

'When I was at university,' Apostle mimics me in a high, whiny voice. It was a mistake to remind them that I have higher education and they do not. 'You? Working for the SBU? For whom? Who was your supervisor? I don't believe it!' Apostle continues. He spits out the words in bursts of saliva. Sportik tenses up beside me and I am afraid he and Apostle will come to blows. I see him sizing up Mongol, Apostle and Fedot, as well as those who are hanging back. Fedot is a tall, sly redhead from Kherson who follows the mob. He'll blow whichever way the wind blows.

'Everything is secret at the SBU. I can't tell you anything about it,' I say. I too am assessing the line-up. Sportik and I would be no match for the ten of them. I want to defuse the situation without losing face.

'I am not leaving. I will command this platoon,' I say sternly, fixing my gaze on Apostle. 'I could discipline you for insubordination, but I won't. I'll give you a day or two to think about it. If you don't want to serve under my command, you don't have to. If you want to transfer to other units, you may. That's true for all of you.'

Sixteen of twenty men in my platoon move to other units, though some, including Mongol and Fedot, ask to return a few months later. In a petty show of pique, they take nearly all the unit's equipment with them, including tools and household items. I am left with only my assault rifle, a BMP tracked fighting vehicle and the Gaz-66 truck which I travelled in from Klynove. The BMP and Gaz-66 are broken down and need serious repairs.

I am devastated, all the more so because I know everyone in the platoon and thought of them as friends and brothers-in-arms. But when I crossed into their masculine territory, I became unprofessional and unworthy. Had they decided after a few weeks or months that they did not want to serve with me, I might have accepted it. But they just assumed that the role of a woman was to do paperwork. They did not even give me a chance.

It is the greatest crisis of my military career. When Illia and I discuss it, I am determined to keep my composure. I fear he will think less of me if I fall apart.

'The bastards,' I say. 'Can you believe there is such blatant sexism in a war in 2017?'

'Forget it, Pooka. They don't deserve to work with you. You'll be better off finding other soldiers.'

For the first two months, I have only four men in a platoon that is supposed to number twenty; two of Illia's friends and two drone pilots I've recruited. Drones have not yet come into wide use for reconnaissance, but I know intuitively how important they will be. I believe the shortage of manpower – starting with my own unit – can be compensated only by technology. My platoon's strength builds gradually, reaching a maximum of fifteen. I never forget the soldiers' mass defection at the prospect of being commanded by me, or Illia's support when I needed him most.

A year after I process death benefits for soldiers killed in the Battle of Svitlodarsk, the town is again a flashpoint. Our battalion is rotated back to what has become known as the Svitlodarsk Bulge, a crescent of territory projecting south-eastwards from Bakhmut and Svitlodarsk towards Debaltseve, which we lost to Wagner mercenaries and Russian-backed separatists in 2015.

My reconnaissance platoon maintains an outpost high on a hill, with sweeping views of the Svitlodarsk Bulge. Later, when we have drones, being on a hill will become a disadvantage, because it makes you an easy target for artillery. But before we had drones, we had eyes. Our position comprises a dugout big enough for two people, linked by a trench to a foxhole at the highest point on the hill, from where we survey enemy movements with binoculars and night-vision equipment. Usually, one soldier rests while the other watches from the lookout.

Because I have only four men in my unit, I sometimes replace them in the outpost for the night so they can go back to base. It ought to be manned by two soldiers, but I like being alone on the hillside and my men are grateful for the time off.

We cannot take vehicles to the outpost because they would be too exposed to enemy fire, so we walk three or four kilometres, often carrying ammunition and rations in backpacks. I go there early one winter evening to relieve my two soldiers, who promise to return at seven o'clock in the morning. There is snow on the ground and icy rain falls. I am soaked by the time I arrive. The dugout is covered with wood and several layers of foliage; it is dry and surprisingly warm. I make tea in an aluminium mug on a camp stove.

Every hour I make my way through the trench to the observation point, which is really just a foxhole at the highest elevation. From there I report by walkie-talkie to battalion headquarters, 10 to 15 kilometres away. In our code, four-five-zero means calm. Four-five-one signifies gunfire. Four-five-two indicates the enemy is firing mortars or grenades. Four-five-three means heavy artillery.

Sometime after 10 p.m. I hear a gun firing. It is not directed at me, but it is not far away. From the observation point I see bright sparks of machine-gun fire in the darkness and say on the radio: 'Four-five-one.' I determine the location of the machine gun so that headquarters can direct mortar fire from an infantry position. I act as a spotter, saying 'ten metres to the left, thirty metres to the right' over the radio frequency. The machine gun eventually stops firing on our positions. Our mortars may have hit it.

I am in the foxhole, which is more exposed than the dugout, when I hear loud explosions near me, mortars and grenade launchers from the Russian lines. They have identified my position and they want to destroy it. 'Four-five-two. Four-five-two,' I say over the radio. I am being shelled.

Headquarters want to know where the shellfire is coming from, so they can launch a counter-attack. But the explosions are almost continuous, and I cannot see where they are coming from because I am under fire. I try to guess the approximate direction. The barrage continues.

The bombardment lasts for less than an hour, but it is one of the longest and most deafening hours of my life. Mentally, I have been sectioned into two people. A rational, almost robotic Yulia attempts to identify the source of the fire and maintain radio contact with headquarters. The human Yulia registers significant explosions all around, knows that red-hot iron is flying over, and that if she does not squat at the bottom of the foxhole it will slice through her flesh like butter. The knowledge I have accumulated of weapons, strategy, Russian and Ukrainian politics and history vanishes in an instant. I am a hapless creature tormented by vengeful furies, obsessed by the thought that if I am killed or wounded no one will rescue me or remove my body.

The name Svitlodarsk means 'gift of light' in Ukrainian, because there is a large power plant in the town. It is becoming a sinister word to me. The soldiers whose deaths I processed the year before. This ordeal on the top of the mountain. 'Svit' like slit throat. 'Darsk' like Darth Vader.

My comrades arrive early the next morning to find the earth

ripped up around our position. I find the casing of an exploded 82-millimetre mortar bomb at the bottom of a large crater a few metres from my foxhole. I have had a very close call.

The night above Svitlodarsk is an exception to the almost enjoyable adrenalin rush of being under shellfire. Time speeds up. Your fate hangs in the balance. You feel you are gambling with your life. Will this be your turn or not? The most terrifying thing is aerial bombing. With artillery, you hear the shell, you can guess approximately where it will explode, and you have time to take cover. With a fighter bomber, you don't hear the rocket or missile that hits you. Even when the jets fly very low and close to the front line, you have only a fraction of a second's realization before the missile explodes.

*

The Minsk accords created all sorts of gentlemen's agreements, if one can use such a term in wartime. They prevented us from using full force to eliminate the enemy. The war is fiercer this time around. We knew each other's front lines well then. We could see each other's armour, but by and large we did not fire on it. Since 2022, as soon as we detect a vehicle, we destroy it. General Yurii Sodol, the commander of Ukrainian forces in the east, told lawmakers in April 2024 that an armoured vehicle is targeted and destroyed within thirty minutes of advancing to the front of the front line.

Under Minsk, we did not make preventive strikes, but we responded when the enemy opened fire. Both sides observed a ceasefire from midnight on New Year's Eve until dawn the next morning. Because Moscow is in a different time zone, their midnight came an hour before ours. They marked the beginning of the ceasefire with sprays of red tracer bullets at 11 p.m. Ukraine time.

Winter temperatures in Donbas are often below freezing and troops on both sides cut firewood for heating. In the earlier phase of the fighting, there was an informal understanding that Russian and Ukrainian snipers would not fire on soldiers who were cutting firewood to keep themselves warm. Despite these small *politesses*, 14,500 people were killed in Donbas between 2014 and 2022. Since the full-scale invasion, any soldier within range of any weapon will be killed.

At the end of January 2018, Illia and I coordinate requests for twenty-four hours' leave. We are no longer stationed at the same base, and we miss each other. We haven't time to go farther than Svitlodarsk. With its coal- and gas-fired power plant and one of the tallest chimney stacks in Ukraine, Svitlodarsk has always been a dreary place. Most of the 11,000 pre-war inhabitants have fled. There are no restaurants or cafés, no scenic walks. We check into the town's sole, Soviet-era hotel, ironically called the Mir, meaning 'peace'. They give us the 'family suite', two cockroach-infested rooms with mouldy wallpaper and rusting metal twin beds with broken springs. We buy fruit, bread, cheese and sausages at the local supermarket and retire to the Mir.

The hotel is dreadful, but it is warm and there is some water. I am with my husband who loves me. I tell myself one needs nothing more to be happy.

I tell Illia about my frightening night at the nearby observation post. He shakes his head at my foolishness for going there alone and regales me with his most recent exploit.

'Three weeks ago, a comrade and I were hungry for adventure.

A Russian PKM machine gun on the front line is harassing our unit. It wounds several of our men. We fire shells and mortars at it, but the emplacement is dug into a cranny, and we can't get at it. So one night we decide to steal it.'

'You *stole* a Russian machine gun?'

'Yes!'

'Was anyone killed or wounded?'

'The two of us who stole it weren't even scratched, but I can't say the same for the Russians. We crawled the last hundred metres, through frozen undergrowth, at three o'clock in the morning. Their lookout had fallen asleep. We lobbed grenades on the Russians and in the ensuing panic we grabbed the machine gun and ran like hell back to our lines. Now we use the PKM against *them*.'

Illia glosses over the enemy casualties. He is laughing.

'My husband is a daredevil,' I say. 'Why do you get to have all the fun? You should have taken me with you.'

'All right,' he says. 'Next time I will. We'll steal an infantry fighting vehicle.'

As soon as I return to my platoon, I begin collecting data on enemy BTRs (armoured personnel vehicles) in the Svitlodarsk area. We choose two accomplices for the raid we are planning, which I expect to be my most daring feat of arms, something we will be able to tell our children about later.

Illia broaches the subject with the battalion commander. 'Strictly speaking, it's against the rules,' the commander says. But he will turn a blind eye and wish us luck. If we succeed, we will be rewarded. If we fail, he will say he knew nothing about it. Our raid never happens.

In the meantime, I cannot sleep that night in the Mir Hotel, thinking about recent events and our new plan. The lumpy mattresses and poking springs don't help. Illia offers to tell me a story.

'Odin is the leader of all the Viking gods,' my husband begins. 'He lives in a silver tower with his reconnaissance ravens, Hugin and Munin. They fly all over the world like drones, then return to headquarters at Valhalla. Hugin embodies thought and he sits on Odin's left shoulder. Munin represents memory and he sits on Odin's right shoulder. The ravens murmur what they have seen into the All-Father's ear. For his own expeditions, Odin uses an eight-legged horse called Sleipnir as his armoured personnel carrier. His pet wolves, Geri and Freki, look like the wolf on the Georgian Legion emblem.

'Odin sees everything, knows everything,' Illia continues. 'He gave one of his own eyes to Mímir, the keeper of the well called Mímisbrunnr, so that he could drink from its waters and everything hidden would be revealed to him. He hanged himself in Yggdrasil, the tree of life, for nine days and nights to enable him to visit other worlds and decipher the secret language of runes. Odin heals the sick and calms storms. He casts spells over women so they fall in love with him. He can adopt the form of any animal or person.

'Half of all warriors who die in battle go to Valhalla, where they eat and drink mead and wine with Odin,' Illia continues. 'If anything should happen to me, darling Pooka, know that I am laughing and feasting and having a glorious time with Odin and the warriors.'

Illia intends his tale to be humorous, but it is serious at the same time. We are surrounded by violent death, which makes thoughts of an afterlife attractive.

I take a photograph of Illia from a crooked angle. He is lying back in bed, and you see his bare chest in the foreground. His bushy Viking beard takes up much of the frame. His eyes stare at the ceiling. The date stamp in my telephone tells me we spent our last night together on 27 January 2018.

Svitlodarsk Bulge. 22 February 2018

Three weeks later, fighting flares again around Svitlodarsk. Illia's unit is in the sector. I ask my drone pilots to reconnoitre the area and I study their footage to summarize enemy movements. I hear a report on the battalion's radio frequency that two of our soldiers have been wounded in shelling between Svitlodarsk and Luhansk. They do not give names or call signs on the radio, but for some reason I think it might be Illia. I look at his WhatsApp to see when he last checked his phone.

'Are you all right?' I text my husband. He does not reply.

I contact the communications engineer. 'Is Illia your guy?' she asks. One of the men in my platoon is also called Illia and I'm uncertain which one she means.

'Which Illia?'

Illia Serbin, my husband, has sustained a shrapnel wound to the chest. 'Pray for him,' the communications engineer tells me.

I run to the commanding officer, who is stationed in a nearby building. 'Now. I must go now. Give me a vehicle. Armoured or not. I don't care. I must save them.'

'Calm down, Lieutenant,' the officer says. His voice is weary and condescending. 'The platoon is pinned down under enemy fire. I cannot risk a vehicle and a medic until the shooting dies down. Have you forgotten that we lost a woman doctor and an ambulance near Svitlodarsk last month?'

Mila, my close friend and a medic in my company, has

heard the news and rushes into the commander's room. 'Please, Captain. He is Yulia's husband. Let me take a Humvee or a BTR. Let me go now.'

'I said no. No means no,' the commander says. He is irritated. Mila and I exchange desperate glances and leave the room.

A vehicle finally sets out, but it breaks down and a second vehicle is dispatched to replace it. The rescue takes two hours. I wait at Svitlodarsk clinic. The surgery lasts many hours, until 10 p.m. or midnight. Time is dislocated. My brain is on fire. Illia greets me in Tamara's apartment. Illia waves goodbye at Kyiv train station, seals our engagement with my grandmother's ring, makes love to me in our honeymoon cabin, teaches me how to shoot... He cannot die. He must not die. Please, God, don't let him die.

The head doctor walks into the waiting room. She looks at me and I know that my husband is dead. I know it and I do not know it. I sit down and try to reason. There were two wounded soldiers. The doctor has made a mistake. It was the other soldier who died. There is still a live soldier on the operating table. That must be Illia. He must survive.

I ask to see Illia before he is taken to the morgue. I peel back the black plastic bag. His eyes are closed. There is a gash across his chin and a tracheostomy tube stuck in the top of his chest. I am shocked to see my strong, athletic husband naked and helpless. He was a rock for me, a waterfall that surrounded me with waves of love and understanding. I slip the wedding ring from his finger and hug him. An orderly stands a few feet away, apparently indifferent to my sobbing. When I have finished, the orderly pulls the black bag over Illia's head and pushes the hospital gurney down the corridor.

Three years earlier, an invisible thread tugged at my heart when Illia Serbin boarded the train in Kyiv. Now I imagine my own chest blown open, a mirror of my husband's wound. My heart is wrenched from its cavity and thrown into the black bag beside Illia's heart. My life rolls away on a clanking trolley.

Two days later, a coffin is delivered to Tamara's apartment near Kyiv. The mortician has sewn up Illia's wound and dressed him in his uniform. His face looks peaceful. He even has a slight smile. But the image of him wounded and helpless on the hospital trolley will stay with me for ever.

I should have disobeyed orders, hijacked a vehicle, gone to save him. I did nothing. He would have come to me on the battlefield. He would have saved me. It is my fault he died.

The funeral in Kyiv is packed with soldiers in uniform, many of them from the Georgian Legion. Illia's parents did not even know where he was serving, but somehow the army has notified them, and they attend the funeral. I have seen them only once before. Illia was so uncomfortable that he cut short our visit. His father insists on making a stupid speech about this being a political war. His father and mother demand two-thirds of Illia's death benefits, which they receive, contrary to his wishes.

Illia's comrades order a bronze plaque to mark the place where he was fatally wounded. I am touched that they care so much about him, but I fear the Russians may seize the territory and I cannot bear the thought of them vandalizing the plaque or urinating on it. In 2020 I ask the comrades to send the plaque to me. I place it under the walnut tree in Baba Lyuba's garden, the tree that was planted on the day I was born, where Illia and I decided to join the army together. The Russians seize Svitlodarsk in the spring of 2022 and still occupy it.

I have Illia cremated and take his ashes to Mariupol, where he had been happy during his first tour of duty in the army. His best friend, Javier, the medic-who-kills-cats, meets me at the station. We scatter his ashes on grey rocks at the seashore near Shyrokyne, where Illia once served.

I had neither the time nor energy to read for eight months after the 2022 invasion, but now I read as much as I can, because I fear my brain will go soft in the combat zone. I devour contemporary fiction, mysteries, Ukrainian classics. Javier and I keep in touch by sending each other photographs of the covers of books we are reading.

The Harry Potter novels are the books that most marked my childhood and the childhood of many in my generation. Since Illia died, I think often of the scene where Dumbledore, the headmaster at Hogwarts School of Witchcraft and Wizardry, discovers Professor Snape's secret love for Harry's long dead mother, Lily.

In Harry Potter, when you love someone, you share their Patronus, a unique animal aura that protects you. As Dumbledore and Snape argue over Harry's future, a luminescent silver doe races through the room and walls and Dumbledore says incredulously, 'Lily – after all this time?'

'Always,' Snape replies.

Lily married someone else, Harry Potter's father. Seventeen years have passed since her death. Snape discreetly protected Harry because he still loved his mother. 'Always' is a key word in *Harry Potter and the Deathly Hallows*, and it has become the key word in my life. When you truly love someone, you love them always.

Illia Serbin was the kindest, most intelligent and dignified person I have ever known. He taught me what a real relationship between a man and a woman can be, as equal partners. He showed me what it means to be a true warrior.

I dream of Illia only once after his death. We are in a hangar filled with tyres and equipment at his base near Mariupol. He wears a tracksuit and is smoking a pipe. He sits down beside me and tells me that he no longer loves me.

'That's a lie. I don't believe you... Can I go with you?' I ask him.

'No, Pooka, it is too early. You cannot,' he replies. My husband stands up and walks away.

I think the dream means that Illia wants me to let him go, wants me to live my life without him. At night I pray that he will return to me in another dream, but he does not. I console myself with the thought that he is eating, drinking and laughing with Odin in Valhalla.

IX

Sisters-in-Arms

When women speak, they have nothing or almost nothing of what we are used to reading and hearing about: How certain people heroically killed other people and won. Or lost. What equipment there was and which generals. Women's stories are different and about different things. 'Women's' war has its own colours, its own smells, its own lighting, and its own range of feelings. Its own words. There are no heroes and incredible feats, there are simply people who are busy doing inhumanly human things.

Svetlana Alexievich, *The Unwomanly Face of War*, 2017

The training ground in Kharkiv oblast. May 2018

The army has received a NATO grant for training. The battalion commander, a lieutenant colonel, has summoned unit commanders on short notice to designate enlisted men for courses on new weapons systems. Attending staff meetings with higher-ups is one of my least favourite tasks as a commissioned officer. I have limited tolerance for bureaucracy at the best of times. As usual, I am the only woman at the meeting. We are seated around a table in a conference room in a prefabricated building. One rarely has the opportunity to express grievances in the army, so I have prepared my speech.

'Colonel, I am happy to discuss candidates for the training programme, once my men have been given a rest. I have repeatedly asked permission to give them a short break, but received no answer. We need to address the lack of rotation and leave time in general.'

There is an awkward silence. 'Lieutenant, that is not the subject of today's meeting.'

'I know, Sir, but normal channels of communication do not seem to function.'

'The Armed Forces of Ukraine are short-staffed. May I remind you that we are at war with Russia?' the lieutenant colonel says. 'Rotation and leave are granted on a case-by-case basis.'

'Sir, the men in my platoon have not had a day off in months. Morale is low. They need to see their families. After all, that is why they are in the army – to protect their families.'

The military is an institution and institutions have no feelings. Lack of rest and recreation is a chronic problem that will become more severe during the full-scale invasion. I think the army should value my attention to the needs of subordinates, but the lieutenant colonel doesn't see it that way.

'I'll be the judge of morale in my battalion,' he says. Then he mutters: 'You just need a man.'

I cannot believe he said that. I have not recovered from Illia's death and the phrase is like a punch in the face. *Be calm. Never show weakness*, I can hear Illia saying. I want to cry and scream at the same time, but I manage to say what I must say.

'Sir, that is the most disgusting, sexist remark I have ever heard.'

I resist the impulse to storm out of the meeting. *Stand your ground. Nothing would make him happier than for you to leave.* The colonel moves on to the next officer. When the meeting breaks up, several of my colleagues tell me what a pig he is. They are apologetic, as if they are somehow collectively responsible for sexism in the army.

It takes nearly six years for the army to seriously address the problem which I have raised repeatedly. On 14 March 2024, Colonel General Oleksandr Syrskyi, commander-in-chief of the Armed Forces of Ukraine, announces on his Facebook page that 'despite the quite difficult situation across the front line, we have managed to launch the process of rotating and replacing battalions and units that have been performing combat missions on the front line for a long time. This will allow us to stabilize the situation and positively affect the moral and psychological state of our soldiers.'

Since Illia's death, it doesn't feel right to continue in the same way with the same battalion in Donbas. I request a transfer to Kyiv so I can live with Tamara and, I hope, sort out my plans for the future. I am eventually offered a position as a supervisor at Ivan Bohun Military Lyceum. Female cadets are to be admitted for the first time in the autumn, and the director wants me to take responsibility for them, among my other duties as an administrator.

The lyceum staff discuss the imminent arrival of twenty-five teenage girls, aged fifteen and sixteen, at a meeting in late summer.

'How are we going to integrate them in the student body?' asks the director, an army major-general.

The lyceum is prestigious. During my three years there, I hear rumours of bribes being paid for admission. Many of the students are from military families.

The director initially proposes distributing the girls evenly through the (until now) all-male classes. 'You can't put boys and girls together!' an instructor, an army officer, objects. 'They're teenagers. Their hormones are rampant. The girls will distract the boys from their studies. They'll be canoodling in the trenches during war games. Girls will get pregnant, and the parents will hold the school responsible. Think of the lawsuits.'

Again, I cannot believe what I am hearing. It gets worse.

'I don't know why we let girls in anyway,' says one of the older instructors. 'The army is no place for women. Everyone knows that cadets must be male, by tradition.'

No one looks at me during the discussion. It is as if I have become invisible, and I think of the aptly named Invisible Battalion, the advocacy group I have been working with in my spare time. A handful of Ukrainian women have produced a documentary film by the same name. I take it to towns and cities across the country for screenings, then talk to audiences and media, as a female veteran of the war in Donbas. The film tells the story of six women in the combat zone. They are medics, a sniper and an assault soldier, Andriana Arekhta. She and I become friends through the project and through Veteranka, the women's veterans' group which she co-founded in 2015.

During her time in Donbas, Andriana is listed in army records as a seamstress, because women are banned by law from combat positions. Other women in combat roles are listed as cooks, cleaners and accountants. As a result, they and their families have no access to indemnities if they are killed or wounded, nor are they eligible for normal veterans' benefits. Andriana and I and our sisters in Invisible Battalion meet with members of the Verkhovna Rada, urging them to vote for the 2018 Amendments to Certain Laws of Ukraine on Ensuring Equal Rights and Opportunities for Women and Men during Military Service. We tell them that war has no gender, that it is a disgrace to treat women soldiers this way. The legislation they approve opens sixty-three combat positions to women.

To achieve real equality in the armed forces, we will have to do much more campaigning after the war. We will be able to argue that 5,000 of the 62,000 Ukrainian women in the army and defence ministry have served in combat positions. That may be a tiny fraction of the nearly one million soldiers in the Armed Forces of Ukraine, but our contribution deserves recognition.

Andriana is the only Ukrainian woman to have participated in an assault group. She is twelve years older than me, but we have a lot in common. When she was younger, Andriana wanted to be a translator of English. She earned a master's degree in public administration at Kyiv-Mohyla Academy, where I did my bachelor's degree. Like me, she participated in the Maidan revolution.

Though I have been a soldier for most of my adult life and have spent years in combat zones, I have never found myself face to face with the enemy on the battlefield, other than those we have taken prisoner. It is the only aspect of warfare that I have not yet experienced, and I want to live through it at least once. I never forget the story Andriana told me before the 2022 invasion.

'When the war started in 2014, I asked to join the Aydar battalion,' Andriana told me. 'There were so few women soldiers that the army had no boots in women's sizes, so I wore sneakers into battle. My baptism of fire was an assault on a village in Luhansk. In the course of the assault, I found myself facing a Russian soldier. I was shooting from the corner of a building, and he was about five metres away. Our eyes meet. We take aim at each other, but neither of us fires; the Russian because he is so surprised to see a woman facing him; me because I am not morally prepared to kill a human being. Another Ukrainian soldier shoots the Russian dead and saves my life.'

Andriana is strong and intelligent and an inspiration to me. She met her husband, Max, a Ukrainian army officer, on the front line and they have a little boy called Makar. She continued fighting until the fifth month of her pregnancy in 2015.

Since the full-scale invasion started, Andriana has twice gone to Capitol Hill in Washington to ask for weapons for Ukraine. She calls this the Toyota and Mitsubishi war because so many soldiers are forced to drive soft-skinned vehicles into battle. She tells US congressmen that Ukraine is losing some of its best soldiers because we have no armoured personnel carriers. 'We are driving civilian cars and trucks on the front line, while NATO countries have stockpiles of armoured Humvees and Bradleys. The armoured vehicles that NATO sends us are twenty years old. They come with no spare parts and break down after a few days.'

Andriana's words are premonitory. In December 2022 she is found unconscious, without a pulse, in the wreckage of the civilian car she was driving on the front line in Kherson oblast.

She hit a mine and is in critical condition with a broken arm, shoulder, jaw and ribs, and damage to her spine, stomach and lungs. She is airlifted to Odesa for medical treatment and has been in and out of hospital ever since.

*

At Ivan Bohun Lyceum, it quickly becomes apparent that the instructors, the male cadets and their parents don't want classes to be mixed. *The important thing is that the girls be exposed to military life. They can decide later if they want to continue*, I think to myself. I propose organizing the first-year class as a military company comprising four twenty-five-strong platoons, three male platoons and one female. I don't like the idea of segregating teenagers in a military high school by gender, because the Ukrainian army is not segregated. But it seems the only way of saving our pilot programme. My colleagues at the lyceum eagerly endorse my suggestion.

A girl called Apollinaria, with long blonde hair, comes to see me one afternoon in my office at Ivan Bohun. She addresses me in Russian.

'What can I do for you?' I ask her.

'Lieutenant, I want to be an army officer, like you. I applied to Ivan Bohun, but they rejected my application.'

'Why did they turn you down?'

'I failed the Ukrainian language test.' She looks down as if ashamed. 'I'm from Sievierodonetsk, in Luhansk. We always spoke Russian in my family.'

Russian forces will capture Sievierodonetsk in June 2022 after a six-week battle during which 90 per cent of the city's buildings

*will be destroyed or damaged. It is a stone's throw from the
front-line village where I am stationed in 2024.*

I look intently at Apollinaria, remembering how difficult it
was for me to speak Ukrainian when I began university at
Kyiv-Mohyla.

'Why do you want to be an army officer?' I ask her.

'I hate the Russians. I saw what they and their separatist
friends did to my city in 2014. I'm Ukrainian and I want to
defend my country.'

'I'll see what I can do,' I tell her.

Another female student is expelled the following month for
poor grades, opening up a place. I plead Apollinaria's case with
the admissions committee. She is very motivated and works
hard. In 2021 she applies to study reconnaissance at the military academy in Odesa. They turn her down, saying the course
is not open to women. She is now qualifying to become the
commander of a mobilized infantry unit – the course I took – in
Lviv. I am touched when Apollinaria says that I am her role
model. I have no doubt that she will succeed as a soldier, though
it will be difficult for her.

Anzhelina, another student who I took under my wing, is
now studying to become a communications officer at the
Zhytomyr military university. She writes to me from time to
time asking for advice. I always tell my students, as well as the
men under my command, that they must defend their rights
in dealings with higher-ups. 'Be gentle but firm, rational and
polite,' I told Anzhelina recently, when an instructor found fault
with her thesis.

I am at least seven years older than my female students and
I cannot help feeling protective of them, especially those who
go to the trouble of keeping in contact. I am proud of them,

and I learn nearly as much from them as they learn from me. When they ask for advice, I tell them what Illia told me: never, ever show weakness. If you want to succeed in the military, you must be better than a man. Sometimes they ask if it's all right to be feminine. I tell them that I collect *vyshyvanka*, which are not only beautiful but part of our heritage, that I feel different when I wear traditional dress, not the way I do in camouflage. I tell them that when I was deployed to Donbas I left behind make-up, nail polish and civilian clothing. It may sound harsh, and it may be mere coincidence, but the women I've seen wearing make-up in combat zones were not good soldiers.

Contrary to what you might expect, the female cadets stand their ground and defend their opinions more than the males, who rarely resist. When there is a perceived injustice, young men tend to accept it while young women rebel.

I am also fond of Anya, a former cadet from Lviv. Unlike Apollinaria and Anzhelina, she has decided not to join the military, though her father is a soldier. Since the full-scale invasion, Anya has been an active volunteer, collecting donations for equipment for her father's unit.

I often wonder why some young women persevere and go on to a military academy after the lyceum, while others chose the path of least resistance. I have always chosen difficulty, which has made my life a lot more interesting, albeit trying. Everything is more difficult for women anyway, especially when they refuse to comply with stereotypes. Because of social conditioning and invisible barriers, because of sexism. When I showed *Invisible Battalion* around Ukraine and at Ivan Bohun, I was struck by the fact that everyone loved the film and agreed with its message. No one thinks of him- or herself as sexist, not even army officers who make disgusting remarks about women.

People mean well, but they betray their innate bias. 'Aren't you afraid?' I've been asked a thousand times, as if fear in battle were a female characteristic.

Sergeant Andriy and some of the guys in my platoon are philosophizing over a bottle of wine one evening. I ask them: 'If you could have extraordinary powers, what would you chose?'

'I would like to improve myself every day, to become better than I was yesterday,' Andriy says.

I believe that choosing the difficult path, taking the most difficult decisions, is the only way to achieve this. I tried to impart that to my female charges.

By November 2022, Veteranka has recorded the deaths of more than 100 women soldiers, and many more wounded. Female fatalities include Inna Derusova, a combat medic since 2015 who was killed in an artillery bombardment in north-east Ukraine while caring for wounded soldiers on the second day of the invasion. Sergeant Derusova was the first woman to be posthumously awarded the Hero of Ukraine medal. She was fifty-one years old.

In March 2023, a report by the Ukrainian Veterans Foundation finds that only 8.9 per cent of officers are women, and none hold senior military positions.

Since the invasion, quite a few male Ukrainian soldiers have been sent on coveted training stints in the US and Europe. I know of no women who have been sent abroad. Some combat positions are still closed to females. For example, we are not allowed to be navy divers because of a silly argument about it being harmful for women to hold their breath and the risk of internal bleeding. More than two years after the February 2022 invasion, the military is just starting to provide uniforms and flak jackets designed to fit women's bodies.

Before 2022, Invisible Battalion was researching sexual harassment in the military. We supported legislation to address the problem, in particular more severe penalties for offenders. We created an anonymous chatbot for male and female soldiers to report sexual harassment, and a course for soldiers on gender sensitivity. There are still incidents, but we have suspended research and advocacy for the duration of the war, because if we lose this war, there will be no equality for anyone in Ukraine.

Since October 2023, the government has required women with medical training to register at recruitment centres. Potential female army medics are not yet being called up, but they undergo medical exams and carry their draft cards. This is a step in the right direction. I want equal rights and equal duties. Women should be drafted, just like men.

When the war is over, I will continue working with Invisible Battalion, the Institute for Gender Programmes and Veteranka. Yet I do not consider myself a feminist. Perhaps the label was appropriate for women of my mother's generation. I am not radical. I just want every individual to be treated with respect, regardless of their gender, for men to show respect to women. I don't know if you can call that feminism.

X

My Father

How good it is that I've no fear of dying
Nor ask myself how ponderous my toil
Nor bow to cunning magistrates, decrying
Presentiments of unfamiliar soil,
That I have lived and loved, yet never burdening
My soul with hatred, curses or regret.
My people! It is to you I am returning.
In death I somehow find my fate.
I turn my pained but goodly face to living
And in filial prostration I begin.
I meet your eyes in fair thanksgiving
And join my kindred earth as closest kin.

> Vasyl Stus, 'How Good It Is', 1972,
> translated by Marco Carynnyk

Maidan Nezalezhnosti. 4 a.m., 30 November 2013

I am in bed in Tamara's apartment when Berkut riot police surround the nine-day-old student encampment on the Maidan.

Dressed in Robocop gear, they charge the students, many of whom are sleeping, firing tear gas. Young men and women are pushed to the ground, kicked with army boots and beaten with truncheons. Even those who sit still and put their hands above their heads in a sign of surrender are beaten.

Tamara and I hear about the violence the moment we wake up in the morning. I sit beside her on the sofa watching terrible images, tears flowing down my cheeks.

'So this is what it is like to live in a dictatorship,' I tell my mother. 'We are forbidden to associate with Europe, forbidden from speaking. Innocent protestors are pounded by the Berkut. Yanukovych will pay for this.'

I rush to the Maidan as soon as classes at Kyiv-Mohyla are over. When I'd left the previous day, we were just a few thousand students on the square. The Vilnius Summit, where Viktor Yanukovych formally renounced Ukraine's Association Agreement with the European Union, had just ended. We were afraid the protests would die out, but today our numbers have multiplied. We are tens of thousands, and more will soon join us. The country is furious with Yanukovych for physically attacking the country's youth, as well as its political and economic future.

Suddenly I see a familiar face in the crowd. 'Tato! What are you doing here?'

Mykola appears tired and excited at the same time. He pulls me by the hand through the swarm of people and we talk, standing face to face and leaning against a wall.

'Are you okay?' he asks, looking me up and down to assure himself that I was not injured in the pre-dawn attack by the Berkut.

'I'm fine. I was at Mama's house when it happened. I went to class this morning and I just got here. I'm kind of sorry I missed the action.'

'Don't be sorry. Count yourself lucky,' Mykola says. 'It was shocking.'

'Were you here?'

Mykola nods yes, and I can see that he is proud. 'I came over last night with my Afghan friends.' He doesn't mean Afghan citizens, but the *Afgantsy*, Ukrainian veterans of the Soviet war in Afghanistan, who have an unfortunate reputation for substance abuse and psychiatric problems. Mykola has a special affinity for them, and says their negative reputation is unfair. He was conscripted a little too late to be sent to Afghanistan and served instead with the Soviet army in Hungary in 1989/90. That was a momentous period. The Soviets pulled out of Afghanistan in February 1989 and the USSR began to crumble. Ukraine's declaration of independence in August 1991 was the final blow that finished off the Soviet Union four months later.

I ask Mykola what he's doing on the Maidan. When I joined the civil disobedience campaign with Vidsich the previous year he had argued with me. I can barely believe that he of all people is a protestor.

'I know what you thought,' Mykola says. 'Your stodgy old father was stuck in his post-Soviet ways. Well, Tato gave it a great deal of thought, and I've seen the light. Yanukovych is a thug and a Russian lackey. Ukraine must free itself of Russian domination. We are better off with Europe. If I had any remaining doubts, they evaporated in the early hours this morning, when I saw the Berkut laying into kids your age and beating them to a pulp.'

'They didn't hurt *you*?'

'For some reason, no,' Mykola says. 'At the age of forty-two, I probably look old enough to be an SBU agent or a government official. I helped a couple of terrified students who couldn't find their way off the square. One of them was bleeding. I know every nook and cranny of this city and I led them down a narrow side alley and up the hill to the monastery, where the monks took them in.'

I tell him I'm proud of him.

Mykola glows. I suspect his conversion to the political opposition stems in part from a desire to make amends. I think he feels guilty for my and Bohdan's disrupted childhood. As I grew up, his adultery stopped bothering me. I don't exactly forgive him, but I realize that things happen in life, and it no longer seems to matter. Besides, he has broken up with Larysa, the second wife he left my mother for, though he's still trying to win her back. I think she's had enough of his boozing and womanizing.

'I am in charge of the nineteenth self-defence *sotnya*,' Mykola boasts.

'And I am in the women's sixteenth *sotnya*, so my wayward father and I are comrades in a way.' I'm surprised we didn't run into each other sooner.

'Yulia,' he says, shifting to a more serious tone, 'I saw what happened overnight. I am talking to the guys from Praviy Sektor and Svoboda. They have weapons and they are determined to overthrow Yanukovych. There will be more violence before this is over. Promise me you'll be careful.'

I promise, and ask him not to worry. It's all for the good cause.

We smile warmly, embrace and return to our respective *sotni*, more moved than we let on by our impromptu reconciliation on the Maidan.

*

In February 2014, the violence spirals out of control. I am at home with Tamara one night when the phone rings. It is Mykola's younger brother, Uncle Dima.

'Your father has been injured near the Maidan,' Dima says. 'If I take him to hospital, they won't care for him. Can I bring him over?'

I ask Tamara. 'Of course,' she says. 'What happened?'

My parents are on reasonably good terms. Like me, Mama has learned not to expect anything of Mykola, and to be pleasantly surprised when he comes through. She would never turn away the wounded father of her children.

'A stun grenade exploded next to him,' Dima says. 'He's unconscious. They put him with the bodies of dead protestors, but someone noticed he was breathing, and – God knows how – they rang me. Try to get a doctor to come to the house if you can.'

Tamara rings my childhood nanny, Viktoria, who by good fortune knows a GP through our old church. The Baptist doctor arrives soon after Dima staggers in with my half-conscious father leaning heavily on his shoulder. We lay Mykola on Bohdan's bed for the doctor to examine him.

'He has suffered a serious concussion. He needs a month's rest,' the doctor says.

The next morning, Mykola gets up, has breakfast with me and Tamara and takes the bus and metro into the city with me. He wants to return to his *sotnya*.

March 2014

Ukraine emerges from the Revolution of Dignity in a state of chaos, confusion and uncertainty. Yanukovych has fled to Moscow. Most of the Ukrainian officer corps have also defected to Russia. We have a caretaker government until new legislative and presidential elections can be held.

Vladimir Putin seizes the opportunity to orchestrate a take-over of Crimea by the pro-Russian minority. On 27 February, Russian special forces seize government buildings in Simferopol and the Russian flag is raised over the Supreme Council of Crimea and the Crimean Council of Ministers. Lawmakers in the Crimean assembly vote at gunpoint to elect as the top official in Crimea Sergei Aksyonov, the leader of a pro-Russian party so unpopular that it had won not a single office in local elections. In a rigged election on 16 March, Crimea votes for reunification with Moscow. Putin annexes the Ukrainian peninsula the following day.

In the meantime, pro-Russian separatists have begun agitating in eastern Ukraine. At a small demonstration in Donetsk City on 1 March, an advertising salesman called Pavel Gubarev proclaims himself the 'people's governor of Donetsk' and declares an independent 'Donetsk People's Republic'.

Mykola and I meet at a café near Kyiv-Mohyla Academy. I haven't seen him since he was knocked out by the stun grenade. My father rails against the iniquity of the *Moskali*, a pejorative term for Russians, who gobbled up Crimea in less than three weeks and are now starting on Donbas.

He says passionately that if we don't react quickly, we'll lose the entire country – everything we fought for over three months on the Maidan. But the military is in chaos, with almost no officers and clapped-out Soviet equipment. We talk about the volunteer groups that are springing up, some reputable, others less so. The government doesn't know whom to send to the east. Most of the Berkut followed Yanukovych into exile. The authorities had to dissolve what was left of the organization, after the way they attacked protestors on the Maidan. The Minister of Internal Affairs has replaced the Berkut with a new National Guard, and Tato has volunteered to join it. They offered him his own platoon and the rank of master sergeant because he had experience in the Soviet army.

'That's great, Tato. You are doing the right thing.' I don't say it, but I hope that military discipline will put order into his unsettled life.

'What are you going to do now, Yulia? Why don't you join up and come to Donbas with me? It would be the logical continuation of Maidan. If the National Guard won't take you as a woman, one of the volunteer battalions will be glad to have you. They're trying to fill the void left by the army. Everyone is a Ukrainian patriot now. The country needs us.'

I tell him I am only eighteen years old, that I need to complete my university degree. I probably wouldn't be of any use to the military anyway, and if I joined up, I might never make it back to university. I tell Mykola that I'm already contributing in my own way, by doing volunteer work for the SBU intelligence agency.

The SBU lost a lot of people when Yanukovych fled, and they are trying to reconstitute the service on a shoestring budget. A friend of my friend Mykhailo, who was with me on the Maidan, works for the SBU. They appealed for student volunteers to monitor the Russians online and on social media. At home in the evening, I scour Google and Twitter and the Russian network vk.com for information about the Russians in

Donetsk and Luhansk. Anything I can find about enemy troop movements, their barracks, hospitals, et cetera. I'm teaching myself how to search for information, how to identify satellite images of barracks and vehicles. I have a hunch the skills I am developing will prove useful later.

Mykola wants to know how I communicate with the SBU. I tell him I have only the email address where I send everything – the equivalent of a dead letter box in old movies. They usually don't reply, but a few days earlier I received a message saying they had saved a Ukrainian jet thanks to information I sent, so I know my material is being read.

'My daughter, the spy!' Mykola says.

'Tato, it's all open sources!'

'Will you come to my oath-swearing ceremony?'

'I wouldn't miss it for the world.'

Novi Petrivtsi village, near Kyiv. April 2014

Mykola's class is the first to complete two weeks' training at the National Guard School. The authorities stage an elaborate ceremony to celebrate their departure for the east, because stopping the Russian incursion in Donbas is a high priority for Ukraine's caretaker government.

It is sunny and chilly on the parade ground. General Serhii Kulchytski, a charismatic, blond, blue-eyed officer from Lviv, western Ukraine, who served with the Soviet armed forces but became a Ukrainian patriot and refused to flee with Yanukovych, has been appointed head of the military and special training directorate at the National Guard. Kulchytski sits on the reviewing platform beside Petro Poroshenko, 'the chocolate king', oligarch and politician whom everyone expects to become Ukraine's next president in elections scheduled for May. Poroshenko owns a nationwide chain of sweet shops called Roshen: his family name shorn of the first two and last two letters. Officials bustle about, practically genuflecting before him.

Master Sergeant Mykola Mykytenko leads the column of national guardsmen across the parade ground. Every soldier swears an oath of allegiance in front of the general and the future president. Mykola stands ramrod straight, without twitching or moving a muscle, for close to ninety minutes. I think he may have found his calling at last. Perhaps the military will give him the sense of purpose he never found in the odd jobs he did until now.

After the ceremony, the guardsmen and their families repair to large tents filled with tables laden with hors d'oeuvres. Mykola's entire family is there: his mother Lyuba, his brother Dima and Dima's wife Halyna, his ex-wife, me and Bohdan. Bohdan is in cadet training and is furious at being told to wear his uniform, which is too big. Despite the war, the mood is almost happy, positive, uplifting. Mykola and his comrades are eager to defend their country on the eastern front. No one imagines there is at least a decade of war ahead of us, that tens of thousands will die and more than 100,000 will be wounded. On the day of Mykola's oath ceremony, the war is still an adventure. Everyone feels certain we'll drive the Russians out of Donbas in no time.

29 May 2014

General Kulchytski is flying an Mi-8 helicopter to the National Guard base at Mount Karachun, near Slovyansk in Donetsk oblast, when it is shot down by pro-Russian separatists. Six national guardsmen and six special forces officers from the Ministry of Internal Affairs are killed with him. Kulchytski is the highest-ranking Ukrainian officer killed in the war so far. His death is considered a national tragedy.

Mykola is stationed at Mount Karachun. He disobeys orders and heads out for the site of the helicopter crash with four men from his platoon in a BTR armoured personnel carrier. The co-pilot is still alive. Mykola pulls him from the smouldering cockpit. Under sporadic mortar fire from separatists and Russians, he and his men retrieve from the wreckage the bodies of Kulchytski and the other dead soldiers and head back to base. Because the vehicle is packed with dead and wounded, Mykola rides on top. The BTR hits a mine and Mykola is thrown to the ground. He lands on his head.

'Come to the hospital quickly, in case he does not survive,' the doctor who telephones me from Kharkiv says. 'It's a miracle that his neck was not broken.'

Uncle Dima, Aunt Halyna, Bohdan and I travel to Kharkiv to see Mykola in the military hospital. We are the same group who attended his oath ceremony a few weeks earlier, minus Tamara and Baba Lyuba.

Mykola is wrapped in bandages like a mummy. We crowd around his bed. For a man who was almost killed, he is in surprisingly good humour. I think he is touched that we care enough to make the 1,000-kilometre return journey.

'How do you feel, Tato?' Bohdan asks.

To our amazement, Mykola pulls himself out of bed and walks a few steps, his limbs stiff and flailing like a robot's. There's a plaster cast around his neck and he cannot move his head. 'I feel great,' he says with a sardonic laugh. 'I finally got to ride in a military helicopter, because I was wounded.'

We help him back into bed. 'Tell us what happened,' I say.

'I'll start at the beginning. The terrorists moved into Slovyansk on 12 April. They took over the town hall and SBU headquarters. Their leader is a mean Russian bastard called Igor Girkin, who goes by the *nom de guerre* Strelkov [meaning 'shooter']. Girkin is a weedy little guy with a thin moustache and no humanity. He's a colonel in the FSB, and he led the takeover of Crimea in March, almost without firing a shot, just through intimidation.

'When Girkin and his henchmen took over Slovyansk, he installed a puppet mayor, the same modus operandi he used in Crimea. After a bogus referendum on 12 May, Girkin declared himself the "Supreme Commander" of the "Donetsk People's Republic". Our agents in Slovyansk say he's torturing prisoners in the basement of the SBU building and that he has ordered several executions.'

Ukrainian forces will drive Girkin and his men out of Slovyansk on 5 July 2014, after nearly three months of occupation. He is dismissed from his position after the separatists he commands bring down Malaysia Airlines Flight 17 over Donbas the following month, killing 298 passengers and crew. In November 2022, a Dutch court convicts Girkin and two other men on 298 counts of murder and sentences them in absentia to life imprisonment.

In the meantime, Girkin has become an enthusiastic supporter of the full-scale invasion of Ukraine. In 2022, he joins a hardline volunteer unit for a time. Like the founder of Wagner and attempted coup leader Yevgeni Prigozhin, Girkin rails against the incompetence of the Russian army. He is a prominent 'milblogger', a war commentator who supports the invasion but regards the military's approach as timid. He calls for a full-scale mobilization, criticizes Putin and speaks of running for president in 2024. In July 2023, Russian authorities arrest him on charges of extremism. In a post on the Telegram messenger service in January 2024, Girkin calls Putin a 'lowlife' and a 'cowardly bum'. On 25 January he is convicted of inciting extremism and sentenced to four years in a Russian prison. His sentence bans Girkin from access to the internet.

*

Mykola has bottled up the excitement and adventure of his deployment in Donbas. In hospital and facing months of rehabilitation, he cannot stop talking.

'It's important for Ukraine to liberate Slovyansk,' he says, 'It's symbolic, because it was the first town taken by the terrorists. We've got them under siege, and we're attacking day and night, with artillery and assaults from the base on Mount Karachun.'

'Tato, are you fighting Russians or Ukrainians in Slovyansk, aside from Girkin?' I ask. 'I mean, is Girkin the only Russian? The Russians deny they are fighting in Donbas.'

'The officers and commanders are all *Moskali*,' he says. 'They're on the second line of defence, and they control the artillery. The men in the trenches are mostly Ukrainian collaborators, so they are the ones we capture. Prisoners always claim they're Ukrainian, but we know how to tell from their accents. For example, you know we stress the "o" in Slovyansk; Russians put the stress on "ansk". Another trick is to ask them to say *palianystia* – you know, the round Ukrainian bread. They cannot pronounce it!'

Mykola continues talking. We want to hear about the helicopter crash.

'General Kulchytski was flying supplies and reinforcements to the base,' Mykola says. 'He could have stayed in an office in Kyiv, but he risked his life to be with us, and we guardsmen loved him for it. He piloted his own helicopter. The chopper was only a kilometre or two from our base when they hit it with a surface-to-air missile. The commanders couldn't make up their minds to send an evacuation squad under enemy fire. We didn't know if there were any survivors, but we had to go regardless. We couldn't just abandon the general on the field of battle. While the higher-ups argued, I got four guys from my platoon, and we headed out in the BTR. I may get court-martialled for it, or I may get a medal. It doesn't matter. I told the driver to go as fast as he could, and we were bouncing down the mountain track while mortars exploded around us. We got to a clearing where the helicopter was burning. There were bodies scattered everywhere. Some were charred and others had been torn apart by the explosion. We jumped out and I ran to the wreckage, looking for survivors. I heard the co-pilot moaning. He was still strapped in his seat, which lay beside the chopper. I undid the buckles, lifted him under the arms and dragged him to safety. Then I went back for the others.'

An army doctor pops his head in. 'Master Sergeant Mykytenko is lucky to be alive,' he says. 'That fall from the BTR would have killed most men. He's making an amazing recovery, but he cracked a vertebra, which will be painful for a very long time. We're sending him to Kyiv for follow-up treatment.'

Having Mykola as a father was always a challenge. He was temperamental and unpredictable, but that day in Kharkiv hospital, I felt incredibly proud of his sang-froid and courage at Mount Karachun.

The next four and a half years are not kind to Mykola. His neck and back give him pain and he is invalided out of the National Guard. He takes the death of Illia very hard. Several times he signs six-month contracts with army units who are less demanding about a recruit's medical condition. Like many Donbas veterans, Mykola wants to fight on the front line and avoids military engagements that would require time at a desk or in training.

*

At some point after his injury on Mount Karachun, I am forced to admit to myself that my father is an alcoholic. Bohdan is the only person I can talk to about it, and we soften our judgement with words like 'borderline'. After all, Mykola still *functions*. On the infrequent occasions when I spend time with him, I usually smell alcohol on his breath.

The summer after Iliya is killed, Mykola, Bohdan and I spend a few weeks at Baba Lyuba's dacha in Zhytomyr oblast. I use my third of Illia's death benefits to build a small grocery store next to the house. Bohdan runs it, with the wife he later divorces. At the beginning of the 2022 invasion, Tamara will go to Lazarivka to manage the shop with Bohdan. The highway is extremely dangerous, so they use back roads to reach big supermarkets where they buy supplies for resale to locals.

During our summer 2018 visit, Mykola takes down a bottle of Mykulynetsky Ukrainian whiskey from the cupboard above the refrigerator several times a day. If he joins us for breakfast, he pours whiskey in his coffee. When I am washing dishes with Bohdan or helping Lyuba prepare food, he throws back his head and swigs a long draught before screwing the top on the bottle and putting it back in place. Every time we buy groceries, he places two or three bottles in the basket. I sometimes make a feeble protest, along the lines of 'Tato, do we really need so many bottles?' but Mykola pretends he doesn't hear me. Bohdan and I exchange glances.

Mykola behaves as if his brazen, excessive consumption of alcohol is invisible to us, or the most natural thing in the world. Through a strange, inverted logic, I sometimes offer him a drink before dinner or before we go out for a walk, because I feel sorry for him, or want to please him, or think he is anxious or in pain. *He has been fighting on the eastern front. Doesn't he deserve a drink?* Or I tell myself he is upset about General Kulchytski, or Illia, or any number of dead comrades. We have all been damaged by the war. We just deal with it in different ways.

I am reading on the living-room sofa one hot summer evening after Lyuba and Bohdan have gone to bed. Mykola places a bottle of Mykulynetsky and two glasses on the coffee table before sitting down opposite me. It is hot and the windows are open. Grasshoppers chirp in the garden.

'Join me for a drink, Yulia?' Mykola asks.

'No thanks, Tato.' I set down the novel I am reading, splayed upside down on the coffee table. A fussy professor at Kyiv-Mohyla flashes through my mind. 'You should respect books!' he always said scoldingly, even about the cheapest paperbacks. 'You'll break the spine!'

Mykola pours himself a full glass, sinks down in the armchair and stares at the ceiling, clutching the whiskey over his stomach. Sometimes when he drinks, he wants to argue, but tonight he is in his other drinking mode, clammed up and non-communicative. He must want company, or he would not come to sit with me. I don't want to hurt my father's feelings or drive him away, but I may not find a better opportunity to talk to him.

'Tato, there is something I've been wanting to talk to you about...'

'You're upset about Illia, aren't you? So am I,' he says. 'I don't know how you endure it.'

'Of course I'm upset, but that's not it,' I reply. I pause before blurting out, 'It's about your drinking.'

Mykola holds the glass of whiskey up to the light as if appraising a precious gem. 'What about it?' he asks.

'You drink too much. Bohdan and I worry about you.'

'Do I?' he asks snidely.

'Tato, I cannot help counting the whiskey bottles. You're putting away three or four every week. You're going to destroy your health. You'll wreck your liver.'

'A Russian artillery shell will kill me first.'

'Frankly, Tato, it's no fun to be with you when you drink.'

Mykola's eyes tear up. His jaw sets and he looks angry. 'My friends don't think I drink too much. Bohdan hasn't said anything. My mother doesn't complain.'

'Maybe your friends are alcoholics. Maybe they don't dare raise the subject,' I say, feeling more like Mykola's parent than his daughter.

'You're making a big deal out of nothing, Lieutenant.'

'Don't you Lieutenant me,' I snap back. 'Tato, it's because we love you. Please try to stop drinking. It makes you depressed and it keeps you from sleeping.'

'I sleep fine,' Mykola says. I know it's not true. I hear him wandering around the dacha at night.

'Believe me, you'll feel better. You'll be happier, I am certain. Will you promise me that you'll try to stop drinking?'

Mykola stares for a long moment at the ceiling before

answering. 'I promise', he finally says, before emptying the glass of Mykulynetsky in one draught.

Kyiv Central Hospital. January 2020

Mykola is hospitalized in the psychiatric ward for post-traumatic stress disorder Because he cannot drink in hospital, I truly enjoy his company. There is a Christmas tree in the reception area on his ward where I take a selfie of us. It is cold, even inside the hospital, and we are both wrapped up. I have braces on my teeth which make me look younger than my twenty-four years. I make an 'okay' sign with the thumb and index finger of my free hand. Mykola wears a dark green army jumper. His beard is greying.

'Are you okay, Yulia, without Illia?' he asks.

Nearly two years have passed. I am a supervisor at Ivan Bohun Military Lyceum, where I command the first women's class, among other duties. It's an important responsibility, but I feel adrift. Though I am dating a cadet in Lviv, we are just going through the motions. It's too complicated to explain to Mykola, who has his own problems.

'It's hard. I keep going,' I summarize. 'I have a boyfriend. He's younger than me. It's not the same.'

'You are very strong, Yulia. You're a true soldier. You say, "It's no big deal," but I can tell there's a lot going on behind your calm demeanour. Illia was an amazing guy. You won't find another one like him.'

I feel a fleeting temptation to cry on the shoulder of my Tato, as I did as a little girl when my tummy hurt in Lazarivka. It would not help me or Mykola, so I change the subject.

'What about you, Tato? I haven't seen you since Baba Lyuba's funeral.' My paternal grandmother died in 2019. It was a huge blow to all of us, including Tamara, whom she continued to treat as a daughter-in-law after the divorce. Lyuba helped all those close to her, but especially her errant son Mykola. Tears well up at the mention of his mother's name.

'I miss her,' he says. 'My mother was the only person who loved me totally, unconditionally. The world is an empty place without her.'

I steer our conversation towards politics. I want to know why my father went from thinking of the Russians as brothers to hating them at present.

'Putin – *khuylo*!' he replies, using the Ukrainian word for 'dickhead', which is even more obscene in Ukrainian than in English. The slogan and popular song started as a football chant in Kharkiv, two weeks after Putin annexed Crimea in 2014. Sixty thousand fans gathered in Kharkiv stadium for a match between FC Metalist Kharkiv and FC Shakhtar Donetsk. They started shouting these two words and carried on shouting as they marched through the streets after the match

'I don't hate the Russian people, but I think they are victims of Putin's propaganda. If the government changed, maybe they would stop fighting,' Mykola says.

The ATO – the famous 'Anti-Terrorist Operation' to which Mykola has devoted the past six years of his life – was rechristened the JFO, for 'Joint Forces Operation', in April 2018. The rationale was that we weren't really fighting 'terrorists' in Donbas, but the Russian military. Mykola doesn't mind the change of name. He suspects it has something to do with NATO's increasing influence in Ukraine. Joint Forces Operation has an American ring to it, and the US started delivering Javelin anti-tank missiles on the very day we changed the name. We're not supposed to use them until or unless the separatists launch an all-out offensive. The Javelins will prove incredibly helpful in the first days of the full invasion.

Mykola, like many in the military, is wary of Volodymyr Zelenskiy, who is elected president of Ukraine in April 2019. The German president Frank-Walter Steinmeier's 'formula' has been kicking around since 2016, but on 1 October 2019, Zelenskiy endorses the plan for a ceasefire and referendum in Donbas. An opinion poll shows that a majority of the residents of Donetsk and Luhansk want to remain part of Ukraine, but with a special status.

The separatists in Donbas hail Zelenskiy's signature of the Steinmeier Formula as 'a victory for Russia', which indicates it must be bad for Ukraine. The accord would mean the loss of some Ukrainian territory. Ukrainian army units would be stood down and the separatists would be rewarded with autonomy if they win the referendum. The plan is never fully implemented because Putin and Zelenskiy cannot agree on the sequence of events.

The Donbas veterans are furious and stage at least four 'No to capitulation' protests in two weeks following Zelenskiy's signature of the agreement. The number of demonstrators rises to 50,000 on 14 October.

'We managed to stop the withdrawal from Zolote with our protests,' Mykola says, referring to several villages grouped into a town in the Sievierodonetsk district of Luhansk. 'We couldn't do anything about Petrovske in November.' Petrovske is another town that Ukraine relinquished under the Steinmeier Formula.

Mykola accuses Zelenskiy of giving Ukrainian land to Russia. He is most upset about the Svitlodarsk Bulge. 'Your husband died defending it, Yulia! And now Zelenskiy wants us to withdraw? We aren't even allowed to shoot back when the Russians fire on us. On my last tour in Donbas, they docked our pay if we retaliated! The Ukrainian government punishes us for defending the motherland! Could there be a greater offence to Donbas veterans? We are no longer allowed to fight.'

Mykola says the new rules created under the Steinmeier Formula have divided veterans from active soldiers. 'Soldiers received pay rises and started getting bonuses for not firing back, but the best people left the army. The veterans are furious and the others don't care what happens, as long as they get their pay cheque.'

The mood in the National Guard has changed. 'It was more dangerous five or six years ago, but it was exciting,' Mykola says. 'People cared. They've lost their motivation. The politicians are caving in, and the fight is going out of us. I tried to see Zelenskiy, but the president's office just ignores me.'

'Despite everything, you look well, Tato. I think it's because you've stopped drinking. Promise me you won't start again when you leave hospital?'

'Life is hard, Yulia. A man needs a little comfort. I'll do the best I can.'

'I cannot ask for more than that,' I say and kiss him goodbye.

Sunday, 11 October 2020

I am visiting my boyfriend, Mykyta, in Lviv when Bohdan calls me. I am alarmed, because he usually sends text messages. 'Yulia, are you sitting down?' he asks in a strained voice.

'What is it? Tell me what's wrong,' I say. A chill slices through me. 'Has something happened to Mama?'

'No. It's Tato.'

This is not the first time our father has generated bad news. Tato leaves Tamara for Larysa. Tato is wounded on the eastern front. Tato becomes an alcoholic. My life has so often been disrupted by Tato's problems that it is almost a relief to hear that he is the one in trouble, not Tamara.

'Don't get upset, Yulia,' Bohdan continues. I have never heard his voice like this.

'What is it? Just tell me!'

'Tato set himself on fire last night, around three o'clock in the morning, on the Maidan. He is burned on over 90 per cent of his body. Doctors in the hospital burn unit say he is not going to survive. In the ambulance, before he lost consciousness, he repeated Baba Lyuba's phone number. Uncle Dima has her phone since she died, so they called him. Dima is with Tato now.'

On the train to Kyiv that evening I am in shock, angry and upset with Mykola. I interpret his act as a sign of weakness. He always told me to be strong, but he gave up. How could he do this to me, just two and a half years after I lost my husband? *Self-immolation.* I say the word over and over. *Self. Selfish. Immolation.* Could there be anything more destructive, more devastating for his children? *Mykola, how could you?*

I call Dima from the train station. 'Don't come to the hospital,' he begs me. 'There's no point. He's in a coma. He wouldn't know you were there. I don't want you to see him like this.'

'Dima, I don't understand. What happened? Why?'

'I talked to him last night, five or six hours before he did it. He sounded normal. He talked about going in for treatment and about helping Bohdan in Zhytomyr. There was no indication...'

Because I have been active in Vidsich and Veteranka for years, my telephone number is easily available to journalists. I am inundated with phone calls from reporters wanting to know about my father. I stop answering. An unscrupulous journalist invents a story about Mykola having done this because of a failed romance, which is rubbish and infuriates me. There are also statements from officials in the Orthodox Church, saying that my father's act was sinful, that he wasted his life. For the moment, I am too overwhelmed by Mykola's impending death to fight back.

Mykola dies three days later, on 14 October, the Day of Defenders of Ukraine. I suspect he chose the date of his self-immolation to mark it.

I go with Dima and Bohdan to the police headquarters. They will not allow us to bury Tato until we sign the death certificate which states he died by suicide. Dima has kept up contacts from his past employment in the police, so the officers are more understanding than they might be otherwise. They show us CCTV footage of Mykola's last protest on the Maidan. Distressing as it is, I feel we must watch it.

Maidan Nezalezhnosti. 3.02 a.m., 11 October 2020

On his Facebook page, Mykola posts an image of the victory column commemorating independence. His words are inaudible on the CCTV footage, but we have seen the Facebook post and know his last words by heart: 'It is 3.02 a.m. and I want Ukraine to be independent.'

The police video shows Mykola distancing himself from the teenagers who loiter around the fountain. He sets down his rucksack and takes out a jerry can. He shows no sign of agitation. He moves deliberately, unscrews the cap on the jerry can, douses himself from head to toe in petrol and strikes a match. There's a 'whoosh' sound as flames engulf him. I have the impression that he is trying to stand tall, as he did on the parade ground at his oath-taking ceremony, but the flames are more powerful than he is. They pull and twist his body in a contorted dance of death as they consume it. The teenagers scream and run towards the human torch. One is filming with his smartphone. Another propels Mykola with his feet towards the fountain. A third tries to dunk him in the water.

'Let me die,' Mykola cries out. 'Let me die and be with my mother.'

One of the teenagers posts the video on the Telegram messaging service. With police help, we track them down and ask them to remove it, which they do. They are disturbed by what they have witnessed. By an incredible coincidence, one of them is a friend of my boyfriend Mykyta.

'Please don't let this video become public,' I beg the police.

'Of course not,' the officer says. 'It must be very painful for you.' He hands me the rucksack containing Mykola's belongings. We find a photograph of the Ukrainian dissident poet Vasyl Stus in his wallet. Someone gave Mykola a book of Stus's poetry when he was in hospital the previous January. Mykola found the work inspiring. The photograph of Stus even looks like my father. Every Ukrainian knows the first line of Stus's most famous poem, 'How good it is that I've no fear of dying'. The poem comes to mean a great deal to me, especially after the invasion, because it helps to explain the courage of my husband, my father and the Ukrainian nation.

'I want you to do a blood test on my father's remains,' I tell the police officer. 'I want to know if he was under the influence of drink or drugs when he struck that match.' In the video, Mykola looks as if he is in command of his senses, but I need to be certain.

The substance abuse tests come back negative. Mykola was

of sound mind when he immolated himself on the Maidan. The shame and anger that I felt when I learned of his act evolve into something resembling pride and admiration. It took courage for my father to do what he did. I have no doubt that he meant his death to be a political statement.

We hold Mykola's funeral on the Maidan on a bleak October day, in pouring rain. The Covid pandemic is still on. Most of the mourners wear surgical masks. We huddle together under umbrellas, around a wooden casket perched on chairs. It is draped with a Ukrainian flag signed in black marker by Mykola's brothers-in-arms. A bouquet of yellow daisies sits on top of the coffin. There are numerous uniforms in the crowd, veterans of the war in Donbas who demonstrated with Mykola as part of the 'No to capitulation' movement.

About 400,000 Ukrainians fought in Donbas between 2014 and 2020, more than half of them volunteers like Mykola. Russian propaganda attempts to discredit them as fascists, misfits and a danger to society. I want to honour Mykola as I ought to have honoured him when he was living. I must do everything in my power to ensure that his bravery is not forgotten.

'The death of Master Sergeant Mykola Mykytenko was not a suicide,' I say, standing before his casket. Somehow, amid the grief and formalities, I have found time to plan what I want to say. The words flow easily, with conviction.

'My father sacrificed himself to warn Ukraine of the dangers of capitulation. He and other veterans were alarmed when President Zelenskiy gave in to Russian pressure and signed the Steinmeier Formula one year ago. They saw Ukraine withdraw from the line of contact and cede territory that our soldiers had paid for with their lives, including the Svitlodarsk Bulge, where my husband Illia was killed. My father loved Illia like a son, and could not bear to see this land, which was holy to him, occupied by the Russians.

'Last July, army commanders left Medic Sergeant Yaroslav Zhuravel to die in Donbas, in blazing heat, without food or water. He was part of a rescue team sent to retrieve the body of a Ukrainian officer, with the agreement of the Russians and international observers. But the Russians fired on the rescue party, wounding Sergeant Zhuravel.

'Master Sergeant Mykytenko was sickened by what happened. If he had been there, he would have sent those commanders packing. He would have crawled to rescue that wounded soldier, just as he risked his life to retrieve the dead and wounded from General Kulchytski's burning helicopter.

'My father was a brave man, and, I realize today, a hero. The place and manner of his death prove that it was a political act. No place in Ukraine is a more potent symbol of the rejection of Russian domination than Maidan Nezalezhnosti. Master Sergeant Mykytenko suffered a concussion from a stun grenade here in 2014, when he led the nineteenth *sotnya* during the Revolution of Dignity. A few days ago, he gave his life here, for Ukraine. We gather today to pay homage and say farewell to him.

'Had Master Sergeant Mykytenko simply wanted to kill himself, there are far less painful ways to do it. As my father was consumed by flames, he shouted, "Zelenskiy prevents us from fighting." In a Facebook post minutes before his self-immolation, he said, "I simply want Ukraine to be independent." If we let Putin have Donetsk and Luhansk, he will not stop until he controls all Ukraine. My father was a soldier, not a politician, but he saw this clearly. He wanted his death to be a warning of the consequences of capitulation.'

'*Slava Ukraini!*' Glory to Ukraine, the mourners shout in unison.

Dima drives me and Bohdan back to Tamara's apartment that night.

'Yulia, do you remember how we argued seven or eight years ago?' my uncle asks.

'Of course, Dima. It doesn't matter now.'

'It matters to me. I was once a policeman. I believed in law and order. I believed in authority, and I thought you students were troublemakers. I felt that way when you started demonstrating, and during Maidan. I didn't like Yanukovych, but I thought he was our president so we should stick with him until we could vote him out of office. I thought Mykola was excitable and that he joined the protests to please you.'

'I thought the same thing, Dima. There was an element of truth to it in the beginning. Tato admitted as much. But it didn't take long for him to become a true believer.'

'It took me a lot longer,' Dima continues. 'I started to change my mind when the Russians took Crimea and invaded Donbas. Yulia, you gave a great speech at Mykola's funeral. It made me understand that all these years you and Mykola were right. You were his daughter, the commissioned officer, his comrade-in-arms and his hierarchical superior. He was so proud of you, and tonight I am proud of you too.'

My father's younger brother concentrates on driving through the darkness and rain while he talks. It has been a day of intense emotion. I want to thank Dima, but there's a lump in my throat and I fear that if I speak I will start crying. So I reach over and squeeze his hand on the steering wheel.

A few days later, I hold a press conference at the Ukrainian media crisis centre, in Ukrainian House on Khreshchatyk Street, between the Dnipro river and the Maidan.

'President Zelenskiy, my father asked repeatedly to see you in the months before his death,' I say in the video which I release at the press conference. 'You were too busy to see him. Now I ask you to see me, as an army veteran, as the widow and daughter of brave soldiers, and as a proud citizen of Ukraine.'

I tell the journalists what I said at Mykola's funeral a few days earlier – that his death was a political statement rather than a banal suicide.

'Master Sergeant Mykytenko's death is not the first such act of bravery,' I remind them. 'Fifty-two years ago, Vasyl Makukh, a Soviet veteran of the Second World War who defected to join the Ukrainian Insurgent Army, immolated himself in this very street. Makukh had survived ten years in Soviet labour camps and was sentenced to internal exile when he returned to Ukraine. He was a schoolteacher and he self-immolated because the Soviets were wiping out the Ukrainian language, and because they invaded Czechoslovakia, a sister country. "Long live free Ukraine," Makukh shouted before dying.

'Fifty-one years ago, the Czech student Jan Palach self-immolated in Prague in protest at the Soviet occupation of his country.

'Nine years later, in January 1978, the Ukrainian dissident Oleksa Hirnyk, an engineer by profession, burned himself to death near the tomb of our great poet Taras Shevchenko, in protest at the Soviet suppression of the Ukrainian language, culture and history.

'Ladies and gentlemen of the press,' I conclude, 'for three hundred years Ukraine's history has been one of Russian and Soviet invasions and colonization, deportation, mass arrests, torture and imposed famine. Today, Russia has amputated independent Ukraine of Crimea and the east of our country. By ceding territory and ordering our troops not to fight, our government is complicit. My father died to tell you this. Today, Master Sergeant Mykytenko has joined the ranks of Makukh, Palach and Hirnyk. He has joined the pantheon of patriot heroes.'

One would expect the self-immolation of a war veteran on the most important square in Ukraine to merit national attention. Mykola's death and my press conference are covered by independent media, but state media mostly ignore it, I believe because it raises awkward questions for Zelenskiy. The president's office has my telephone number, but no one answers my appeal for an appointment to see him.

Vladimir Putin invades Ukraine sixteen months after Mykola takes his own life. I set aside the documentary I am making about my father, which was to have been shown on the second anniversary of his death, to rejoin the army. The world is impressed by Zelenskiy's determination and refusal to leave Ukraine. I am waiting to see how the war ends before I pass final judgement. I have not forgotten that Zelenskiy was ready to give in to Putin in 2019.

Ukraine was not ready for the 24 February 2022 invasion because Zelenskiy had neglected the armed forces, leaving them in a demoralized, ill-prepared and ill-equipped state, as my father and other veterans warned. My father immolated himself to draw attention to our country's vulnerability. When the war ends, there will be a presidential election. These things will be remembered, and if they are not, I will be there to remind my compatriots of what took place.

XI

The Miracle of Courage

At the beginning of these adventures, there is solitude, darkness, the impossibility of foreseeing the consequences for oneself and for others. Courage is a leap into the unknown, taken by the light of a dark lantern. There are no more prophets, no dogmas, no signs to show the way, only the example of those who have preceded us on an endless path, in a peregrination that expresses the best of what we are.

François Sureau of the Académie Française,
discourse on courage, 1 December 2023

Zakytne, a small village on the Siverskyi Donets river, Donbas. March 2024

The shelling gets worse and worse. For weeks, the Russians have pounded us with 203-millimetre shells almost daily. They've taken a few trenches and dugouts but no hamlets or villages yet. Maybe they want to mark the second anniversary of the invasion. Maybe they're fired up because of Putin's impending re-election. Media talk mostly of the fall of Avdiivka and of an expected Russian play for Kupyansk, but we are being attacked the length of the thousand-kilometre front line. The Institute for the Study of War, a think tank in Washington, says Russia has seized an additional 505 square kilometres of Ukrainian territory since October 2023.

Zakytne has become a small hub for transport and logistics. Russian drones have doubtless seen a lot of movement, personnel, equipment and vehicles. If they were firing 152-millimetre shells it would be more bearable, but the 203s are very loud and it is like a never-ending earthquake. The ground shakes. The walls shake. The noise reverberates in our heads.

The explosions usually start a reasonable distance away, then move in closer as the gunners correct fire. The cycle takes about an hour, from the first explosions to the last ones that crash around us, followed by a few hours' respite. We ignore the shelling for as long as possible, then run in our flak jackets and helmets to the basement of a nearby house, because ours doesn't have a proper shelter. The thought of a direct hit is always there in the back of your mind. We've seen too many dead and wounded not to imagine our own bodies mangled and bloodied.

The Russians usually start with artillery to soften up our defences, to force our infantry into dugouts and shelters. Then, while they are still shelling, they drive two or three BMPs across the grey zone, followed by fifteen or twenty foot soldiers. Or they send infantry but no armour. We eventually manage to stop them with a combination of our own artillery and FPV drones.

We're fighting Storm Z troops now, penal units created in

April 2023 on the model of Prigozhin's Wagner militia. Like Prigozhin before them, the Russian defence ministry promises reduced sentences and good money to *zeks* – Russian slang for prisoners – who are willing to serve as cannon fodder in Donbas. Regular troops who drink or do drugs are punished by transfer to a Storm Z unit. All risk being shot by barrier troops if they try to retreat or surrender. I saw a video streamed by a Russian soldier who says their commanders shoot wounded men who return from an assault. He uses the verb *obnulit*, to nullify in prison jargon.

Ten nights ago, the Russians sent a larger than usual group of about fifty *zeks* running across a field towards our base. I saw them on the relay from the night-vision drone and alerted the artillery gunners and FPV pilots, who attacked them. With a combination of Soviet-era and new Western weapons – the American cluster munitions are particularly effective – we kill about fifteen Russians and wound another thirty. Watching the battle on my laptop in the dugout, I see men blown into the air, falling onto the moonscape of churned earth and splintered trees. Our FPVs score direct hits, tearing men to pieces and burning them alive. It does not affect me. I am doing my job. I am not the one who fires the shells, though I have guided the artillery. This is shared work, shared responsibility. I do not know the names of the Russians, nor do I want to know them. If I had time to think about it, I would say that by killing the assaulting *zeks* we are saving the lives of our comrades. If we don't kill them, they'll kill us.

The survivors finally turn back. More Russians arrive to help the walking wounded. I see them stagger back towards the Russian line. All those who lie on the ground, whether dead or wounded, are abandoned. Ten days have passed, and they are certainly dead now, drained of blood, frozen, food for rats and vultures. The Russians do not return for them. It's unlikely Russian commanders would risk able-bodied men to pick up single-use soldiers. Our attitude is different. Ukrainian officers do their utmost to retrieve dead and wounded soldiers from the battlefield, though at such close range it would be a suicide mission.

The walls of our billet are only one brick thick. I watch them sway with each successive explosion and become obsessed with the idea that the entire unfinished structure, the house we have inhabited for the past year, since Wagner troops drove us out of our previous base at Zvanivka, is about to collapse on top of us and bury us alive. The houses where the rest of my platoon are stationed are no better. If we don't leave soon, we may all die. After a sleepless night I call the company commander.

'Requesting permission to withdraw from Zakytne, sir.'

'Permission granted.'

Pulling out of Zakytne feels awful, like an eviction. There are twenty-five of us in the platoon and we have one pick-up truck, a minivan and two vehicles to move ourselves and our equipment during lulls in the shellfire. A second platoon begins moving out just after we do. We pack the drones, generators and Starlink terminals first, then go back for personal belongings and weapons. We must leave behind the wood-stoves that were purchased for us by civilian donors, and sizeable stocks of trench candles and tinned food. It galls me to think the Russians may soon be squatting in our house and using our supplies. I am particularly sorry to leave the wood-stoves because they've kept us warm, and I don't know if we'll be able to get new ones next winter. This is the first time I have thought of next winter and it gives me a sinking feeling to know we'll probably still be in Donbas.

We spend two nights at company headquarters in Slovyansk, which is not really a headquarters but a series of abandoned or rented houses dispersed throughout the city, so the Russians cannot kill too many of us with one strike. The company commander and I study the maps and reconnaissance data before choosing a new base, eight kilometres from Zakytne and 15 kilometres from Lyman. I don't want to publish the name of the village as long as we are stationed here. The Russians want to retake Lyman. They are trying to fight their way through the forest to get there, but it's not easy because both sides have dug in. We hold half the forest at present. The Russians have the other half. I'm not sure you can still call it a forest. The trees have been decimated by artillery fire and look like burnt sticks.

6 March 2024

I find a suitable house for myself, Sergeant Andriy, Petro, Ruslan and Shorty. It has wood panelling and a stone wall in the main room, which gives it the feel of a mountain cabin. If we have time and fuel to use the generator to power the pump, we even have running water, albeit ice cold. Our new village has views of lakes and forest. It was occupied by the Russians at the same time as Lyman, for five months in 2022. Before leaving, the Russians truffled it with landmines.

Serhii, our new landlord, stops by while we are moving in.

'Be very careful,' Serhii says. 'The previous owners wanted to go and live with relatives in the west last year. They'd had enough of war. They'd got as far as the edge of the village in a civilian car when they hit an anti-tank mine. Killed them both. Sasha and Yuriy. Good people.'

So there will be no leisurely walks by the lakeside. We must restrict movement to roads which have been cleared by army sappers. Within days we will resume rotating to the new dugouts we haven't built yet, so we can launch our drones and watch the Russians continue to eat away at our corner of Donbas.

The previous times we moved, I found billets for all twenty-five soldiers in my unit. This time I tell the boys to find their own houses. I must stop mothering them. They have to fend for themselves, make their own decisions. In the event, they find houses easily. Property in front-line villages is not at a premium, especially with the Russians advancing.

On the night we move in, I catch sight of myself in a mirror over the living-room fireplace. I am not a vain woman, but I am shocked to see how tired and old I look, in my knit khaki cap. I think of the narrator in *All Quiet on the Western Front*: 'I am young ... but I know nothing of life except despair, death, fear...'

But our plight cannot be compared to that of Remarque's First World War soldiers. They joined up as schoolboys, egged on by a patriotic teacher, and quickly realized that the slaughter was absurd. Our refusal to accept Russian occupation is an act of resistance, and resistance is in itself a positive and hopeful thing. Unlike most wars, this conflict has a clear cause, profound meaning and stakes of enormous importance. If Putin is allowed to win, Ukraine, a country of forty-four million people, will cease to exist. The security of Europe and the entire world will be in question.

The weeks of shellfire, the tough decision to redeploy and the rushed move have taken a toll. I am too experienced to be afraid, but the anxiety is always there, more for my men than for myself, the fear that one of them will be killed or wounded. I dread the cycle of identifying remains, notifying the family, seeking consolation with my brothers-in-arms when there can be no consolation. There are dark circles under my eyes. I see Sergeant Andriy looking at me in the mirror and turn to him.

'It's not your fault,' he says.

'I know. It's the fault of bad luck, not enough men and weapons, fickle allies, Putin's bloody Russian war machine... But it still feels terrible to lose a position.'

'We'll take it back,' he says.

'Well, maybe. Some day.'

18 February 2024

In an interview broadcast on German television five days after he is appointed commander-in-chief of the Ukrainian armed forces, General Oleksandr Syrskyi states the obvious, that Ukraine has moved 'from an offensive to a defensive operation'.

For the first two years of the full-scale invasion, we were high on anger, adrenalin and a sense of unity. At times we almost thought we were invincible, when our soldiers took back the entire region of Kharkiv in September 2022, and much of Kherson oblast two months later. Ukraine's military planners thought our forces should remain lithe and mobile. But the Russians outsmarted us with the impenetrable fortifications of the Surovikin line. Our inability to break through to the Sea of Azov persuaded many of our Western backers that we are losers, that they and we should cut our losses and strike a deal with Putin.

The failed counter-offensive also made us understand how badly we need a Surovikin line of our own. With our new defensive war footing comes the realization that Ukraine has badly neglected its own defensive fortifications. Efforts are being made around Avdiivka – too late to save the strategic town on the outskirts of Donetsk City – and endangered Kupyansk. Zelenskiy talks about a 2,000-kilometre line of fortifications, three layers deep. We hear that the army is using heavy equipment to excavate deep, wide trenches with sloping walls to trap Russian tanks. In front of the trenches, they place dragon's teeth, 'Czech hedgehogs' made of metal beams, and minefields. They install chain-link fences around artillery emplacements and the entrance to dugouts to detonate FPV drones before they hit their targets. Ukrainian army engineers are reportedly building reinforced trenches for soldiers, covered with canvas so that FPV drones cannot see inside.

We can, alas, do little to protect ourselves from the glide bombs that the Russians increasingly use to attack our dugouts and bunkers. They can be countered only by fighter aircraft and air defence missile systems. Ukraine has pleaded since February 2022 for NATO to 'close the skies' over Ukraine. It took eighteen months for our allies to finally agree in August 2023 to send F-16s, which we only begin to receive one year later. Western countries have donated a handful of Patriot air defence missile batteries. The first launchers did not arrive until the spring of 2023 and are insufficient to protect our cities and our front lines. The long-awaited $61 billion military aid package voted through the U.S. Congress on 21 April 2024 should help eventually, but Putin is determined to exploit our vulnerability in the meantime.

I and my colleagues see no sign of the new Ukrainian fortifications showcased in foreign media. There is a lot of grumbling in the ranks about the inadequacy of our defences. Ukraine has good third and fourth lines of defence, but they are 30 to 50 kilometres from the line of contact, too far back to be of use to us. We would have to retreat dozens of kilometres to be protected, which would mean a huge loss of territory. Building defences so far back serves no rational purpose. Five kilometres from the front line, we have no fortifications to retreat to. With every position the enemy takes, we find ourselves within one or two kilometres of them. We fall back and hastily dig new foxholes, which are faster to dig than trenches and less vulnerable to artillery fire.

If our commanders had shown foresight, this would not be happening this way. It may be too dangerous to send private contractors to the combat zone, but they could train soldiers to operate diggers and earthmovers. Unfortunately, our military has only a tiny fraction of the construction equipment available to the Russians, who were able to use civilian civil engineering companies to build the Surovikin line. The incompetence of a military hierarchy who have never built fortifications is the only explanation for the lack of defensive measures. Someone should be punished for this.

When the war is over, I want to start an advocacy campaign to reform the army. The first step will be to change the way rank is attributed. The Ukrainian army promotes men simply because they have been in the army for a long time. We have a lot of senior officers who are inexperienced, incompetent armchair warriors. These are the men who bungled fortifications on the eastern front.

This is one reason why I want Ukraine to join NATO, because

I am not certain we will be able to reform our military on our own. Joining NATO might clear out unprofessional soldiers and higher-ups and instil greater respect for women, as well as providing us with higher standards of weapons and technology.

I want to be useful in the army for as long as the war lasts, though I have no ambition for a military career. I would love to be promoted to captain, but it doesn't matter if I'm not; I'll probably make captain when I'm in the reserves. If there is a peace agreement, I will leave active duty. There will be a lot of work with the veteran community after the war; thousands of men with serious health problems, many of them amputees. I would like to return to the job I was doing when the 2022 invasion started, helping veterans reintegrate in civilian life – work that is close to my heart. Before the full-scale invasion, we were fighting sexism and harassment in the military. We also had plans for an advocacy campaign to raise awareness of the high suicide rate among army conscripts, apparently due to bullying by unprofessional officers. So many issues have been set aside because of the war.

When Zelenskiy tried to make peace with Russia in 2019, the veterans of Donbas cried 'capitulation'. My father died because he could not bear to see Ukraine sacrifice land for peace with Russia. But I have seen the human cost of this war, and the near impossibility of taking back our lost territories. Civilians may be less prepared to accept the loss of some territory than the military. The military is reasonable. If a real peace could be achieved, with security guarantees, with Ukraine free to join Europe and NATO, I believe the military could be persuaded to accept a negotiated settlement. It would be like drinking poison, but I would lay down my weapon. But if Ukraine is occupied by Russia and the war ends without an agreement, I will use my savings to buy a gun and join the resistance.

Sooner or later, we will be forced to sign some sort of peace agreement. I hope it will take our interests into account, but it will not be the end of the war. This artificial peace will merely be the precursor to another war. Russia will use the time to gather strength and attack again. Putin will not rest until he conquers Kharkiv, Odesa and possibly Kyiv. He thinks of them as Russian-speaking cities, and therefore Russian. I fear I will not see a peaceful Ukraine in my lifetime, that this war will go on for as long as Putin's regime is in power. That will likely be Ukraine's problem rather than NATO's. They have not suffered at the hands of Russia the way we have.

I know I contradict myself, alternating between talk of peace and fighting to the death. The conflict is also within us, between a yearning to return to normality and our determination to remain independent. The most important thing is that Putin not be allowed to install a subservient government in Kyiv.

Since the failure of the counter-offensive, we hear a lot about 'Ukraine fatigue' in the West. We are endlessly reminded that Russia is the biggest country in the world, with seventeen million square kilometres of territory, twenty-eight times the size of Ukraine. We know they have three times our population, that their economy is ten times greater than ours, that they have the world's largest inventory of nuclear weapons. Because we are outmanned and outgunned, some see our defeat as inevitable. Like Pope Francis, they tell us to 'raise the white flag'.

Some argue that the combined economy of the European Union is nearly ten times greater than Russia's, that NATO has three times as many soldiers as Russia, more than three times as many ships and five times as many aircraft. This might be convincing if Ukraine was a member of the EU and NATO, but neither will let us join for as long as the war continues. Neither organization is as strong as the sum of its parts. At best we can hope that Russia's aggression against Ukraine has shaken the EU and NATO out of their lethargy.

The Russians are not unbeatable. They occupied Afghanistan for ten years and gave up. We have been fighting them for ten years already. And we have something they do not have, for all their size and power: our love of freedom. I do not understand why Russians do not rise up against Putin, who deprives them of freedom. I think they have the mentality of serfs.

Our need for security guarantees is the main motivation for joining NATO. Armchair strategists suggest we should accept the loss of territory in exchange for NATO membership, which would, in theory, 'sanctuarize' the territory we now hold, with the promise of NATO intervention in the event of renewed aggression by Moscow.

Though it is heresy to say so, it is obvious that we will probably lose Crimea, most of Donbas and, I fear, the parts of the Kherson and Zaporizhzhia oblasts currently occupied by Russia. The possibility of joining NATO is not sufficient reason to sacrifice 18 per cent of Ukraine, but if we have no choice but to lose territory, NATO membership would be a consolation. It is difficult to imagine under what circumstances Putin would accept Ukraine joining NATO.

Our history with NATO is as old as independent Ukraine. In 1991, we joined the North Atlantic Cooperation Council which was set up by the alliance as a forum for dialogue with NATO's former Warsaw Pact adversaries. It was mainly to persuade Ukraine to give up the nuclear weapons it inherited from the Soviet Union that Bill Clinton created the Partnership for Peace, as a sort of substitute for NATO membership, in 1994. Ukraine was the first country to join.

Our neighbours in eastern Europe had suffered so much under Soviet rule that they pleaded to join NATO. We pleaded too, but Western leaders were afraid of offending Moscow. George W. Bush wanted NATO to set a date for Ukrainian and Georgian accession at the 2008 Bucharest Summit, but this was opposed by Angela Merkel and Nicolas Sarkozy. Ukraine and Georgia received instead a promise of eventual membership without a deadline, the worst of all possible solutions because it enraged Putin and left us unprotected.

Ukraine continued to build ever stronger ties with NATO. I first met American and Canadian NATO officers at the Hetman Petro Sahaidachnyi National Ground Forces Academy, where I attended officer training school in 2017. The academy is co-located with the International Centre for Peacekeeping and Security on the 390 square kilometre Yavoriv military base between Lviv and the Polish border. The ICPS was created in 2007 to train Ukrainian soldiers in the framework of the Partnership for Peace. Russia's 13 March 2022 attack on Yavoriv, which killed thirty-five people and wounded 134 others, was for all intents and purposes an attack on NATO's presence in Ukraine.

When I was a supervisor at the Ivan Bohun Military Lyceum in Kyiv, NATO officers occupied space in our building and sometimes attended or even gave lectures. I interpreted for them. Their talks were never sophisticated, more like a friendly visit with NATO, just chats with teenagers about the officers' experience and military careers. I also accompanied Ukrainian cadets on visits to military schools in Britain and Sweden, which was not yet a NATO member.

On 25 February 2024, the *New York Times* published a detailed report on ties between US and Ukrainian intelligence, and revealed that the CIA has, since 2014, built twelve secret bases on Ukraine's borders with Russia. These bases are today used by Ukraine to organize secret commando operations inside

Russia. Britain and France are also reported to have sent military and intelligence personnel to Ukraine, to assist us with the weapons they are providing.

Putin attempts to justify the full-scale invasion on the grounds that NATO's presence in our country threatens the very existence of Russia. If he is truly worried about NATO expansion, his plan backfired, because the invasion prompted Sweden and Finland to join the alliance. Finland's accession more than doubled Russia's land border with NATO, but Putin is not yet threatening to invade Finland.

There is one simple reason why Putin refuses to allow Ukraine to join NATO: he wants to control us, and NATO's presence prevents him from doing so. I dare say he also fears the example of a free, democratic Ukraine on Russia's borders.

We want security from NATO, but we also have a great deal to offer the alliance. There isn't an army in Europe that could stand up to Russia as we have. The Ukrainian armed forces now number close to one million men and women, including hundreds of thousands with experience fighting Russia for the past decade. No NATO power can say that. I am puzzled by NATO's reluctance to provide us with the materiel we need, because Ukraine is the ideal place for them to combat-test their weapons. We could also teach NATO a great deal about efficiency in the heat of battle. Their vertical chain of command goes all the way up to headquarters, which slows down any military. The Ukrainian army has learned how to be flexible and react quickly.

Sometimes I have doubts about NATO. It is the biggest, shiniest, most expensive and powerful military alliance in the history of the world, with titanium jets and main battle tanks costing millions of dollars apiece. Yet NATO has gone to war only with lesser powers: with Milošević's Serbia, Islamist Afghanistan and Gaddafi in Libya. When it came to confronting Russian aggression – NATO's *raison d'être* – they shrank from helping Ukraine. When Russia invaded Crimea in 2014, Barack Obama told us not to fight. Boris Johnson, who has been a true friend to Ukraine, says Chancellor Olaf Scholz advised Zelenskiy 'to fold' as soon as possible after 24 February 2022. In the first days of the invasion, we begged NATO to 'close the skies' by imposing a no-fly zone over Ukraine. They were afraid to do even that. I sometimes think that if Russia invaded Poland, NATO would not react until Russian troops reached the outskirts of Paris.

NATO sends a flurry of conflicting signals regarding Ukraine's application to join the alliance. They do not want to give Putin the satisfaction of excluding the possibility of our joining, but they do not want to antagonize him either. There is no unity – and hence no credibility – in the attitude of NATO powers. The once and possibly future American president Donald Trump says he will 'encourage Russia to do whatever the hell they want' to NATO members who do not meet the 2 per cent threshold for defence spending.

On 20 February 2024, NATO's then secretary general, Jens Stoltenberg, said Ukraine has the right to strike Russian military targets inside Russia. But, Stoltenberg added, each ally can decide what conditions it places on the use of the weapons it donates. Britain and France let us use their Storm Shadow/SCALP cruise missiles to target Crimea. On a visit to Kyiv on 2 May 2024, the British foreign secretary, David Cameron, stated explicitly that Ukraine has the right to strike inside Russia. But Scholz has refused to send Taurus cruise missiles which could destroy the Kerch Bridge linking Crimea to Russia. The US has been ambiguous. In late April, National Security Adviser Jake Sullivan told journalists that Ukraine had promised not to fire newly supplied long-range ATACMS (Army Tactical Missile Systems) into Russia. When asked a few days later if Ukraine could use the missiles to strike Russian territory, Defence Secretary Lloyd Austin replied, 'It's up to them on how and when to use it.'

At the end of May, three weeks into a month-long Russian offensive which captured 13 villages in the Kharkiv oblast, President Biden said Ukraine could use US-supplied weapons to shoot down missiles heading for Kharkiv, at troops massing on the Russian side of the border near Kharkiv, and at bombers launching glide bombs towards Ukraine. The US said we could not use their weapons to target Russian civilian infrastructure, or military targets deep inside Russia. In June, the Pentagon said we could strike Russian forces firing on Ukrainian troops anywhere along the border.

The debate over the possible deployment of NATO 'boots on the ground' to Ukraine was equally confusing. On 26 February 2024, President Emmanuel Macron said NATO 'should not rule out' sending troops to Ukraine. Macron made similar statements throughout the spring, prompting firm rebuttals from most NATO members except the Baltic states. The French president doubled down in a 2 May interview with the *Economist*, saying the question of sending Western troops to Ukraine would arise 'legitimately' if Russia broke through Ukrainian lines and Kyiv asked for help. Two years earlier, the same Macron said Russia 'must not be humiliated'. Now he says Russia must be defeated.

When your country has been invaded by a murderous dictator, you overlook the shortcomings of putative allies. If Trump is elected and the US leaves NATO, there will still be strong countries who will keep the alliance going, and we will still want to join. The Verkhovna Rada made joining NATO and the European Union official foreign and security policy objectives in 2017. These were enshrined in our constitution in 2019.

In June 2022, Putin said he has nothing against Ukraine

joining the EU, because it is not a military bloc. He didn't feel that way back in 2014 when we were demonstrating for association with Europe on the Maidan, and he could change his mind again. But the statement shows Putin's disdain for Europe and the greater importance he attaches to NATO.

Ukrainians too place a higher value on joining NATO. I am European through my cultural and historical roots, but the appeal of EU membership is fading. I am not sure what Ukraine would gain from it. Seen from Donbas, the EU looks like a disunited trade zone built on foundations that are ageing badly. Britain has been one of our staunchest supporters in the war and we cannot forget that Britain left the EU in 2020. We also see extreme right-wing nationalist parties – far more objectionable than the so-called 'Nazis' who Putin persists in imagining in Ukraine – progressing across Europe. Many of them are sympathetic to Putin.

It is humiliating to want to belong to a club that does not want you. Polls show that while Europeans continue to support military aid for Ukraine and welcome Ukrainian refugees, they are far more reluctant to let us join the EU. Turkey has been waiting for thirty-seven years and will probably never be admitted. Western Balkan states have waited fifteen years already. We are told it will be at least another six years before we might be allowed to join the EU.

Europe seems to be afraid of Ukraine. They cite our geographical size, relative poverty, competition from our agricultural sector, the cost of post-war reconstruction and spillover from our conflict with Russia. It has taken Europe two years since the invasion to even begin to organize weapons production and procurement to help us. That said, Europe eventually came through on a promise of €50 billion in grants and loans for Ukraine over the next four years, even as US Republicans stalled for six months before authorizing $61 billion in desperately needed military aid.

We are fighting this war for ourselves, but also for the benefit of the collective West. Ukrainians are dying at the hands of Russia so that Europeans and Americans do not have to die. As our foreign minister, Dmytro Kuleba, is in the habit of saying: 'We offer you the best deal: you don't sacrifice your soldiers, give us weapons and money and we will finish the job.' If Europe and the US do not give us the support we need, this will be the last war in which they will not have to fight. Europeans are beginning to realize how much Russia threatens them. That threat and our need for protection coincide. If the European Union transforms itself into a military alliance, Ukraine will be very keen to join it.

For all its failings, there is such a thing as the world community. The Holodomor is not likely to be repeated in the twenty-first century. Our allies may be unreliable, but we are not alone. We will survive, with their help or without it.

Kyiv. 6 December 2022

I have been summoned along with about twenty of my fellow soldiers to the Mariinskyi Palace, the official residence of the president of Ukraine. I was notified on 14 October – the second anniversary of my father's death – that I am to be awarded the Medal of Courage, 3rd Class, for 'individual courage and heroism while rescuing people or valued materials while endangering one's own life'. There is no indication which specific rescue mission I am being rewarded for. Front-line rescue missions are a routine part of my job, and none seem particularly heroic to me.

We wear camouflage, not dress uniforms, because ostentation looks out of place in wartime. Security is extremely tight. We queue outside in the bitter cold, are searched and go through metal detectors, then wait for hours in an annex to the palace. At some point there is an air raid siren and we are ushered down to the basement. None of us are sure the award ceremony will happen. The invitation is marked strictly personal – no family or friends allowed – except for amputee soldiers who cannot move without assistance. Other family members have come to collect posthumous medals on behalf of dead soldiers. About an hour before the ceremony, we are led outside to rehearse. I wear layer upon layer of clothing because it's so cold.

We are finally ushered into the opulent, late baroque palace where Zelenskiy receives foreign heads of state. It was designed by the Italian architect Bartolomeo Rastrelli for Russian Empress Elizabeta Petrovna in 1744. Her niece by marriage, Catherine II, stayed here during a visit to Kyiv in 1787. The palace remained the residence of visiting members of the imperial family until the 1917 revolution. Zelenskiy has proclaimed the reception room where the ceremony takes place the White Hall of Heroes of Ukraine. I see Ukraine's use of this relic of Russian colonialism as an expression of defiance.

When my father died, I asked to talk to Zelenskiy, but this is not the time or place. The president hands me a wooden box and shakes my hand. The enamelled medal inside shows a Ukrainian trident over crossed swords and hangs from a blue, gold, red and white ribbon. General Zaluzhnyi poses for a photograph with me in the anteroom.

I am humbled by the presence of the amputees and the dead soldiers' relatives. I want to talk to them, but I am tongue-tied. Zelenskiy uses the big words. Heroism. Courage. He says the world has under-estimated the power of courage. This seems to be a comfort to the families. Though the mood is more like a requiem than a celebration, the event feels necessary. I have mixed feelings about accepting the medal. I know that undeserving people often receive medals, and that many soldiers are more worthy of a medal than I am.

The ceremony ends. I say a brief farewell to the other newly decorated soldiers, steel myself against the cold and walk alone to the metro station. I stash my pretty medal in its wooden box in a drawer in Tamara's apartment and head back to my platoon in Donbas.

Everyone on the front line thinks about death because we know we can die at any moment. We don't make a big deal of it; it's just death. Another state of being. Another adventure. It's just a body, after all. Everyone has his own scenario on how he or she would like to be remembered, what to do with the body and the government money. I have written a will and prepared letters for Tamara and Bohdan. To be honest, I am not really afraid of dying.

After Illia was killed, I started thinking about the afterlife. I do not practise any religion, though I believe in God, or at least in some sort of higher power. I don't know if heaven will be Valhalla, as Illia said, or the green golf course with fluffy lambs they taught us about in Sunday school. I think it will be a place of eternal rest and peace, where I will be reunited with Illia.

I also believe in accountability: that individuals who do evil will be judged for what they do or do not do. People are able to hide their true character in peacetime. War shines a spotlight on cowardice and courage. Like all wars, the war against Ukraine has unearthed its share of traitors and corruption, but that must not be allowed to discredit the bravery of the majority of Ukrainian people.

I would like to think that courage will be rewarded in heaven, because courage is a miracle, an irrational reaction contrary to human instincts for survival. Perhaps God will pass out medals, like President Zelenskiy.

You either have courage or you do not. It reveals itself only in critical moments, and you do not know until you are tested if you will be paralysed or have the courage to throw yourself into the void, drive yourself beyond your limits, confront and embrace the thing that threatens you, wrestle it and come out the other side victorious. There is nothing so satisfying, and yet once you have done this you have the impression it was nothing really. If you have courage, you do what you must, and you are not afraid of dying. There is some higher goal, some purpose bigger than your own life. Knowing that goal or purpose is the beginning of courage. For me, it is to defend my family, to defend my mother and brother.

Ukraine has been fighting Russia off and on since the Battle of Poltava in 1709. We are in a better situation than in the past, when our ancestors fought Russia alone and without hope of succeeding. The Russians were not able to starve us to death. They did not manage to kill us with imprisonment and exile in Siberia. These memories are deep in the heart of every Ukrainian. We know what we owe to those who went before us. I want to ensure that their lives were not given in vain.

Glossary

A-50 – Ukraine is believed to have destroyed two Russian Beriev A-50 radar airborne warning and control (AWACS) aircraft worth hundreds of millions of euro in January and March 2024, leaving Russia with only seven remaining A-50s. The A-50 helps Russia seek out Ukrainian air defences and coordinate attacks by other aircraft.

Abrams – After months of pleas from Kyiv, the United States finally agreed to send 31 M1A1 Abrams tanks to Ukraine in January 2023. They arrived the following September, were given to the NATO-trained 47th mechanized brigade and were first seen in action against the Russians near Avdiivka on 23 February 2024.

Afgantsy – Ukrainian veterans of the Soviet war in Afghanistan. Yulia's father, Mykola Mykytenko, had friends among them.

AK-47s and AK-74s – Soviet and post-Soviet assault rifles used by both sides in the Russo-Ukrainian war.

ATACMS – Kyiv asked Washington for the Army Tactical Missile Systems (ATACMS) in the early stages of the Russo-Ukrainian war, but the US feared the weapons would escalate the conflict. The US delivered medium-range ATACMS in the autumn of 2023. President Biden secretly authorized the transfer of longer-range ATACMS with a range of up to 300 kilometres in March 2024, after months of debate. Ukrainian forces used them against targets in Crimea and Russian-occupied eastern Ukraine in April and May. The missiles are fired from Multiple Launch Rocket Systems (MLRS) and from High Mobility Artillery Rocket Systems (HIMARS). Some carry cluster munitions.

Baba – An abbreviation of *babusia*, a familiar term for grand-mother in Ukrainian.

barrier troops – Also known as blocking units or anti-retreat forces. The Bolsheviks began using barrier troops comprising agents from the Cheka secret police in 1918. They had orders to shoot to prevent desertion or retreat by front-line Red Army soldiers. The practice was reintroduced on a wide scale during the Second World War, especially against unwilling penal bat-talions created by Stalin. There are numerous reports of Russian use of barrier troops in Ukraine.

Beriev A-50 – Since the beginning of 2024, the Ukrainian air force had reportedly downed two of Russia's nine Beriev A-50 airborne early warning and control aircraft. The Beriev A-50 first flew in 1978. Each aircraft can coordinate up to ten fighter aircraft and costs an estimated $300 million.

Berkut – Ukrainian riot police who acted under the authority of the interior ministry and were used by the pro-Russian presi-dent Viktor Yanukovych to terrorize his political opponents during his 2010–2014 rule. The Berkut were responsible for most of the 108 deaths in the Maidan revolution and were dis-solved and replaced by the National Guard when Yanukovych fled in February 2014.

BM – 27 Urugan – a self-propelled, 220-millimetre multiple rocket launcher manufactured in the Soviet Union between

1975 and 1991. The Urugan (meaning 'hurricane') was the Soviets' first spin and fin stabilized heavy multiple rocket launcher. Russia is believed to possess about 750 Urugans.

BMP – Soviet and post-Soviet armoured fighting vehicles used by both sides in the Russo-Ukrainian war. BMP stands for *Boyevaya Mashina Pekhoty*, Russian for 'infantry combat vehicle'.

Boykos – An ethnic and linguistic subgroup of Ukrainians who along with the Lemkos and Hutsuls live in the Carpathian Mountains straddling Ukraine, Slovakia, Hungary and Poland. Stalin forcibly moved many Boykos to Donbas in the early 1950s because he suspected them of anti-Soviet sympathies, and to give their land to Communist Poland. The Boykos who settled in Donbas are noticeably different from local inhabitants, many of whom are descended from Russians who were brought by the Soviets in earlier decades to work in mines and industry.

Bradleys – The United States has provided more than 300 M2 Bradley Infantry Fighting Vehicles to Ukraine, of which more than 100 were included in the aid package that was finally voted by Congress in April 2024. The armoured, tracked vehicles are highly manoeuvrable and are equipped with Bushmaster chain guns and TOW anti-tank missile launchers. They are considered one of the best combat vehicles available.

BTR – Soviet and post-Soviet armoured personnel carriers used by both sides in the Russo-Ukrainian war. BTR stands for *Bronetransportyor*, Russian for 'armoured transporter'.

Bucharest Summit – George W Bush wanted the April 2008 NATO summit in Bucharest to set a deadline for Georgian and Ukrainian accession to the Atlantic Alliance. The move was opposed by Chancellor Angela Merkel and President Nicolas

Sarkozy because they feared antagonizing Putin. Georgia and Ukraine were promised they would become members one day but were not given a target date.

Budapest Memorandum on Security Assurances – Signed in Budapest on 5 December 1994, the memorandum guaranteed the protection of Belarus, Kazakhstan and Ukraine in exchange for the former Soviet republics giving up their nuclear weapons and adhering to the Treaty on the Non-Proliferation of Nuclear Weapons (NPT). Russia, the United States and the United Kingdom were the initial signatories. China and France gave weaker assurances in separate documents.

Caesar – An acronym for *Camion Équipé d'un Système d'Artillerie*. French defence minister Sébastien Lecornu said on 18 January 2024 that Ukraine had already received 49 of the French-made, self-propelled howitzers, of which France has donated 12. Ukraine has purchased six and France appealed to its allies to help foot the €260 million bill for sixty Caesars, for a total of seventy-eight.

Challenger 2 – The United Kingdom announced in January 2023 that it would provide Ukraine with fourteen Challenger main battle tanks. They were deployed in late March 2023 with the Ukrainian air assault forces' 82nd brigade in Zaporizhzhia oblast and participated in the failed counter-offensive. At 71 tonnes, the Challenger 2 is the heaviest tank in the Russo-Ukrainian war.

Cheka – The first Soviet secret police organization, established by the Bolshevik revolutionary Felix Dzerzhinsky in 1917. Under Lenin, the Cheka carried out mass arrests, imprisonment, torture and executions without trial.

Chornobyl – (Russian spelling: Chernobyl.) A partially abandoned city 90 kilometres north of Kyiv, near Ukraine's border with Belarus, and the scene of the 1986 nuclear disaster. Russian forces ignored nuclear safety regulations when they captured and occupied the nuclear power plant from 24 February to 2 April 2022.

dacha – A country house or cottage in Russian and Ukrainian.

Donbas – An abbreviation for Donetsk coal basin, comprising the oblasts of Luhansk and Donetsk.

dragon's teeth – Pyramid-shaped concrete obstacles invented during the Second World War to slow the advance of enemy tanks. Russia fortified its Surovikin line across south-eastern Ukraine with dragon's teeth. Ukrainian forces are deploying them around Kharkiv, Kupyansk and other eastern cities in anticipation of a Russian assault.

drones – See UAVs below.

Duma – The State Duma is the lower house of the Russian parliament, comprising 450 members elected for four-year terms. The Federation Council constitutes the upper house.

Eurasian Economic Union – The treaty founding the trading bloc of five former Soviet republics was signed by Belarus, Kazakhstan and Russia in May 2014. Putin conceived of the EEU as a rival to the European Union. In 2013, he had offered the pro-Russian Ukrainian president Viktor Yanukovych a $15 billion loan to pull out of an association agreement with the EU and join the EEU instead. Yanukovych's decision to obey Putin sparked the November 2013 to February 2014 Maidan revolution which led to Yanukovych's downfall.

F-16 fighter jets – Since the beginning of the full-scale invasion, Ukraine's Western allies have dragged their feet on urgent requests for artillery, air defence missiles, tanks and fighter aircraft. Denmark pushed hard in the spring of 2023 for F-16s to be given to Ukraine. Four NATO countries – Belgium, Denmark, the Netherlands and Norway – have promised to provide a total of forty-five of the combat aircraft, which are manufactured by Lockheed Martin. Complex maintenance and training requirements have slowed the process and the first F-16s were not delivered to Ukraine until August 2024. Some European militaries are phasing out the F-16 in favour of the newer F-35.

FPV – First-person-view drones cost about $500 each. The FPV pilot wears a visor over his or her eyes and sees everything the drone sees. Ukrainian soldiers rig them to carry explosive charges and use them as kamikaze weapons.

FSB – The Federal Security Service of the Russian Federation (*Federal'naya sluzhba bezopasnosti Rossiyskoy Federatsii*) replaced the Soviet KGB as the main intelligence service in Russia in 1995. Vladimir Putin was head of the FSB in 1998/99.

Fyksyky – A popular Ukrainian television cartoon about a girl called Symirochka who spends her time rescuing a naughty boy from trouble. Tamara and Yulia have a pet cat called Symirochka and the name became Yulia's call sign.

Gaz-66 – The four-wheel drive, all terrain civilian and military truck produced in the Soviet Union and then Russia between 1964 and 1998 is used by Russian and Ukrainian forces in the Russo-Ukrainian war.

glide bombs – In 2023, Russia began rigging Soviet-era **FAB** (*fugasnaya aviatsionnaya bomba* or high-explosive aerial bomb) gravity bombs with satellite guidance systems and wings that pop out in flight, making it possible for Russian aircraft to elude anti-aircraft defences by launching bombs from up to 60 kilometres away. Some sources also refer to more sophisticated **KAB** (*korrektiruyemaya aviatsionnaya bomba* or adjustable aircraft bomb) as glide bombs. Glide bombs weighing between 250 kilos and 1.5 tonnes are far more effective than artillery shells at destroying bunkers and buildings. Russian defence minister Sergei Shoigu said in March 2024 that Russia has a new, three-tonne glide bomb. The Ukrainian military blame the loss of Avdiivka in February 2024 on Russia's systematic use of glide bombs. Scarce US-made Patriot missiles are the best defence against glide bombs. See also **Su-34s and Su-35s**.

Grad missiles – Another Soviet-era weapon being used by both sides in the war in Ukraine. The BM-21 Grad ('hailstorm' in Russian) is a 122-millimetre self-propelled multiple rocket launcher system developed in the 1960s. The rockets are aligned in tubes resembling organ pipes and fired from the back of a combat vehicle. They are sometimes referred to as 'Stalin's organs'.

Hetman – The word is believed to be derived from the Turkic title ataman ('father of horsemen') or from the German word Hauptmann ('captain'). In much of central and eastern Europe it signifies a political or military leader. Commanders of the Zaporizhian Cossacks in present-day Ukraine were called Hetman from the late sixteenth century. Empress Catherine II abolished the title in 1764. It was revived during the 1917-1920 Ukrainian revolution and is evocative of Cossacks who established their own state and fought domination by the Polish-Lithuanian Commonwealth and by Russia. Three Cossack Hetmans who lived between the sixteenth and eighteenth centuries are considered precursors of the modern Ukrainian state: Petro Sahaidachny, Bohdan Khmelnytsky and Ivan Mazepa.

HIMARS – Since the summer of 2022, the United States has given Ukraine 39 truck-mounted High Mobility Artillery Rocket System, considered to be among the best artillery in the Ukrainian armoury.

Hindenburg lights – Home-made trench candles which originated in the First World War and are in use in Ukraine. They are made by pouring wax into a tin can with a wick, surrounded by a spiral of corrugated cardboard, and are used for light and warmth in trenches and dugouts.

Holodomor – (Meaning death by hunger in Ukrainian.) About four million Ukrainians starved to death in the 1932/33 famine caused by Stalin's policy of farm collectivization.

hryvnia – Ukraine's national currency since 1996.

Humvee – The United States has provided more than 3,000 of its High Mobility Multipurpose Wheeled Vehicles to Ukraine. Colloquially known as the Humvee, the light, four-wheel drive military trucks and utility vehicles have been produced since 1984 and have largely replaced the jeep.

HUR – The Main Directorate of Intelligence of the Ministry of Defence of Ukraine (*Holovne upravlinnia rozvidky Ministerstva oborony Ukrainy*) has been responsible for daring attacks in Crimea and behind Russian lines. Its symbol is an owl hovering over a map of the world and driving a sword into a blackened Russia. The symbol of the GRU, the equivalent intelligence agency in Russia, is a bat superimposed on a globe. Owls prey on bats. The HUR is headed by Lieutenant General Kyrylo Budanov, who has survived numerous assassination attempts. His wife, Marianna, survived poisoning with heavy metals in November 2023.

ICPS – The International Centre for Peacekeeping and Security was established on the Yavoriv military base between Lviv and the Polish border in 2007, to train Ukrainian soldiers in the framework of NATO's Partnership for Peace. Russia attacked the base on 13 March 2022, killing 35 people and wounding 134 others.

Il-22 – The 1950s vintage Ilyushin Il-22 is a propeller-driven airborne command post used by Russia. Wagner mercenaries shot down one during their June 2023 mutiny, after which Russia was believed to have about one dozen left. Ukraine destroyed another in January 2024.

International Legion – Also known as the Ukrainian Foreign Legion. Three days after Russia's 24 February 2022 full-scale invasion of Ukraine, Foreign Minister Dmytro Kuleba announced that President Zelenskyy had created an International Legion comprised of foreign volunteers to help Ukraine's Territorial Defence Forces fight Russia. Kuleba later said that 20,000 volunteers from 52 countries had enlisted by 6 March 2022. But an investigation by the New York Times one year later said there might be as few as 1,500 volunteers in the International Legion.

Invisible Battalion – An advocacy group formed by women in the Ukrainian military, of which Lieutenant Yulia Mykytenko is an active member. Invisible Battalion is also the title of an award-winning documentary film made in 2017 to raise awareness of women's second-class status in the military. A campaign by Invisible Battalion led to passage of a law in 2018 opening combat positions to women.

IRIS-T – Germany had delivered three IRIS T air defence missile systems to Ukraine by February 2024. Five more are promised for a total of eight.

Ivanovets – Ukraine sank the Russian missile corvette with sea drones off the coast of Crimea on 1 February 2024.

JAS 39 Gripen – Sweden's accession to full NATO membership on 7 March 2024 opened the way for the transfer of JAS 39 Gripen fighter jets, manufactured by SAAB AB, to Ukraine. Ukrainian pilots tested the Gripen (which means 'Griffin' in English) in the autumn of 2023. The Swedish aircraft is a light, single-engine, supersonic, multi-role fighter with modest strike capability which would complement the much-awaited deployment of heavier US-made F-16 strike fighters.

Javelins – The United States provided Javelin shoulder-fired anti-tank missiles to Ukraine for training well in advance of the full-scale invasion. The Ukrainians proved adept at destroying the first and last tank or armoured personnel carrier in a column, then destroying all the armour in between. The Javelins attained almost cult status in Ukraine.

Joint Forces Operation – or JFO was the name given in 2018 to Ukrainian forces fighting Russians in Donbas. The JFO was previously known as the ATO for Anti-Terrorist Operation. The change of name signified recognition that Ukrainian forces were mainly fighting Russians rather than Ukrainian separatist 'terrorists' in the east of the country.

Kalibr cruise missiles – A family of Russian cruise missiles developed by NPO Novator and deployed since 1994. There are ship, submarine and air-launched versions of the missile. Sonic Kalibrs, with a double propulsion system, are better at evading air defence systems, while the subsonic variety have longer range. The Kalibr can carry a 500-kilo conventional or thermonuclear warhead. Kalibr missiles have been widely used by Russia against military and civilian targets in Ukraine.

kiptar – A traditional Ukrainian sleeveless waistcoat.

Kornet – Russia's best anti-tank guided missile.

Krab – A self-propelled, tracked gun howitzer designed in Poland but equipped with a South Korean chassis and a British turret. Poland donated eighteen Krabs to Ukraine in 2022 and promised to sell Ukraine an additional fifty-six.

Lancet – A Russian loitering munition, also known as a suicide, kamikaze or exploding drone, which is controlled remotely to wait for the opportune moment to crash into a target and destroy it. Russian forces mostly use ZALA Lancet drones, developed by Zala Aero, which have led Ukrainians to build chain-link cages around their artillery to prevent easy destruction.

Leleka-100 – An Unmanned Aerial Vehicle (UAV) used for reconnaissance or to carry loitering munitions. It was commissioned by the Ukrainian armed forces in 2021 and has been widely used in the Russo-Ukrainian war. With a two-metre wingspan, the Leleka looks like a miniature aircraft.

Leopard – As of mid-February 2024, Germany had sent thirty Leopard 1 main battle tanks and eighteen Leopard 2 main battle tanks to Ukraine. Germany had been reluctant to send either, but followed the lead of the United States and Britain in January 2023 after they agreed to send Abrams and Challenger tanks. Germany also agreed to allow the re-export of Leopard tanks owned by third countries. The Leopard 1 is no longer in production and fires a different calibre shell from the Leopard 2.

M777 – Australia, Canada and the United States have donated close to 200 British-made M777 155-millimetre towed howitzers to Ukraine. By mid-2023 about a third of them had been damaged or destroyed.

Magura – The Ukrainian-made Magura Unmanned Surface Vessels or sea drones, which look like pilotless boats, have proven extremely effective at sinking Russian warships in the Black Sea.

Maidan – Maidan Nezalezhnosti or Independence Square in Kyiv was the scene of the 2004/05 Orange Revolution and the 2013/14 Euromaidan Revolution of Dignity, both of which drove the pro-Russian president Viktor Yanukovych out of office. The name is usually shortened to Maidan, a Persian word meaning 'square'.

Mavic – Inexpensive Chinese-made drones with four rotors which are widely used by Ukrainian troops for reconnaissance. The Mavics cost between $1,500 and $2,000 for daytime drones, and at least $2,400 for those with night vision.

Milblogger – A service member or civilian with a close relationship to the armed forces who writes a blog about the ongoing war, often from front lines. Russian milbloggers, who usually post on the encrypted Telegram channel, have been a major source of information about the Russian side of the conflict in Ukraine. They tend to be enthusiastic supporters of the invasion who criticize Russian generals and the defence ministry for what they see as incompetence. The Kremlin has mostly tolerated such criticism, though Igor Girkin, the former FSB agent turned milblogger who was convicted in absentia by a Dutch court of responsibility for downing Malaysia Airlines flight 17, was sentenced to four years in prison and deprived of access to the internet after making derogatory remarks about Putin.

Minsk accords – In 2014/15, France and Germany mediated two agreements intended to end the war in Donbas. Ukraine signed the Minsk Protocol or Minsk I agreement after losing close to 400 soldiers in the August 2014 battle for Ilovaisk. The fighting continued and Russian forces defeated the Ukrainian army at Donetsk International Airport and Debaltseve. The February 2015 Minsk II Accord was supposed to lead to a ceasefire, disarmament and local elections in Donbas. Russia and Ukraine never agreed on the details of its implementation. Two days before the full-scale invasion of 24 February 2022, Vladimir Putin declared that the Minsk accords 'no longer existed'.

MLRS – see ATACMS and BM-27 Urugan.

Moskali – A derogatory term used by Ukrainians for Russians.

Moskva – The sinking of the guided missile cruiser *Moskva*, the flagship of Russia's Black Sea fleet, by two Ukrainian-made Neptune anti-ship missiles on 14 April 2022, was one of the most symbolic Ukrainian victories of the war so far. The *Moskva* had demanded the surrender of Ukraine's Snake Island on the first day of the full-scale invasion. A Ukrainian border guard famously replied, 'Russian warship, go fuck yourself'.

NATO – Independent Ukraine has maintained close relations with the North Atlantic Treaty Organization since it joined the North Atlantic Cooperation Council in 1991 and the Partnership for Peace programme in 1994. At the 2008 Bucharest summit, NATO leaders promised that Georgia and Ukraine would become NATO members but did not say when. NATO–Ukraine cooperation paused under the pro-Russian presidency of Viktor Yanukovych from 2010 until 2014. In 2019, Ukraine enshrined the aspiration to join NATO in its constitution. Vladimir Putin claims that NATO's presence in Ukraine forced him to stage the full-scale invasion in 2022.

Nebesna Sotnya – Most of the 'heavenly hundred' (in fact 108) civilian protestors who died in the Euromaidan revolution

were killed by Berkut riot police in the final days of the protests which drove Viktor Yanukovych from power. They are
commemorated at the National Memorial to the Heroes of the
Heavenly Hundred and the Revolution of Dignity Museum.

Neptune – The Ukrainian-designed and manufactured subsonic
anti-ship missile was developed in 2021 and was first used after
the full-scale invasion. Two Neptunes sank the Russian Black
Sea flagship *Moskva* in April 2022. Ukraine has developed a
land version of the same missile.

NLAW – The Next-generation Light Anti-tank Weapon is a
shoulder-held weapon developed in Sweden and manufactured
in the United Kingdom. As of 15 May 2023, the United Kingdom
had supplied more than 5,000 NLAWs to Ukraine. Smaller and
lighter than Javelin missiles, the NLAWs are the most numerous
anti-tank missiles in the Ukrainian arsenal.

Nord Stream pipelines – The network of natural gas pipelines
running under the Baltic Sea from Russia to Germany comprising Nord Stream 1, which entered service in 2011, and Nord
Stream 2, which was completed in 2021 but never entered
service. Russia shut down Nord Stream 1 six months after the
22 February 2022 invasion, on the pretext of maintenance.
Germany withheld permission for Nord Stream 2 to open one
day after the Duma recognized the independence of the separatist regions of Donetsk and Luhansk on 21 February 2022. The
US had long opposed the pipelines on the grounds they created
dangerous dependency on Russia. Four underwater explosions
on 26 September 2022 made the pipelines inoperable. A joint
investigation by *Der Spiegel* and the *Washington Post* reported
that General Valerii Zaluzhnyi, then commander-in-chief of
Ukraine's armed forces, ordered British-trained saboteurs to

destroy the pipelines. Zaluzhnyi, who is now Ukraine's ambassador to London, denied this.

North Atlantic Cooperation Council – NATO established the Cooperation Council in 1991 to facilitate dialogue with its former Warsaw Pact adversaries. It was a precursor to the Partnership for Peace, a sort of substitute for NATO membership which was created by Bill Clinton in 1994 to persuade Ukraine to give up the nuclear weapons it inherited from the Soviet Union.

Nova Poshta – A private nationwide delivery company which is used to ship equipment, food and supplies to the front lines.

Novocherkassk – Ukraine used cruise missiles to destroy the Russian landing ship on 26 December 2023 in the port of Feodosia on the south-eastern coast of Crimea. Ukraine said the *Novocherkassk* was carrying Iranian Shahed drones. Three days later, Russia unleashed two days of drone and missile attacks which killed forty Ukrainians.

oblast – 'Province' or 'region' in Russian and in Ukrainian. Ukraine is divided into twenty-four administrative oblasts. Russia occupies parts of the oblasts of Luhansk, Donetsk, Zaporizhzhia and Kherson, but none in entirety. In June 2024, Putin said he would make peace with Ukraine if Kyiv would give up these four oblasts and promise not to join NATO.

obnulit – Russian prison jargon meaning to kill or nullify, used to describe the shooting of wounded soldiers who return from an assault.

Olenivka prison massacre – On 29 July 2022, an explosion in a Russian-operated prison in Donetsk oblast killed more than fifty Ukrainian prisoners of war and wounded about a hundred. Most of the prisoners had survived the Russian siege of the Azovstal complex in Mariupol. Ukrainian officials said

Russia bombed the installation to destroy evidence of the ill-treatment of prisoners. Russia claimed the Ukrainians fired a HIMARS rocket at the prison. Independent investigations indicated that the explosion was probably caused by a bomb placed inside the building.

ostalgie – The German term for nostalgia for the former Soviet bloc. A similar phenomenon exists in Ukraine.

Paladin – The British Ministry of Defence announced in October 2023 that it would send its Terrahawk Paladin stationary air defence system – reputed for its ability to shoot down Iranian Shahed drones – to Ukraine. Not to be confused with the highly mobile M109 Paladin self-propelled howitzer, which has been provided to Ukraine by the US and at least four other NATO countries.

Party of Regions – The pro-Russian Party of Regions was founded in 1997 and banned in 2023. The POR was strongest in Russian-speaking regions of eastern and southern Ukraine. Its candidate, Viktor Yanukovych, was president of Ukraine from 2010 until he resigned and fled to Russia in the wake of the Euromaidan revolution in 2014.

Patriot – Patriot truck-mounted surface-to-air missiles have constituted the main air defence system in the United States since the mid-1980s. It took Volodymyr Zelenskiy until December 2022 to persuade Joe Biden to provide Patriot systems to protect Ukrainian cities. Germany, which had earlier refused, followed suit. Ukraine has reportedly deployed one battery in Kyiv and one each in the south and east.

Pion – (Russian for 'peony'.) The S7 Pion self-propelled gun is used by Russian forces to pound Ukrainian front-line troops with high-calibre 203-millimetre shells.

PKM – An improved variant of the original Soviet PK belt-fed, general purpose machine gun, introduced in 1969 and still produced in Russia. The 'K' in PK signifies its development from the Kalashnikov assault rifle. The PKM is a standard front-line infantry and vehicle-mounted weapon and is used by both sides in the Russo-Ukrainian war.

pochekun (**singular**) and *pochekuny* (**plural**) – Ukrainian slang for a 'waiter'; someone who sits on the fence or waits to be 'liberated' by Russian forces, represented by a meme of a fat, bear-like creature twiddling its thumbs. See also *zhdun/zhduny*.

Praviy Sektor – Several far-right paramilitary groups united under the banner of Praviy Sektor (Right Sector) at the beginning of the Maidan protests in November 2013. Praviy Sektor claims to represent the legacy of Stepan Bandera, who headed a faction of the Organisation of Ukrainian Nationalists (OUN) during the Second World War. Its members have fought in Donbas since 2014 as a volunteer corps and were integrated into the regular Ukrainian armed forces in 2022.

Prometheus – The leading online education platform in Ukraine, run by the non-profit Education Equality Institute, offers more than 250 courses and teaches more than 1.8 million students. The defence ministry has posted lessons for drone operators on Prometheus. Other programmes include lessons on Information Technology to help Ukrainians displaced by the war develop job skills.

Revolution of Dignity – also known as Euromaidan. The confrontation between pro-western Ukrainians who see Ukraine's future with the European Union and Moscow's supporters came to a head in three months of protests from November 2013 to February 2014 in which 108 civilians were killed. The Revolution of Dignity culminated with the flight of pro-Russian president

Viktor Yanukovych, followed by the Russian invasion of Crimea and Donbas. See also **Eurasian Economic Union.**

SCALP cruise missiles – see **Storm Shadow/SCALP.**

SBU – The Security Service of Ukraine (*Sluzhba bezpeky Ukrainy*) is Ukraine's main intelligence and counter-intelligence agency, under the authority of the president of Ukraine.

Sergei Kotov – A Russian patrol ship which Ukraine claims to have sunk with marine drones in the Black Sea near Crimea in March 2024.

'Slava Ukraini! Heroyam Slava!' – A patriotic greeting or exclamation in wide usage since Russia's 2014 invasion of Ukraine, meaning 'Glory to Ukraine! Glory to our heroes!' Typically, one person or group chants 'Slava Ukraini!', to which another person or group responds, 'Heroyam Slava!'

sotnya (singular) and *sotni* (plural) – Protestors in the November 2013–February 2014 Maidan revolution organized themselves in units which they called *sotni*, the term used for its combat troops by the Ukrainian Insurgent Army (UPA) which fought the Soviets and Nazis in the Second World War. The Cossacks used the same term centuries earlier for 100-strong units.

Starlink – Two days after the full-scale Russian invasion, the Ukrainian government asked Elon Musk's SpaceX company to activate their Starlink satellite internet service over Ukraine, to replace communications disrupted by Russian attacks. Because Starlink functions with small, portable satellite dishes, it cannot be shut down by attacks on communications centres. Musk provided the service to Ukraine free of charge until June 2023 when the US Department of Defence agreed to pay for it. Starlink is used by Ukrainian civilians, government and military.

Steinmeier Formula – Frank-Walter Steinmeier, then Germany's foreign minister, now president, proposed elections in Russian-occupied parts of Donbas in 2016 as a way of implementing the stalled Minsk accords. The formula required that some Ukrainian army units be stood down, and offered autonomy to separatists in Donbas if they won a referendum. President Volodymyr Zelenskiy endorsed the formula in October 2019 but faced fierce opposition from Donbas veterans who formed the 'No to capitulation' movement.

Storm Shadow/SCALP – Ukraine has used the Franco-British cruise missiles with a 550-kilometre range to strike the Russian Black Sea fleet and well beyond Russian lines. France has given about fifty of the missiles, which it calls SCALP-EG, and President Emmanuel Macron promised about forty more in January 2024. The United Kingdom has provided an unspecified number of the same missiles, which it calls Storm Shadow.

Storm Z – Penal military units comprising Russian prisoners. From April 2023, the Russian defence ministry followed Yevgeny Prigozhin's example and began recruiting prisoners to fight in Ukraine, in exchange for pay and reduced sentences.

Su-34s and Su-35s – The Su-34 is the Russian air force's best supersonic strike plane and is used to fire glide bombs from up to 60 kilometres away. Supersonic Su-35 superiority fighters escort the Su-34s. In an episode dubbed 'the Sukhoi massacre,' Ukraine shot down four twin-seat Su-34s and two single-seat Su-35s in three days in February 2024, presumably with its dwindling stock of US-made Patriot missiles. The Oryx defence analysis website reports that Russia has lost twenty-five of 150 Su-34s and six of 120 Su-35s.

Surovikin line – Defensive fortifications build on the orders of Russian General Sergei Surovikin, also known as 'General

Armageddon', in south-east Ukraine in 2022/23. The three-layer, 120-kilometre line of defence in Zaporizhzhia oblast comprises tank traps, dragon's teeth, and up to five landmines per square metre. It is one of the principal reasons why the 2023 Ukrainian counter-offensive failed.

Svoboda – The ultra-nationalist far-right party founded in 2004 as a successor to the Social-National Party of Ukraine peaked in the 2012 parliamentary elections when it won 10.45 per cent of the vote, gaining thirty-seven seats in the 450-strong Verkhovna Rada. Svoboda (which means 'freedom' in Ukrainian) played a part in the Euromaidan protests, but its support dropped there-after. The party holds one parliamentary seat at present.

T-90 – Russia's main battle tank. Russia is believed to have lost more than 2,000 tanks, two-thirds of those it went to war with in 2022. Those losses include dozens of top-of-the-line T-90s. Destroyed tanks have been replaced with hundreds of T-72s, T-62s and even T-54s and T-55s, which are fifty to seventy years old. The Russian Uralvagonzavod and Omsktransmash tank factories have stepped up production dramatically and are reportedly upgrading or producing enough tanks to keep up with losses. The small number of Abrams, Challenger and Leopard 2 tanks deployed or promised by the United States, Britain and Germany is nowhere near the number deployed by Russia.

tato – Ukrainian for papa or dad.

Taurus cruise missiles – President Volodymyr Zelenskiy wants German-made Taurus cruise missiles to enable Ukraine to destroy the Kerch Bridge linking Crimea to Russia. Chancellor Olaf Scholz said on 26 February 2024 that he was reluctant to send the Taurus because its range would be sufficient to strike Moscow and because German servicemen would be required to operate them. Germany 'will not become a party to the war, neither directly nor indirectly', Scholz wrote on social media.

temniki – As President Leonid Kuchma's chief of staff from 2002 until 2005, the future oligarch Viktor Medvedchuk issued secret memoranda known as *temniki* (directives) to Ukrainian television editors, dictating what they could and could not report. Human Rights Watch denounced Medvedchuk's *temniki* as 'informal state censorship'.

Territorial Defence Forces – During the 2014–2021 war in Donbas, the reserve battalions of the Ukrainian army were comprised of part-time veterans and civilians in volunteer militias. More than one hundred thousand Ukrainian men and women joined the TDF in the wake of the full-scale invasion of 24 February 2022, when the TDF were officially organized as a branch of the armed forces. They ensure local defence and can be integrated into the regular army in the event of mass mobilization. Zelenskiy's **International Legion** (see separate entry) is part of the TDF.

titka – Aunt or aunty in Ukrainian.

Tsezar Kunikov – A large Russian landing ship sunk by Ukrainian-made Magura drones off the coast of Crimea in mid-February 2024.

UAVs – Unmanned Aerial Vehicles or drones have never been so widely used as in the Russo-Ukrainian war. Manufactured in China, Iran, Russia and Ukraine, hundreds of thousands of drones, perhaps millions, have been purchased for as little as $500 each. Some are used for reconnaissance only. Others are equipped with an explosive charge and used to destroy armour and tanks costing millions. Remotely controlled UAVs are also used to attack advancing ground troops or stationary soldiers in dugouts, foxholes and trenches. Their omnipresence in Ukraine has been a major factor in freezing front lines. Progress in electronic jamming could make UAVs obsolete, though electronic countermeasures are also being developed.

Ukrainiskiy Vybor – A right-wing, pro-Russian NGO founded by the oligarch Viktor Medvedchuk, 'Ukrainian Choice' campaigned against the conclusion of an Association Agreement between Ukraine and the EU by broadcasting crude, misleading television advertisements. Medvedchuk and his wife, the television presenter Oksana Marchenko, were imprisoned after the full-scale Russian invasion and exchanged for the defenders of the Azovstal steel plant in September 2022.

UPA – The Second World War Ukrainian Insurgent Army (Ukrayins'ka Povstans'ka Armiia), which fought the Soviets and the Nazis. Some UPA units in western Ukraine cooperated with Nazi authorities in 1944, against the orders of their leadership.

Verkhovna Rada – Ukraine's 450-strong unicameral parliament.

Veteranka – The Ukrainian women's veterans' association, founded by female soldiers in 2015, has worked tirelessly for equal rights for women in the army. Veteranka successfully lobbied the Verkhovna Rada to pass the 2018 law allowing women to fight in combat positions. Their humanitarian and military aid hub in Kyiv distributes armour, medical and technical equipment and food to front-line units, and supports women, children and disabled people affected by the war. Veteranka makes uniforms and other necessities designed for women soldiers and helps to rehabilitate veterans.

Vidsich – The Ukrainian word for 'rebuff' is a civil society group founded by students at Kyiv-Mohyla Academy in 2010 to oppose close ties with Russia.

Vilnius Summit – President Viktor Yanukovych was to have signed an association agreement with the European Union at the Eastern Partnership summit in the Lithuanian capital, Vilnius, on 28/29 November 2013. Yanukovych's announcement on 21 November that he would not sign after all sparked the Euromaidan revolution. Yanukovych had twice visited Vladimir Putin in the preceding weeks and was under pressure to join Putin's Eurasian Economic Union instead. Putin used carrot and stick to sway Yanukovych, offering cheap Russian gas and a $15 billion loan if Ukraine backed out of the agreement and threatening to occupy Crimea and Donbas if he did not.

vyshyvanka – Ukrainian traditional embroidered clothing which is often worn as a symbol of patriotism.

Wagner Group – The private military company founded by Yevgeny Prigozhin in 2014 was secretly funded by the Russian government to fight dirty wars in the Middle East and Africa with official Russian deniability. Prigozhin recruited prisoners to fight in Ukraine and used them in human wave assaults. After his mercenaries seized the ruined city of Bakhmut, Prigozhin, who had long criticized the Russian defence ministry, ordered a march on Moscow on 23 June 2023. The mutiny lasted only one day but Prigozhin and his right-hand man, Dmitry Utkin, died two months later when Prigozhin's private jet exploded en route from St Petersburg to Moscow.

Warsaw Pact – The 1955–91 defence alliance maintained by the former Soviet Union and seven satellite countries in central and eastern Europe. The Warsaw Pact was established to counterbalance NATO. After the fall of the Soviet Union, Russia opposed the enlargement of NATO to former Warsaw Pact members, all of whom nonetheless joined the Western alliance.

zachistka – The Russian word for cleansing was used in

intercepted Russian communications during the occupation of Bucha, which resulted in the deaths of 458 civilians. Bucha saw some of the worst atrocities of the Russo-Ukrainian war, including rape, torture and summary executions. Revelations of the atrocities at Bucha and other towns west of Kyiv put an abrupt end to negotiations between Russian and Ukrainian representatives in Turkey.

zek – Russian word for prisoner, used by Ukrainians to refer to soldiers in the Storm Z penal military units.

zhdun (**singular**) **and** *zhduny* (**plural**) – Russian word for a 'waiter', used for Ukrainians in Crimea who hope for the victory of Ukrainian forces and the return of the peninsula to Ukraine. See also *pochekun/pochekuny.*

Acknowledgements

I first interviewed Lieutenant Yulia Mykytenko in August 2023 for an article about women in the Ukrainian army which was published in the Weekend section of *The Irish Times*. It was a sunny summer day. Yulia wore a khaki T-shirt and sat in front of the unfinished brick house which she shared with soldiers from her platoon on the front line in Donbas. I was in Kyiv, working with interpreter/fixer Nazar Yatsyshyn. The moment the Zoom interview ended, I turned to Nazar and exclaimed, 'What an amazing woman!'

The idea for this book popped into my head like an epiphany several weeks later, after I had returned to home base in Paris. I discussed it with Nazar in Lviv, and with my agent, Jonathan Williams, in Dublin. Neil Belton, the director of the Head of Zeus imprint at Bloomsbury, embraced the project with enthusiasm.

I was thrilled when Yulia agreed to tell me her story. The miracle of modern technology enabled three of us – Yulia in Donbas, Nazar in Lviv and me in Ireland – to spend more than twenty-four hours together over five months.

First thanks must go to Yulia herself, whose courage has been an inspiration to me. This book could not have been written without Nazar's first-rate interpreting and encyclopedic knowledge of Ukrainian language, culture, politics and history.

I am immensely grateful to Jonathan and Neil for their untiring support and editorial advice.

I wish to thank the Ukrainian women's veterans' association Veteranka for making the initial contact with Yulia.

I am grateful to Ruadhán Mac Cormaic and Conor Goodman of *The Irish Times* for sending me to Ukraine, and to Mary Minihan for commissioning the article on women soldiers.

My brother, Robert Cochran, looked after my home in Paris while I worked in the peaceful seclusion of Ireland. He read an early draft and delivered painful but invaluable criticism.

My thanks, too, to Lesia Davydiuk, Irena Kozymka, Yurii Lysenko, Mykhaylo Nazarenko and Yuriy Rubashov for helping me to source Ukrainian poetry for the epigraphs.

Text Credits